1994

THE NEW GOVERNANCE
Strategies for an Era of Health Reform

AMERICAN COLLEGE OF HEALTHCARE EXECUTIVES MANAGEMENT SERIES

Anthony R. Kovner, Series Editor

Russell C. Coile, Jr.

THE NEW GOVERNANCE
Strategies for an Era of Health Reform

MANAGEMENT SERIES
American College of Healthcare Executives

98   97   96   95   94   5   4   3   2   1

Library of Congress Cataloging-in-Publication Data

Coile, Russell, C.
   The new governance : strategies for an era of health reform / Russell C. Coile, Jr.
      p.   cm. — (Management series / American College of Healthcare Executives)
   Includes bibliographical references.
   ISBN 1-56793-007-7 (hardbound : alk. paper)
   1. Hospitals—United States—Administration.   2. Health services administration—United States.   3. Health care reform—United States.   I. Title.   II. Series: Management series (Ann Arbor, Mich.)
   [DNLM: 1. Hospital Administration—trends.   2. Delivery of Health Care—organization & administration.   WX 150 C679n 1994]
RA971.C6849   1994   362.1′0973—dc20
DNLM/DLC for Library of Congress   93-44914 CIP

The paper used in this publication meets the minimum requirements of American National Standard for Information Sciences—Permanence of Paper for Printed Library Materials, ANSI Z39.48-1984. ∞™

Health Administration Press
A division of the Foundation of the
   American College of Healthcare Executives
1021 East Huron Street
Ann Arbor, Michigan 48104-9990
(313) 764-1380

To Nancy Coile,
my wife and partner,

with special appreciation to
Dr. Stuart Wesbury
for his leadership and support,

and to Thomas C. Dolan
for his leadership to the field

and to
Charles Ewell, Ph.D., Laura Walker,
and my colleagues at the Governance Institute,
La Jolla, California

Contents

Foreword

What's right with health care? We hear all the bad things—costs, short-ages, weaknesses in the system, unfairness, poor quality, and many other criticisms. Some are valid, and some are inspired by people who may have other agendas in this huge and most important human service industry, the American health care system. Can it be that these criticisms and the resulting changes are the natural course of events for a field that is in a state of constant change and evolution?

We must remember that hospitals and health care as we know it are barely 50 years old. This industry has grown faster than any other segment of our economy. With so many changes and outside influences, it is natural to be dissatisfied with some aspects. However, in the United States we still enjoy—and expect—a very fine level of health care. The real challenge before us is to know how to change in an ever-changing environment. Russell C. Coile, Jr., offers guidance in this book. He has identified what is happening and how changes are affecting the health care system. In doing so, he helps those of us who are not professionally trained in health care to better understand the changes and how they will affect the future and our ability to lead our organizations.

More than ever before, it is critical that community leaders learn more about health care and work with health care organizations in meeting the needs of the community. Even with the many state and national regulations, the delivery of health care is essentially local, administered and directed by the community.

My experience for many years as a hospital trustee and a participant in the merger of eight hospitals in St. Paul, Minnesota, has given me unique insight into the changing world of hospitals and health care. This book provides an insight beyond experience and should be read by trustees, physicians, employees, managers, and those in the public sector charged with making policy and laws that will affect all of us. Each chapter is important and enlightening, but I recommend particular attention be given to the final chapter, which presents what recognized futurists of health care believe the coming decade will bring. These insights and projections, supported by informed analysis of the earlier chapters, will provide the reader with a better understanding of what to expect in the future and how to elicit positive changes to our American health care system.

Roger P. Foussard
Chair
HealthEast Hospitals
St. Paul, Minnesota

Preface and Acknowledgments

In the past 10 years, I have worked with thousands of board members and medical staff leaders in 500 hospitals and health systems across America, from Portland, Oregon, to Portland, Maine. In every situation, it is *leadership* in the face of change that has kept these institutions vital community resources. This book is dedicated to the infusion of leadership that these community and medical staff leaders bring to their institutions and emerging systems.

As an independent advisor to hospitals, physicians, and health organizations, I am indebted to a number of my colleagues for inspiration and support. If I have a gift, it is the ability to listen to the best and brightest minds in American health care and to communicate their fresh ideas and innovative successes to others. Forecasting the future is most effectively done through metaphors and models. There are a number of "model-builders" I want to recognize and thank for their inspiration.

A special thanks is due to Stuart Wesbury, Ph.D., the long-time president of the American College of Healthcare Executives, whose early enthusiasm was a critical factor in creating this book. My real appreciation is expressed for Ed. Kobrinski, who stewarded this book to completion at Health Administration Press. Thanks are also due to Gene Handley, Ph.D., James Drury, Walter Wachel, and Joyce Flory, who, through their work at the American College of Healthcare Executives, provided me opportunities to work with trustees in educational programs and to write about the challenges of governance in the *Healthcare Executive*.

It is a continuing pleasure and inspiration to work with Charles Ewell, Ph.D., Laura Walker, James Orlikoff, Bill Mohlenbrock, M.D., Bob Rosenfield, and the Fellows of the Governance Institute in La Jolla, California. The Governance Institute and its new Medical Leadership Institute have primed the trustees and medical staff leaders on the challenges that will face hundreds of hospitals and health systems in the decade ahead.

For working with new ideas, there are few peers to Kathryn Johnson, Judy Berger, Bob Stein, Susan Anthony, Annette Gardner, Pat Dean, and the creative staff of the Healthcare Forum. From "mega-managing" to leadership and mastery, to healthy communities, the Forum has been in the forefront of change. Kathryn Johnson and the Forum board are an innovative force for reshaping American health care through transformational leadership.

One of American health care's most trusted advisors is Don Arnwine of Arnwine and Associates in Irving, Texas. Don was a vanguard leader in the creation of Voluntary Hospitals of America. Following his advice, hospitals and emerging systems across America are today making the changes and building the new organizations required for the coming era in health care.

Many of America's health care trustees owe their leadership to Lee Kaiser, Ph.D., Will Pfieffer, M.D., John Horty, Sandra Gill, Spence Meighan, M.D., and the excellent faculty of the Estes Park Institute. Their programs from Florida to Hawaii have trained thousands of new trustees in governance.

In a field where you are only as good as your forecasts, my futurist colleagues Lee Kaiser, Clem Bezold, Ph.D., Jeff Goldsmith, Ph.D., Gerry McManis, Michael Annison, and Roger Selbert have been frequent sources of future-minded insights. There is no higher source of spirituality in reshaping American health care than Lee Kaiser. Clem Bezold's future scenarios are the best in the U.S. health field, and he is single-handedly responsible for keeping American futurists connected to the International Futurists Network. Jeff Goldsmith's critical thinking frequently tests my assumptions. His description of "driving the nitroglycerine truck" is a vivid metaphor of reshaping America's hospitals and systems for the future.

Creating healthy environments is a special mix of design and spirit. Much is owed to Robin Orr, Derek Parker, Wayne Ruga, Debra Levine, Jayne Mailkin, Cindy Liebrock, Jim Ray, and my colleagues on the board of the National Symposium for Health Care Design. In the creation of future-relevant designs, it is a special pleasure to work with Derek Parker, Roger Dyer, Ken Schwartz, and Jeni Wright of Anshen + Allen in San Francisco and Anshen Dyer in Great Britain. Our "21st century hospital" project in Norwich, England, hopes to create a new model within Britain's National Health Service.

My theories on reshaping health systems are infused with insights from academia. One of the health industry's premier health services researchers is Stephen Shortell, Ph.D., at Northwestern University's Kellogg School of Management. His work on strategic leadership, hospital-physician relations, and health system integration is absolutely at the forefront of managing tomorrow's health organizations. Dennis Pointer, Ph.D., at the University of California–San Diego understands organizational change better than anyone, and he is a major intellectual contributor to leadership of these new systems.

Philip Reeves, Ph.D., of my alma mater, the George Washington University, has introduced strategic planning to thousands of health care management students in a book I was privileged to coauthor. Robert Myrtle, Ph.D., of the University of Southern California has brought the discipline of systems thinking to health care administration in the United States, the Far East, and Latin America.

A special recognition is due the "model-builders" in some of the best of American health organizations: Boone Powell, Gerry Bryant, Al Swinney, and the senior management team at Baylor Health System, Dallas, Texas; Tim Hanson, Roger Green, Doug Fenstermacker, Ann Schrader, Bob Beck, M.D., board chair Roger Foussard, and the management group that restructured HealthEast of St. Paul, Minnesota, for the twenty-first century; John King and his integrated management group at the Legacy Health System, Portland, Oregon; Sam Tibbitts, Dennis Strum, and Terry Hartshorn, who are creating the model of the integrated health organization at UniHealth America in Burbank, California; Rod Wolford, former CEO of Alliant Health System in Louisville, Kentucky, for his commitment to quality; and Alan Guy of Fort Sanders Health System, Knoxville, Tennessee, for sharing a strategic vision widely with managers and medical staff.

I want to make special reference to Dan Lang, M.D., Medical Director of Valley Presbyterian Medical Center in Van Nuys, California. As editor of the *Medical Executive Reporter*, Dan's leadership and wisdom in hospital-physician relations have been an inspiration to doctors and administrators across southern California and the West.

Finally, this book is dedicated to the trustees of America's community hospitals and health systems. With governmental pressures and a price-competitive marketplace, these health organizations have been a tremendous testimonial to America's voluntary health system. They deserve our gratitude for their stewardship. The future will bring universal access and national health reforms. Trustees will be challenged to reshape their institutions to meet changing needs. Some of the choices will be painful. The 1990s may be the last, best hope for a voluntary health system. America's health care trustees must be pathfinders and visionaries to create the twenty-first century health systems of the future. I wish them well.

Introduction

Welcome to the Future:
The Twenty-First Century

Remember the landmark film "2001: A Space Odyssey"? Not so long ago, the futuristic visions of that famous work seemed as impossibly distant as the next millennium itself. But the year 2001 is now less than a decade away, and some of the wildest imaginings of yesterday have become reality. Nowhere is this more true than in health care, where the pace of both scientific and social change is unprecedented and accelerating. What will health care look like in the 21st century? And how can health care leaders make themselves ready to guide their organizations through such uncharted waters?

—Kathryn E. Johnson (1992)

These are changing times! A new millennium is approaching; the twenty-first century is upon us. For America's hospitals and health systems, new patterns of organization, alliance, management, administration, and governance are emerging. The nineties will be filled with change, but the future is not mere fate or our destiny. There are many possible futures—at the national level, at the state and regional levels, and at the institutional level for hospitals and multihealth systems.

The concept of a voluntary system and trusteeship is deeply rooted in America's culture and history. Some experts frankly question whether nonprofit boards are capable of making the tough business decisions that a competitive health market demands. These same critics were wrong in predicting that for-profit hospitals and chains would dominate the U.S. health care industry: the proprietary systems in 1990 controlled less than 15 percent of America's hospitals and are shrinking, not growing. The resiliency of the voluntary model of governance and leadership, then, has been underestimated. Yet, to face the challenges of the 1990s much work must be done to renew the concept of voluntary governance and trusteeship.

The New Governance was written to give hospital and health system trustees the information (trends) and new directions (strategies) from which they can make informed choices and decisions to guide their institutions in the next century. By anticipating what's ahead, each health care organization can build its preferred future.

As outlined in Chapter 1, the governance of American hospitals is realigning in order to effectively address the coming changes. Hospitals and health systems are restructuring their boards to become more businesslike on the "corporate model," and the role of trustees in directing and overseeing their health care organizations is undergoing significant change. A more business-oriented director will emerge on the boards of many of the nation's leading hospitals and health systems in the 1990s.

Facing health care's future does not require a crystal ball. Instead, trustees and their managers can read this book, confer with experts, develop their own forecast, and obtain second opinions on the future from other experts. Most of the important trends for the U.S. health system in the next ten years can be seen and predicted.

The term "farsight" is used by futurist Selwyn Enzer of the University of Southern California's Center for Futures Research to describe the process of anticipating the future. Foresight in managing and strategic planning can identify the forces that will drive each health care organization. How will hospitals and the health field respond to the trends? First, hospitals must believe in "futures management" to guide their institutions toward a preferred future. Second, hospitals need an anticipatory management style that monitors the environment and adapts continuously. Third, hospitals must be value-driven, ensuring that customer satisfaction and the community's health are the primary goals. Fourth, hospitals need a "bias for action" and willingness to take risks, with innovative solutions to changing problems. Fifth, hospitals need a global outlook that allows them to see beyond their boundaries and to collaborate with competitors.

To assist trustees in meeting these challenges, *The New Governance* is comprised of 13 chapters and is organized in the following way: Chapter 1 explores the book's purpose of helping to create the "board of the future." The changing roles, composition, tasks, decision processes, and authority of hospital boards are projected. Tomorrow's boards must become smaller and more business-oriented, with more members from within the institution, and tomorrow's health care trustees must become professional directors.

Chapters 2–6 lay out the future environment for hospitals and the U.S. health system. Chapter 2 reviews the trends and makes predictions for a decade of change. Managed care—HMOs, PPOs, and OWAs (see Chapter 3 for a definition)—will fundamentally restructure payment in the health field. Chapter 4 addresses the conflicts created between emerging technologies and limited resources. Chapter 5 profiles the health care cost-management strategies of major employers and their effect on hospitals. Chapter 6 outlines the reform proposals that will reshape national health policy in the 1990s and dramatically alter America's health system.

Chapters 7–12 prescribe effective strategic responses to the changing health care environment. Chapter 7 prescribes the blueprint for building tomorrow's community care networks. Chapter 8 envisions new relationships between the three major stakeholders in tomorrow's health organizations—the hospital, the board, and the physicians. Chapter 9 outlines new organizational options for integration of physicians. Chapter 10 explores the revolution occurring in clinical care and customer service. Chapter 11 discusses the hospital of the future's three-pavilion design of a campus for acute, long-term, and ambulatory care. Chapter 12 examines the future of public health and the role of the hospital.

Chapter 13 looks forward to the year 2000, forecasting scenarios for health care in the next century.

A New Paradigm for Tomorrow's Hospitals

It is not too soon to plan for the health organization of the twenty-first century. The hospitals of the future are being built today. Design and construction of health facilities typically takes five to seven years, but these new and remodeled facilities will have a useful life of 20–30 years and more. Tomorrow's hospitals will be voluntarily organized into local and regional health systems. Networks are intended to develop regional distribution systems for managed care contracting. Physicians will become closely integrated with their hospitals, contracting together for managed care and collaborating in clinical care networks—for example, cancer, heart, and trauma. In the integrated medical campus model, 25–35 percent of a hospital's medical staff will practice on the hospital campus.

A new paradigm will influence the governing of tomorrow's hospitals and health systems. A paradigm shift occurs when the fundamental assumptions and arrangements are in transition to a new order. These realignments will last through the 1990s, but every hospital and health system will be affected by this new paradigm for hospital governance.

As John Naisbitt (1982) recognized in *Megatrends: Ten New Directions Transforming Our Lives*, we are living in "parenthetical times"—the transition between the old giving way to the new. While the new pattern is far from clear, the lines of change can be predicted, as shown in Table I.1.

Predicting Health Care's Future, Reviewing Its Past

Think futuristically. During this decade the American health industry will witness the following events (Coile 1991).

Table I.1 New Paradigm* for Health Care by the Year 2000

Health System Characteristic	Present	Future
Health system	Voluntary/pluralistic	Private-public mix
Ownership/control	Nonprofit independents	Regional systems
System goal	Disease treatment	Health maintenance
Disease focus	Acute intervention	Chronic maintenance
Organization	Hospital as hub	Integrated care system
Governance model	Nonprofit voluntary	Nonprofit corporate
Marketplace	Competitive	Collaborative
Provider role	Hands-on treatment	Case manager
Patient role	Care-seeker	Therapeutic partner
Payer role	Claims review/pay	Managed care
Government role	Payer/regulator	Standards/subsidies
Health information	Decentralized paper	Computer networks
Health financing	Maximize payment	Clinical efficiency
Quality assessment	Credentials/procedures	Clinical outcomes

*This table was inspired by Marilyn Ferguson's *The Aquarian Conspiracy: Personal and Social Transformation in the 1980s*, Los Angeles, CA: J. P. Tarcher, 1981.

- The United States will spend $1 trillion and 13.5 percent of the gross national product (GNP) on health care by 1995; spending will reach $1.6 trillion and 16.4 percent of the GNP by the year 2001.
- Scientists will decipher most of the genetic code.
- Medicine will discover a vaccine and perhaps a cure for AIDS.
- Economic pressure will close 300–400 small and rural hospitals during the 1990s; 100–200 new hospitals will open.
- Congress will expand Medicare to cover long-term care.
- More women than men will enter medical school by 1995.
- Hospitals will install telemonitors on every inpatient bed.
- Ambulatory and long-term care together will be more than 50 percent of hospital revenues by the mid–1990s.
- More than 75 percent of doctors will practice in groups.
- Three out of four hospitals will belong to a multihospital network, alliance, or system.

The 1980s were often called "turbulent" for America's health care providers (Coile 1986). The 1980–1982 recession led to congressional adoption of a new Medicare payment plan for hospitals. Government adoption of diagnosis-related groups (DRGs) transformed the health care market, slowing the rise of Medicare spending but leading to massive cost shifts to private insurers and employers. Employers, pinched by recession, shifted from indemnity insurance to health maintenance organizations (HMOs) and preferred provider organizations (PPOs). Hospital competition heated up, with a wave of marketing and advertising. Capital spending increased, as hospitals competed with new facilities and high-tech equipment. Physicians began to organize into groups, engage in discounting, and become more involved in managed care (Coile 1990).

The ten greatest influences on the hospital industry at the end of the 1980s were:

1. Double-digit inflation (and growth). Hospital spending expanded at rates consistently above 10 percent all through 1989 (Coile 1992). Declining Medicare length of stay began to bottom out, which restabilized length of stay and rising admission rates. Hospitals raised prices, too. With higher volumes, operational profitability doubled in 1990, from 0.9 to 1.8 percent by year's end, outperforming the bleak estimates of other hospital surveys that hospital finances would barely break even.

2. The age wave. The aging of America showed signs of becoming the engine that would propel the U.S. hospital industry upward (Dychtwald 1989). As proof, more than 50 percent of 1989 hospital days were Medicare days. Longer lengths of stay and rising Medicare admissions continued to offset the declining use patterns of those under age 65.

3. Ambulatory hospitals. The expansion of ambulatory care continued as revenues became more strategically significant, rising to 22 percent of total hospital dollars. Visits increased, but the rising intensity of diagnostic and treatment procedures was the underlying driver.

4. National health policy. The debate on national health policy began with no early consensus in sight. In 1990 the Pepper Commission reported an ambitious plan to extend universal health coverage and since then many other plans have been introduced, but none have resolved the payment issue. Providers predictably struggled to articulate principles for a future health policy, leading the American Hospital Association (AHA) to call for the creation of community care networks that would become accountable for tens of thousands of consumers (Davidson 1993).

5. Physician regulation. Physicians were the top target of government, insurance, and managed care plans. Third party review organizations proliferated to more than 300 in 1990, and physicians learned to "game the system," boosting their revenues more than 12 percent in 1989 (Coile 1991).

6. Quality control. The quest to measure health care quality began in the mid-1980s. Pennsylvania released the first public report of comparable

quality data based on MedisGroups. A federal agency, the Agency for Health Care Policy and Research (AHCPR), has been created that will concentrate its full efforts on outcomes research.

7. The managed care era. Managed care plans (HMOs and PPOs) have spread on a national basis. While cost reimbursement and indemnity insurance plans in health care are now almost gone, three of four indemnity health policies sold in 1990 were managed indemnity. Now buyers manage their health care expenditures. The percent of managed care in inpatient revenues for the average hospital climbed from 15–25 percent at the end of the 1980s toward 30–45 percent by the mid-1990s (not including government, another form of managed care).

8. Labor shortages. Finding and retaining qualified staff was a continual challenge for U.S. hospitals. Money eased labor shortages in some hospitals by the close of the 1990s, but only temporarily. Reports from the AHA showed nursing vacancies worsening in 1990. Despite immigration expansion by Congress in 1990, labor shortages are likely to continue to be a chronic problem for hospitals in the nineties.

9. Consolidation. Consolidation and rationalization occurred, but not to the extent many experts had forecasted. Hospitals strengthened their profitability by 1990, so economic pressures for mergers abated. Instead of mergers, hospitals put their energy into developing clinical and managed networks.

10. The access crisis. The number of medically uninsured Americans grew by approximately 1 million per year during the 1980s. Access problems have worsened in states like California, Michigan, and Texas. The Pepper Commission report documented the problems of the 33 million medically uninsured Americans but offered no solution or payment source. The access issue will have to become a top-three public issue before it finally gets the public attention—and resolution—it deserves. National health reform was still three to five years from solution as America entered the 1990s.

Looking Forward: Every Trustee Is a Futurist

Trustees should be their own futurists. Trustees should look for trends and design locally appropriate strategies in response. Remember that health care is a *local* business. Compare the macrotrends in this book with your own forecasts. Local hospital trustees, not outside experts, are most likely to be right about the future of their local markets. Take all expert forecasts with a grain of salt, and chart a preferred future for your own hospital and health system, guided by local values and community needs.

References

Coile, Russell C., Jr. 1991. "Health Care 1991: Top Ten Trends for the Health Industry." *Hospital Strategy Report* (January): 1–8.

———. 1992. "Health Care 1992: Top 10 Trends for the Health Field." *Hospital Strategy Report* (January): 1–8.

———. 1986. *The New Hospital: Future Strategies for a Changing Industry.* Rockville, MD: Aspen Publishers.

———. 1990. *The New Medicine: Reshaping Medical Practice and Healthcare Delivery.* Rockville, MD: Aspen Publishers.

Davidson, Richard. 1993. "Networks and Our Next Step: Communicating the Hospital Community's Vision on Reform." *Hospitals* (20 January): 22.

Dychtwald, Ken. 1989. *Age Wave: The Challenges and Opportunities of an Aging America.* Los Angeles, CA: Jeremy Tarcher.

Johnson, Kathryn E. 1992. "A Healthcare Odyssey." *Healthcare Forum Journal* 35 (May/June): 8.

Naisbitt, John. 1982. *Megatrends: Ten New Directions Transforming Our Lives.* New York: Warner Books.

1

The New Governance: Creating the Board of the Future to Manage the Hospital of the Future

The hospital of the future needs the board of the future! Smaller, smarter, savvy and strategic . . . that is the profile of governance for progressive hospitals and health systems. Hospital boards are changing, but not fast enough. The shift toward "corporate" boards for America's hospitals and health systems needs to accelerate.

—Russell C. Coile, Jr. (1991)

The 1990s is a window of opportunity for ambulatory care, managed care contracting, hospital-based medical groups, and dominating markets for inpatient specialty centers. The ability to move quickly and decisively is critical to success, *if* the hospital's board is ready.

Effective governance is the key to building the health care organization of tomorrow. A hospital or health system's board of directors is the accelerator of expansion and the brake of restraint. Board policy defines the limits of growth, the speed of change, and the direction of the organization. No dynamic administrator can outrun a board. Neither can a defensive executive hide behind the board to avoid the forces of change. Hospital and health system chief executive officers (CEOs) must heed this message: *The keystone of strategic management is the hospital's board.*

Hospital boards are changing, but maybe not fast enough. In the eighties, almost half of America's hospitals experienced some form of corporate restructuring, according to a 1989 study by Korn/Ferry International (Heuerman 1989). Mergers, reorganizations, and affiliations have resulted in more complex organizations. The result has been to load heavy new responsibilities on the board and create new tensions in the governance triangle of the board, CEO, and medical staff.

Given health care's volatile environment, 70 percent of hospital CEOs report they rely more heavily on their boards now than in the past (Heuerman 1989). These findings should come as no surprise to most hospital administrators, especially the 25 percent of CEOs who say they rely "substantially more" on their boards today than in the past. The survey reported that board leadership is improving in 72 percent of hospitals sampled, and most hospital CEOs are pleased by their board's assistance. In addition, fully 91 percent of health care executives believe their board's input has contributed significantly to better corporate results (Heuerman 1989).

How do CEOs best use their boards? According to the Korn/Ferry study (Heuerman 1989), CEOs value trustee participation in serving as sounding boards for new ideas and direction, strategic planning, financial planning, setting the corporate mission, and communicating with the medical staff.

The pace of change during the 1990s will be continuous. Can today's boards keep up? According to John Witt in *Building A Better Hospital Board* (1987):

> The voluntary hospital organization has been the most successful not-for-profit enterprise created in our society. . . . Will your board be capable of changing how it operates? . . . To keep up with management and medicine, boards will need to move boldly in new directions. The shift to better, stronger boards of directors has already begun, and it will gain momentum in this age when health care is increasingly judged more by its financial performance than by its compassion.

Will the hospital boards of the 1990s effectively manage the challenges of governance? Perhaps. The salient issues for hospitals in the decade ahead are clear from the Korn/Ferry (Heuerman 1989) study—improving profitability, strategic planning, and physician relations, as well as quality and capital. It is less clear that today's hospital boards are equipped and organized to provide needed counsel and leadership for the 1990s. The financial turmoil of today's hospitals suggests that boards of trustees must change if tomorrow's health care organizations are to be successful.

Adopting the Corporate Model

Two surveys of boards of directors indicate that hospital boards are taking on the characteristics of the corporate model. Hospital and corporate boards are growing closer, according to the Spencer-Stuart Board Index for 1990, which reports on 1,000 private sector corporations, and the AHA (Earle 1990). Examples of the trends include creating holding companies (corporate restructuring), involving "inside directors" (hospital CEOs and physicians), and executive compensation contracting for hospital CEOs and senior management linked to financial performance.

In other ways, hospitals and their private sector counterparts show increasing similarities. Hospital boards are becoming smaller, down from 20 in the early 1980s to 16, which is closer to the median size of corporate boards, 14 (Earle 1990). The average age of directors is 61 for both groups. Both types of boards are spending more time on committees, reportedly attending more than 20 meetings per year; both boards are emphasizing similar issues of financial performance, strategic planning, and capital (Earle 1990).

While progress has been made in the direction of corporate governance by U.S. hospitals, the critical factor of lack of expertise on hospital boards continues. Hospital and health system boards should be composed of 9–13 members, with 5–7 outside directors chosen for their expertise in managing large corporations.

Five Most Important Functions of Governance in the 1990s

Function 1: Financial Performance

Are today's hospital and health system boards savvy enough to monitor finances? Overseeing the financials will be the number one responsibility of boards during the 1990s, according to the 1991 Delphi survey conducted by Arthur Andersen and the American College of Healthcare Executives. Analysis of *Trustee*'s content for the past three years alone confirms that trustees are spending an increasing amount of time on financial affairs.

Hospital and health system finances will bear close watching in the 1990s. The 1990s will be a time of mounting financial pressures on hospitals. Indeed, according to Health Care Investment Analysts, the number of "financially distressed" hospitals rose from 10 percent in 1990 to 19 percent in 1992 (Health Care Investment Analysts 1992). The data raise a tough question: Are hospital boards effective in their function of budgetary oversight?

If hospital boards are to be constructive in providing financial stewardship, they must have an informed finance committee that "knows the numbers," and have continuous reporting of reliable, timely indicators of key aspects of financial performance.

A strong hospital finance committee is composed of five to seven trustees with business skills and a knowledge of health care reimbursement. This is probably the most important committee assignment on the board. Monthly finance meetings provide a continuing review of financial performance in the last month, quarter, and budget year-to-date. An informed finance committee regularly looks at scenarios of future financial indicators developed by the chief financial officer (CFO). To avoid surprises, this must be accompanied by forecasts of key ratios and indicators for the next quarter and year forward.

Some hospital and system boards spend too much time on finances, and yet not enough. This is a paradox of "data overload" versus informed financial assessment at the board level. Hard-to-read overheads of computer spreadsheets leave many hospital and system boards bewildered rather than reassured that finances are on track. Ideally, every month boards should review a short set of financial indicators that provide insight into the hospital's financial strengths and weaknesses.

What are the key indicators for board attention? Those who direct multihospital systems have recommended that boards regularly review profitability, liquidity, and capital structure (Ashworth 1989).

The two most important *profitability* indicators are net income as a percentage of gross revenues and return on equity. Both of these indicators should be compared to agreed upon standards and financial targets that the board has set at the beginning of the hospital or health system's budget year. The board should also be looking at the profitability of key payers such as Medicare, and high-profit programs such as cardiology.

Two critical ratios of *liquidity* are the current and acid-test ratios. Because of the tight cash position of many hospitals, the most important financial indicators are the amount of cash available to meet the annual debt service requirements and the number of days outstanding in patient accounts receivable.

For hospitals with a sophisticated understanding of the *capital structure* in financial success, it is essential to continuously monitor the debt-to-equity ratio and total debt to total asset ratio, compared with the hospital's standards and expectations for these critical indicators. At least the hospital's finance committee must understand how the hospital will finance its future needs for operating and development capital—from internal sources (operating profits) and debt (bonds). Given a growing reliance on debt, the impact of debt service on hospital profitability is becoming a critical success factor.

The board's financial accountability. Two financial problems common to today's hospitals can be directly traced to their boards—"slippage" of profitability and the inability to terminate unprofitable programs. When a hospital begins to experience "slippage" in financial indicators, it's imperative that the problems be addressed immediately. Waiting three to six months for additional data can be disastrous when the hospital is losing $100,000–500,000 a month. Experienced hospital finance experts believe that general financial expertise is available on most hospital boards. What is not available among lay trustees is a more sophisticated understanding of health care revenue sources. Boards need to understand the impact of Medicare financing and managed care reimbursement policies, two of the most volatile dimensions of health care financing today.

The inability to terminate unsuccessful programs in a timely manner is the other common financial problem. A good board has to support—that is, invest—in programs that complement or are central to the hospital's mission. The board must also be tough-minded in deciding to downsize, divest, or terminate programs that cannot be self-supporting and that require subsidy. One New England medical center facing a $2 million deficit could not address the underlying problems—a $1 million operating loss in obstetrics and two satellite ambulatory care centers that required heavy subsidies. But the problem was the board. It could not face making difficult choices that would visibly affect the hospital's reputation in the community. Was this hospital's board sufficiently professional? Or should it have been replaced?

Function 2: Competitive Position

Too many hospital CEOs play their strategy cards close to the vest. It is time to bring the board into strategy formation. The changing times demand it. Revolutionary change in health care has created a business environment in which hospitals must chart the future, plot strategy, develop innovative approaches, and monitor the needs of the consumer. But who is responsible for setting strategy and repositioning the hospital? It should be the board, according to Reg Balantyne, CEO of Phoenix, Arizona's Presbyterian Medical Center (Balantyne and Sadowy 1988). The board of trustees taking responsibility for strategy and innovation requires a stretch of the imagination for most hospital CEOs. Balantyne and Hal Sadowy, the Medical Center's vice president for strategic planning, demonstrate the importance of high trustee involvement in strategy and innovation, as shown in Figure 1.1.

Figure 1.1   Trustee Involvement in Strategy and Innovation

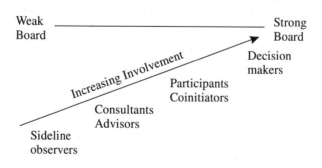

Reprinted from *Trustee*, Vol. 41, No. 4, by permission, April. © 1988, American Hospital Publishing, Inc.

The board's role in strategic thinking can fall anywhere from passivity to dominance. "Rubber-stamp" boards do what they are told, based on the limited information that management spoon-feeds them. At the other end of the spectrum is the strong board, often led by an influential board chair or officers. Neither extreme is desirable, although a strong board is clearly preferable. The middle ground is the most productive arena for a strategic relationship between CEO and board.

Hospital and health system boards can play several key roles in strategy formulation.

- *Trustees are environmental assessors.* Theoretically, no one in the hospital knows the community better than board members, bringing years—often decades—of local experience to the board. They should be tapped to assess the future economic prospects of the market area, its opportunities, and threats, for as the community goes (whether growing or shrinking), so goes the hospital.

- *Trustees are focus group participants.* The board is a representative focus group of community opinion in developing programs and improving services. Test new ideas and directions with the board.

- *Trustees are opinion leaders.* Board members are often leaders of key stakeholder constituencies in the community and represent groups whose opinions are of significance in charting new strategies. Tap into the groups these trustees represent.

- *Trustees are constituency representatives.* Trustees can help sell hospital strategies and plans to the community—for example, a capital campaign, expansion into a new territory, or the need for a parking structure. Use the political clout of trustees.

- *Trustees are strategic advisors.* From their business and leadership experience, trustees can advise on the feasibility of new business strategies such as corporate restructuring, diversification, or opening a "second campus."

- *Trustees are political consultants.* Savvy board members can lend their political expertise to the hospital in terms of strategy such as gaining planning commission approval or state bond financing. Trustees should take high-visibility roles in selling hospital needs to political representatives.

Ideally, trustees present their ideas in a dialogue with management. The best strategy is worked out in frank discussions between the two. The board advises, and management implements.

Managing crises. Crisis management in these turbulent times is increasingly becoming a board function. The solution may not be to "fire the coach." In many instances, the need for change begins with the board of trustees. Management consultants believe that hospitals who want to reposition themselves for change must begin by "leveling the playing field" for key stakeholders—board, medical staff, and management. Repositioning the hospital or system is a team-leadership process as much as a strategic activity. The need for repositioning is widespread as hospitals continue to face considerable fiscal pressure. Operational profit margins were "thin" as hospitals entered the 1990s, averaging under 1 percent during the period 1991–1992. One in five U.S. hospitals are struggling to maintain fiscal viability. In 1991, some 19 percent of U.S. hospitals were characterized as "financially distressed" (Health Care Investment Analysts 1992).

Given the need for repositioning, Chirchirillo and Rindler (1990) recommend that boards

- Form a five-member repositioning leadership committee comprised of two trustees with business skills, two from the medical staff, and the CEO.
- Detect "distressers" among key stakeholders—for example, employee/medical staff dissatisfaction over an expensive advertising campaign conducted while the hospital was laying off staffers.
- Clear the air regarding frequent complaints and breakdowns in key systems such as billing, accounts receivable, ancillary reporting, and medical records.
- Identify factions among the board, such as trustees who are loyal to the CEO.
- Encourage trustee leadership that responds aggressively to the crisis and revitalizes the organization with a positive "can do" spirit.

Most often it has been the board that must be brought up to speed before the hospital can launch into significantly new directions. All parties in the governance triangle must have an equal knowledge of the hospital's internal situation and external realities. In too many instances, boards of trustees are substantially less informed than the medical leadership or administration.

Function 3: CEO Evaluation

CEO turnover in America's hospitals has become an epidemic. Frequent CEO turnover was one of the most visible characteristics of the "turbulent 1980s" for health care. From 1983 when the turnover percent averaged 12.8, America's hospitals replaced their executive with increasing frequency, topping out at 24.2 percent in 1987 (Wesbury, Williams, and Carver 1991). More recent data from the American College of Healthcare Executives (ACHE) in a national survey with the AHA and Heidrick and Struggles,

Inc., (1991) indicates that CEO turnover has restabilized, averaging 12.8 in 1990, after almost a decade of volatility.

CEO evaluation is a critical board responsibility. Fully one-third of departing hospital CEOs were asked to leave by their boards, the ACHE (1991) survey indicates. Reasons for termination included dissatisfaction with performance targets, opposing directions in hospital strategy, differences in leadership style, and personality conflicts. But, on average, two of three CEOs left voluntarily. The ACHE (1991) study lends some insight to turnovers initiated by CEOs who quit or found new positions and were not fired. These CEOs cited the following as reasons for their turnover: value differences between the CEO and board; the CEO was task-oriented, not relationship-oriented; lack of support from board and/or subordinates; lack of clarity about board expectations for CEO; insufficient latitude for CEO decision making; inadequate compensation; and low involvement in other community affairs.

The high level of executive turnover has made it difficult for a number of hospitals to maintain any sustained strategic direction. Many business consultants believe it takes five years to effect major change in a company; that is clearly impossible where CEO durability is barely two or three years.

Contracting with CEOs. To encourage CEO risk-taking, hospitals should offer contracts that make performance expectations explicit and provide sufficient stability to get a long-term commitment from both board and CEO (*Trustee* 1988). Since 1982, the American College of Healthcare Executives has encouraged negotiation of employment contracts, and its recommendations, as described in *Contracts for Healthcare Executives* (1987), for hospital CEO employment contracts are to:

- Provide realistic position descriptions and measurable performance criteria
- State explicitly a term of three to five years; alternatively use a "rolling contract" that runs for a specific period (renewable) without a formal termination date
- List among duties level of authority and reporting requirements; avoid "laundry list" of functions
- State compensation as a minimum, not maximum, and avoid specific reference to future salary increases
- Include termination for cause related to competency and performance; expect to see more noncompete and arbitration clauses
- Negotiate severance agreement for a term of 12–24 months.

Negotiating employment contracts is now frequently extended to other senior management positions, such as chief operation officer (COO), CFO, and vice president for patient care. Remember that employment contracts are financial agreements, not a substitute for a professional relationship.

Because evaluating a CEO is one of any board's most important responsibilities, it's critical that boards do it equitably or well. But few boards do. A study by one executive search firm (Stefl, Tucker, and Halstead 1989) sheds new light on the responsibility of CEO evaluation. What characteristics do the chairs of hospital boards seek in new CEOs and expect from incumbent executives? This survey found: (1) personal characteristics were most highly rated, including leadership, communication, personal confidence, and self-esteem; (2) a commitment to quality and high personal ethics were the second highest–rated set of factors for CEO evaluation; (3) business management and strategic planning fell in the middle rank of desired characteristics. The board chairs suggested that financial and market skills could be found in strong subordinates; and (4) experience was relatively less important than leadership ability, even over specific experience in marketing, managing joint ventures, and medical staff relations.

Trustees cannot afford to neglect their responsibility to evaluate the CEO—it may be *the* critical success factor in a hospital or system's performance.

Function 4: Clinical Efficiency/Quality

Hospitals boards have the legal responsibility for quality, but do they have the expertise? Probably not. Hospital boards are generally poorly informed or organized to review the quality of a hospital's care or the clinical effectiveness of its medical staff. Most trustees have no clinical background, and hospital data systems provide little useful, comparable information on which to evaluate quality. Boards are, however, much better equipped to judge the cost (efficiency) of the hospital's performance than assessing the quality (clinical effectiveness) of care. This does not mean that boards should abdicate overseeing quality. Rather, they should concentrate on what they can potentially do best: monitor the relative cost of care in their institution yet ensure that quality assurance, medical staff credentialing, and risk-management programs protect patient safety.

Economic credentialing—the board's review of cost as well as quality experience in renewing medical privileges—may be the wave of the future. Focusing on the cost of every physician's care is essential if hospitals are to remain financially viable. Cover stories by *Hospitals* and *Modern Healthcare* have reported the mounting concern by hospital CEOs and trustees that they must hold their physicians accountable for the costs as well as quality of their care. Despite the publicity, there is more "smoke than fire" in the economic credentialing issue so far. Only a handful of physicians have had the renewal of their privileges reduced due to their "economic performance."

Economic assessment of medical staff includes: comparative profiles of the hospital's costs for the 20 most commonly performed inpatient and ambulatory procedures, as compared with other hospitals of similar size and complexity (patient severity); and comparative profiles of performance on each physician's five most frequently performed procedure or admission, as compared with other physicians on the hospital staff and those treating similar patients. The board has a mechanism for such performance evaluation— the organized medical staff. Each clinical department (and its chief) should be held responsible for cost profiles and the periodic assessment of all physicians working in each department. Discussions of economic credentialing are drawing nervous criticism from medical staffs, but soon medical staffs will have to transform from a "guild" to a management organization.

Function 5: Stakeholder Representation

Public and political representation is a primary function of trusteeship on hospital boards. Trustees are representatives of important stakeholders for the hospital. A well-balanced board brings a broad base of viewpoints to decision making. Trustees are liaisons between the hospital and the community. Each trustee represents a different set of opinions, expertise, and values held by segments of the community. Trustees can speak on behalf of the hospital with many community organizations, listening and bringing back their comments. A presentation on the need for a linear accelerator or lithotrypter, for example, is all the more effective when it is made by a lay trustee who knows the clinical contribution of these high-cost technologies. Business trustees can speak to local businesses about the hospital's efforts to manage costs and keep community health expenditures down. The believability factor is high when trustees speak on behalf of the hospital. Spokesperson trustees are highly influential in political representation. A number of trustees have established political linkages. The AHA's trustee advocacy office cites four advantages for trustee involvement in public affairs: familiarity with the political process, community perspective on the board, established political connections, and increased potential for coalitions (McEntee 1988).

Hospitals have discovered the value of using trustees as political advocates. Trustees presumably have a higher interest than paid management or consultants. In fact, trustee involvement in Medicare advocacy is a major reason why Congress has taken a somewhat protective stance toward Medicare hospital payments, despite continuing efforts by the Health Care Financing Administration (HCFA) to cut hospital reimbursement.

A Profile of Governance Today

The average community hospital board has only 14 members, smaller than usually thought, according to a survey of 3,166 U.S. hospitals (Longo et al. 1990). The snapshot of American hospital governance was sponsored by the Hospital Research and Education Trust (HRET) of the AHA with Spencer Stuart, a health care search firm. Conducted in 1989, the survey showed that community nonprofit boards were often larger, averaging 17 members; nonfederal public hospitals and investor-owned hospitals were smaller, averaging 8 and 10 members, respectively (Longo et al. 1990). The survey also found that as a group, hospital trustees are older. A majority, some 51 percent, are between the ages of 51 and 70; 42 percent represent the next leadership generation, ages 31–50. Given the difficult economic and regulatory climate for managing today's hospitals, it is not surprising that 37 percent have business backgrounds. More than one in four hospitals trustees (26 percent) have health care training and experience (Longo et al. 1990).

Seeking, Selecting, and Compensating a Trustee

What qualifications and interests do today's hospitals seek in a trustee? According to Longo et al. (1990), the first criterion is interest and commitment to the hospital (41 percent of responding hospitals). The financial skills (18 percent) and values (14 percent) of the trustee are the next most important factors in selection. Other responses included community involvement and political influence in the community (each 7 percent) and knowledge of health care and its administration and "other" (each 3 percent). Some of the more traditional factors appear to be losing significance: geographic proximity and the ability to represent a constituency are no longer substantial criteria; the time available and the ability to raise money for the hospital were rated barely significant.

The intensely competitive environment of hospitals is clearly a driving factor in selecting a hospital trustee. The criteria listed above were consistently ranked across hospital type, except with respect to for-profit hospitals, which differed in one aspect: investor-owned facilities ranked knowledge of health care and its administration as the third most important consideration in a hospital trustee.

Competency, not loyalty, should be the first criterion for selection of future hospital trustees. U.S. hospitals have their priorities backward when it comes to choosing the best directors to advise the hospital or health system on its future; the current reliance on trustee commitment suggests that board members are being selected based on their loyalty to management. While an effective board-CEO relationship is essential, CEO support by the board should be earned by management performance, not by friendliness with and loyalty to directors.

In a competitive environment, all trustees should have financial business skills. That should be a given. Board members should be selected for their specific expertise and experience. First among these should be a knowledge of health care and the health industry.

Most $50–500 million companies do not function without a paid board of directors. Despite their growth and complexity, most U.S. hospitals and multihospital systems still operate on the voluntary model of governance. According to Korn/Ferry's 1989 national study (Heuerman 1989), fully 97 percent of hospital boards do not compensate their members. However, there can be other benefits of trustee membership: A number of hospitals reimburse travel expenses, provide private hospital rooms and VIP services, pay spouse travel to trustee educational programs, and cover director liability insurance. But few hospitals—only 3 percent—now offer some form of monetary compensation. But these attitudes on trustee compensation may be shifting. More than one-third, some 37 percent, of CEOs surveyed by Korn/Ferry (Heuerman 1989), believe that trustee reimbursement is appropriate. Indeed, the differences are diminishing between hospital and health systems compared with private-sector corporations, especially in the critical issues of financial performance, financial planning, and capital access.

To attract good trustees, hospitals may have to pay them. Already, 67 percent of hospital executives report having trouble locating and recruiting board members, and it's worsening, according to 60 percent of these CEOs (Heuerman 1989). Partly as a result, there is less "new blood" infusing hospital boards. Korn/Ferry's governance survey found that only 31 percent of hospitals added new members in 1988, and 43 percent added only one or two new directors (Heuerman 1989).

Among parent corporations of restructured hospitals and health systems in particular, the switch to corporate boards is being made. Smaller boards with professional directors who have expertise in health care management are considered essential to success in managing their more complex organizations. Trustee compensation may accompany this trend to recruit and retain the high quality of directorship required by tomorrow's hospitals and health systems.

Physicians on Boards

Hospital–medical staff relations are a key dimension of hospital governance. Nevertheless, physicians remained woefully underrepresented on hospital boards, according to Longo et al. (1990). Physician representation on a national sample of all hospital boards averaged only 17 percent of the trustees; for-profit hospitals, however, recognized the benefit of high-level medical participation in governance, averaging 43 percent participation by physicians; community nonprofit hospitals (16 percent participation) and public hospitals (11 percent participation) were much more skittish about physicians on the board.

Although physician participation on hospital boards has been required by the Joint Commission for Accreditation of Healthcare Organizations

(JCAHO) since 1986, the number of doctors among hospital trustees remains limited. This may in part be due to one of the board's functions, overseeing quality through the task of physician credentialing. The granting of medical staff privileges is shifting from an emphasis on "paper" (credentials and adherence to hospital rules) to one of "performance" (admissions, volume, use of ancillary services, and cost of patient care). As this shift occurs, the board's level of expertise in its core business—medical and health services— will be enhanced. Clinical experts will assist hospital boards in evaluating new strategies for improving clinical performance.

The Three-Legged Stool

Who will lead the hospitals and health systems of tomorrow? The CEO? Chair of the board? Chief of the medical staff? Textbook theory of hospital administration has called for a balanced relationship among all three—the classic "three-legged stool" of governance. This model must be renewed in new conceptual framework and built on the foundation of a strong board of trustees.

In *Building a Better Hospital Board*, John Witt (1987) argues for an effective leadership role for hospital trustees, constructed on a modern notion of corporate directorship. This ideal model seldom existed in the past as the American hospital's history shows. Witt reports that from 1900 to the 1950s, many hospitals were founded and led by a strong chairperson or highly motivated community physician. Because hospital administration professionalized and became more widespread during the 1960s and 1970s, most of today's hospitals today are led by CEOs trained in health care management.

This three-legged stool model of hospital governance is obsolete and should be abandoned as a conceptual model for defining the governance responsibilities of board, executive, and medical staff. Frankly, the model probably never truly worked except on paper. As Witt (1987) notes, "Every organization I have ever seen had a strong leader, an individual who claimed 'ownership' of the institution's mission, purpose, or major program." What's needed, Witt reports, is a strong committee.

How has the three-legged stool model failed to govern America's voluntary hospitals?

- Leadership by committee—Most of the nation's nonprofit hospitals are still governed by the same sort of committee that was formed at the institutions' founding.

- Committees spawning committees—If anything has changed in hospital governance in the past 25 years, it is that hospital boards have increased the number of members through committees.

- Not representative of community—Today's hospital boards are the same kind of well-intentioned mix of part-time volunteers drawn from the top social strata of the community as they were 40 years ago.
- Well-intentioned amateurs—What hospital trustees know about governance is typically learned at weekend seminars, and what boards know about the hospital's operating environment is often filtered or diluted by administration.
- Not knowing the business—Physicians and nurses, those who know most about the core business of hospitals, medical care, are usually given only token representation on boards of trustees.
- The fear of inside directors—Other key management representatives—from the areas of finance, operations, and marketing, for example—who would be "inside directors" in private-sector companies are seldom represented on their hospital's board.
- Hospitals as big business—This is hardly an effective leadership model for complex health care organizations where annual budgets of $50–200 million are commonplace and the hospital is often one of the top five employers in the community.

If the three-legged stool won't work, what will? John Carver (1990), president of Carver Governance Design, outlines this framework for a new model of governance. He suggests that hospitals

- Have "cradle" vision—The role of the board should be to hold the organizational vision in a primary position, with systematic encouragement to "think the unthinkable" and to dream.
- Explicitly address fundamental values—The governing board is the guardian of organizational values.
- Force an external focus—The board must be more concerned with needs and markets to guarantee an external responsiveness.
- Enable an outcome-driven organizing system—All functions and decisions must be made against the standard of purpose.
- Separate large issues from small—Ensure that large issues deserve first claim on policy setting and decision making.
- Force forward thinking—Thrust the majority of the board's thinking into the future.
- Enable productivity—Press boards to lead, not react.
- Facilitate diversity and unity—Optimize the richness of diversity in board composition and opinion, and assimilate that variety into one voice.
- Describe relationships to relevant constituencies—Define and represent constituencies.

- Balance overcontrol and undercontrol—Clarify those aspects of management that need tight versus loose control.

Carver (1990) laments the "empty rituals" of governance in both for-profit and nonprofit boards and calls for a new model of governance where vision can be the first order of business. Strong governance requires strong management in a true partnership. Boards need not be mired in the trivial, such as setting goals only for incremental improvement. Governance is long overdue for a rebirth; strategic leadership *is* exciting and accessible at the board level.

Governing the Three Waves of Change

Health care is undergoing rapid transition, driven by societal and economic changes. Cost-based hospital reimbursement and fee-for-service medicine are now in the past. Change is coming in three waves, according to consultant Barry Bader (1986): (1) triggered by Medicare adoption of prospective payment and DRGs in the early 1980s, most hospitals adjust to declining inpatient utilization, increased competition and cost-consciousness, and a growing emphasis on ambulatory care; (2) the rising popularity of managed care plans drives the creation of new forms of alternative delivery systems, multihospital networks, and physician-hospital organizations; and (3) the demands of the medically uninsured and soaring costs of medical care lead to national health reform. The nation faces the questions, What kind of a health care system do we want? and What is the role of government in achievement? New arrangements between buyers and sellers result in a multitiered health care system as hospitals seek to balance business goals and social values.

The governance model for the third wave will be based on ultimate accountability for improving the health status of the community. This model will not replace hospital and health system boards but will provide a coordinating force to improve community health. Bader (1986) suggests four types of models for providing this kind of community governance: *communications*—in its loosest form, it brings hospitals, community health agencies, employers, and government together to seek voluntary solutions to specific health issues using ad hoc task forces; *coalition*—broad-based health coalitions coordinate actions among purchasers, providers, government, and voluntary agencies in taking a problem-solving approach to issues, such as lack of health plan coverage for the unemployed; *multi-institutional health system*—another alternative governance model is the integrated health system, which would take contractual responsibility for meeting all the health and related needs of hundreds of thousands of "covered lives," in a managed competition scenario where a few very large health systems provide all care; and *regional health authority*—in a governmental system, such as the Canadian model, regional authorities have designated public jurisdiction to set health budgets, allocate capital, and coordinate local health care providers.

Looking Forward: Governance Works

Somehow, hospital governance works, but it still needs reform. Because of the efforts of dedicated board members, hospitals and systems grow and succeed despite the limitation of their governance model. Any critique of the current state of hospital governance must recognize the remarkable development of today's health organizations under such voluntary arrangements. The growth of today's $200 billion hospital industry is a tribute to the hard-working trustees of America's mostly voluntary health system. These trustees succeeded despite a governance model better suited to managing a fund-raising event than a multimillion-dollar enterprise.

It is no wonder that hospitals and health systems struggled in the 1980s to adjust to the changing environment of DRGs and managed care—after all, hospital governance in nonprofit hospitals is an anachronism and overdue for structural reform. In no other industry are $100 million companies run by committees of volunteers who are unpaid and undertrained for their functions.

Health system governance is marginally better, but even the best multihospital systems must frequently rely on retirees and others who can give their time. Ideally, health care systems should also involve CEOs of other companies who are actively managing their businesses in today's competitive environment and who would bring those experiences to bear within the health sector.

Corporate restructuring into health systems is a strong first step toward the corporate model in health care. In systems, parent company boards are smaller and usually comprised of more experienced board members. But as Stephen M. Shortell and his colleagues (1990) note, any progress from system development is frequently offset by systemwide confusion over the authority and prerogatives of local hospitals versus corporate offices. Adding another layer of governance and administration has seldom resulted in the intended benefits of system efficiency, centralized management, or consolidated strategy.

The wave of hospital corporate restructuring that took place in the 1970s and the 1980s has not eliminated the need for governance reform. If anything, the development of today's multiunit health organizations and multihospital systems has only accelerated the necessity of refashioning the governance structure. America's voluntary health system badly needs a new governance model to effectively manage the evolution of hospitals and health systems for the twenty-first century.

Strategies

1. **Incorporate a corporate board model**. The need is clear and the time is now. Corporate-style governance for hospitals and health systems is essential to success in the 1990s. A small, knowledgeable board can make quick decisions where time (and timing) is a factor—for example, managed care contracting, technology investment, ambulatory expansion, and merger/acquisition of other facilities. Boards should be restructured with seven to eleven members. Each board member should bring a specific expertise to the decision-making group and provide representation to key stakeholders in the community or market served.

2. **Recruit inside directors**. Every hospital and system board should have at least three to five inside directors, including the CEO, CFO, COO, vice president for patient care/director of nursing, and vice president for medical affairs/medical director. The substantial presence of inside directors ensures that the board is fully informed in all the important dimensions of hospital and system performance. This is critical when many key decisions facing hospital and system boards in the 1990s will require substantial expertise in finance and clinical affairs (medicine and nursing). The presence of inside directors ensures that board strategy is well directed and that policy is implemented quickly and completely. Board–management–medical staff communication issues are minimized and trust is enhanced when these key individuals are policymakers at the board level.

3. **Compensate directors**. By all means, pay "outside" directors and members of the medical staff for their time and expertise. Members of the board need to treat their decision-making responsibilities for the hospital or system with the highest professional attitude. Their expertise will be an important success factor in the board's strategy setting and financial overseeing. This will not fundamentally undermine the leadership of nonprofit corporations. Only in successfully managing health costs and providing quality care can America's hospitals preserve the voluntary nonprofit base of the U.S. health system.

4. **Elect system CEOs to be chairs of the boards**. Electing the CEO to the chair should be a mark of the advancing sophistication of America's health systems. Managing a $100–500 million health care corporation should be a full-time activity. America's health systems must incorporate the concept of the "inside" chair of the board by promoting the president/CEO and delegating operational responsibilities to a president/COO at the system level to ensure appropriate experience and leadership in the external (strategy) and internal (management) dimensions.

References

American College of Healthcare Executives. 1987. *Contracts for Healthcare Executives*, 2d ed. Chicago: The College.

American College of Healthcare Executives, with the American Hospital Association and Heidrick and Struggles, Inc. 1991. *Hospital Chief Executive Officer Turnover: 1981–1990*. Chicago: The College.

Arthur Andersen & Company, and the American College of Healthcare Executives. 1991. *The Future of Healthcare: Physician and Hospital Relationships*. Chicago: The College.

Ashworth, R. B. 1989. "On Budgetary Oversight." *Trustee* (June): 6–7.

Bader, B. 1986. *Three Waves of Change: Hospital Board Responsibilities in the New Health Care Environment*. Washington, DC: Bader & Associates.

Balantyne, R. M. III, and H. S. Sadowy. 1988. "Innovative Thinking: Whose Job?" *Trustee* (April): 28.

Carver, J. 1990. *Boards That Make a Difference*. San Francisco: Jossey-Bass Publishers.

Chirchirillo, A., and M. E. Rindler. 1990. "Hospital Repositioning: The Leadership Imperative." *Trustee* (October): 14–15.

Coile, R. C., Jr. 1991. "The New Governance: Five Most Critical Trustee Functions in the 1990s." *Hospital Strategy Report* 3, no. 11 (September): 1–7.

Earle, P. W. 1990. "Hospital and Corporate Boards: Growing Closer." *Trustee* (September): 20.

Health Care Investment Analysts. 1992. *Distressed Hospitals Quarterly*. Baltimore, MD: The Analysts.

Heuerman, J. N. 1989. "Trends and Changes in Hospital Boards." *Trustee* (October): 28.

Longo, D. R., et al. 1990. "Profile of Hospital Governance: A Report from the Nation's Hospitals." *Trustee* (May): 6–8.

McEntee, C. 1988. "Hospital Trustees: Natural Allies in Political Advocacy." *Trustee* (June): 13.

Shortell, S. M., E. M. Morrison, and B. Friedman. 1990. *Strategic Choices for America's Hospitals: Managing Change in Turbulent Times*. San Francisco: Jossey-Bass Publishers.

Stefl, M. E., S. L. Tucker, and F. A. Halstead. 1989. "What Makes an Effective CEO: The Board's Perspective." *Trustee* (April): 28.

Trustee. 1988. "Encourage CEO Risk-Taking with an Employment Contract." (June): 8–9.

Wesbury, S. A., Jr., A. Williams III, and M. D. Carver. 1991. "CEO Turnover: Study Findings Help Boards Solve the Puzzle." *Trustee* (May): 4–5.

Witt, J. 1987. *Building a Better Hospital Board*. Ann Arbor, MI: Health Administration Press.

2

Health Care Trends in the 1990s:
A Decade of Change for
America's Health Field

For this is the dawn of the Powershift Era. We live at a moment when the entire structure of power that held the world together is now disintegrating. A radically different structure of power is taking form. And this is happening at every level of human society. In the office, in the supermarket, at the bank, in the executive suite, in our churches, hospitals, schools, and homes, old patterns of power are fracturing along strange new lines.

—Alvin Toffler (1990)

The twenty-first century will soon be here. Much will happen before the year 2001. The nineties will be a time of growth and development for America's health field. In the next 10–20 years, an unprecedented level of demand for health services will be driven upward by the aging of the population and life-extending medical technology. National health expenditures are expected to reach $1 trillion by the mid-1990s and continue to rise. By the year 2000, health care may account for 18.1 percent of the GNP, with $1.7 trillion in health spending, according to an estimate by the U.S. Health Care Financing Administration (Waldo 1992).

High technology will be a driving force in health care's future. Hospitals will build high-technological medical institutes for major centers of excellence in cardiac care, cancer, and orthopedics—the diseases of aging. Subspecialties of medicine will have their own second-tier centers of excellence in arthritis, Alzheimer's, diabetes, kidney disease, neurology, and urology. The high-tech approaches will take direct aim at the expanding problems of old age, with applications of new technologies such as artificial organs, joint replacements, and genetically engineered therapies.

In addition, the aging of America will dramatically change long-term care. By the end of the nineties, one-third of nursing home patients will be short-stay patients, using nursing homes for recuperation from acute illness. As the high-tech products go into the home, cancers, pneumonia, and AIDS care will allow many more patients to receive modern medicine in their own beds, and to die there. By the year 2000, as many as 50 percent of the terminally ill will die at home, not in nursing homes or hospital intensive care units.

Health Care Forecasting for the Nineties

As is usually the case with change, it won't be smooth or painless. America has some difficult problems to overcome before a technologically advanced scenario of affordable health care can come to fruition. Managed care must retard the rate of health inflation to an annual rate of 7–8 percent, not the 10– 14 percent or higher experienced in the 1980s. Federal deficits of $250–300 billion experienced in the early 1990s will pressure the federal government to freeze or cut Medicare spending. Trustees should expect additional Medicare payment reforms for hospital capital payments, physician fees, and ambulatory care costs during the next five to seven years.

Additionally, a solution to the 35–40 million medically uninsured must be found. Ideally, a national program will be developed, rather than a patchwork of state laws and insurance pools. President Clinton's health reform proposal made national health insurance a major political issue, but easy or early agreement between Democrats and Republicans is unlikely. By 1995, Congress is likely to mandate employer-paid health benefits for all workers. Also, Medicaid will require reform to create a national system of benefits and eligibility. Provider payments from government, especially Medicaid, must reimburse reasonable costs or hospitals and physicians will refuse to treat public patients. Medicare's DRG hospital payment reform in 1983 financially squeezed many hospitals, some of which are still recovering. Physician payment reform under Medicare, which began in January 1992, struck physician incomes hard, and many fear a backlash, with physicians refusing to treat Medicare patients.

Small, rural, and financially distressed hospitals will continue to be economically vulnerable. It's expected that many more hospitals will close or convert to other uses in the decade ahead. More than 25 percent of hospital CEOs believe their hospitals could fail, according to a 1992 national survey by Deloitte & Touche. The good news is that the predicted failure rate is well below the 48 percent reported in the same survey in 1988, when 75–80 hospitals were closing a year (Deloitte & Touche 1992).

Health Care's Ten Trends for the 1990s

Despite the continuing turbulence in the health care industry, signs of restabilization are emerging. A hopeful forecast is for the 1990s to be a decade of change and growth for most of America's hospitals. The leading trends that will reshape U.S. hospitals and the health industry in the decade ahead are discussed.

Trend 1: Falling Demand, Continued Profitability

As health care enters the era of national reform, the outlook for hospital performance in the short term (1994–1995) looks promising. Beyond 1994, national health reform price controls and market reforms will accelerate declines in acute care demand. Hospitals can retain profitability through efficiency, particularly in managing clinical costs.

The following dimensions of performance will greatly affect health care in 1994–1995—profitability, expenses, staffing, inpatient demand, and ambulatory care. Hospital profitability will continue in the range of 5.5 to 6.5 percent (see Table 2.1). Hospital profits rose in 1992, due to strong revenue growth of 10.2 percent, according to an AHA national survey (1992c). Net patient (operating) margins continued under 1 percent, but total net margin was a healthy 5.5 percent. All these figures were up from 1991 levels (American Hospital Association 1992c).

With economic experts claiming that the recession is winding down, supply, wage, and capital expenses should continue to decrease, at least during the period 1994–1995. Expenses were up by 9.7 percent in early 1992 (American Hospital Association 1992b). As is typical in an expanding economy, supply costs and interest expenses should remain low in the short term but then begin to climb by 1995.

Table 2.1 U.S. Hospital Performance: Forecast of Selected Indicators, 1993–1994

Performance Indicator	1991	1992*	1993–1994†
Net patient margin	(−3.5)%	1.2%	1.5–2.5%
Total net margin	4.3	6.0	5.5–6.5
Inpatient net revenue	7.2§	8.3	7.0–8.0
Outpatient net review	17.3§	16.4	16.0–18.0
Total expenses	10.5	9.8	9.5–10.5
Admissions	(−0.4)	(−0.4)	(−0.5)–(−1.5)
Average length of stay	(−1.0)	(−1.8)	(−1.5)–(−2.5)
Inpatient days	(−0.4)	(−2.1)	(−1.5)–(−2.5)

Source: Russell C. Coile, Jr.'s "Hospital Performance in 1993: An 'Upside' Forecast on the Eve of National Health Reform," *Hospital Strategy Report* 4 (January), published by Aspen Publishers, Inc. © 1992.
*First six months only (January–June 1992).
†Forecast by Health Forecasting Group, Santa Clarita, CA, December 1992.
§Data for first six months only (January–June 1991).

Wage costs were lower because of the recession, but this has a down side. As the economy improves, pressure for wage improvements and easing of tight staffing limits may result in slowly rising labor costs in the mid-1990s. Full-time equivalent (FTE) levels have been rising, by 1.4 percent in 1992, as hospitals shifted from part-time employees to full-time workers (American Hospital Association 1992c).

Inpatient demand continues to slip, after briefly stabilizing in 1990. Hospital days fell by more than 2.1 percent in 1991, slowing somewhat to −0.6 percent in 1992 (American Hospital Association 1992a). Hospital inpatient demand has further to fall in the mid-1990s. Medicare (age 65 and over) length of stay is still at 10.8 days in the mid-Atlantic, compared with 6.9 days in the Pacific region (American Hospital Association 1992a).

Hospital finances are becoming increasingly dependent on expanding demand for ambulatory care. Hospital outpatient visits rose by 6.5 percent in 1992, and it is this growth that is compensating for the loss of inpatient business (American Hospital Association 1992c). Hospital inpatient admits continued to slip by 0.6 percent in 1992, as they did in 1991, when admissions fell to just over 31 million. Patient days fell by 2.1 percent, compared to a loss of 1.4 percent for 1991 when days sunk to under 233 million, and length of inpatient stays dropped another 1.8 percent, a steeper rate than the 1.0 percent of 1991, where stays averaged 7.17. Ambulatory activity more than compensated as outpatient visits soared by 6.4 percent in 1992. As of the end of 1991, some 52.3 percent of all hospital-based surgeries were ambulatory (American Hospital Association 1992a).

As a result of these indicators, hospital boards must closely monitor performance, and management must have contingency plans to adjust to shifting demand. Many hospitals are unprepared for the financial consequences of significant reductions in length of stay. For many, the strategy is to emphase ambulatory care to offset inpatient decline.

Trend 2: Age Wave

The aging of America continues to be the most significant catalyst on America's health system. For example, in 1989, more than 50 percent of all hospital days were covered by Medicare, and by the mid-1990s, the percent of Medicare days in the average community hospital may reach 55 percent. Medicare HMOs are expected to grow rapidly in the 1990s. Only 1 million of Medicare's 33 million eligibles are currently enrolled in an HMO, but successful managed care plans are expanding their marketing efforts. For example, PacifiCare Health Systems, one of the largest Medicare risk contractors in southern California, launched a campaign in 1993 to enroll 140,000 new Medicare members in northern California. Another major Medicare HMO, FHP International, is introducing its Medicare HMO plan in

New Mexico and northern California. FHP already serves 260,000 Medicare HMO subscribers in five states and Guam (Kenkel 1993).

Although those over age 65 are the fastest growing segment of the population, the age wave is just beginning, as shown in Figure 2.1. The share of the population that is elderly will grow to 15 percent in 2010 and 22 percent in 2030. Although they comprise only 12 percent of the population today, America's senior citizens consume 36 percent of U.S. health spending (*Medical Benefits* 1993). The oldest Americans—those over age 85—spend twice as much on hospital care as the "young elderly," ages 65–69. By the year 2010, the number of Americans over age 85 will double.

Figure 2.1 Growth of Population Aged 65 and Over

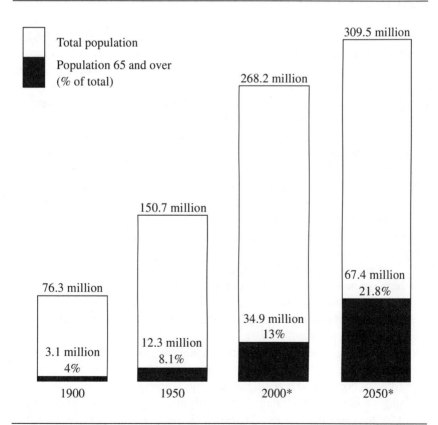

Adapted and reprinted with the permission of Ken Dychtwald, as it appeared in *Age Wave: The Challenges and Opportunities of an Aging America*, published by Jeremy P. Tarcher © 1989.
Source: U.S. Census Bureau reports.
*Projected figures.

In an attempt to contain these expenditures, employers and medigap insurers are trying to improve the health habits of the elderly. A study of 4,712 Bank of America retirees had impressive results—experiencing 20 percent cost reductions in reported health expenses per year for seniors who switched to healthier lifestyles (Fries 1993). The two-year study demonstrates that health promotion intervention facilitates decreasing health costs, while improving health status in precisely those age groups in which the national health economic burden is greatest.

Hospitals too need a plan for elder care services. In many hospitals, older consumers are the most frequent patients and Medicare is the largest payer. Hospitals must plan and invest in their future with establishment of a continuum of elder care services.

Trend 3: Ambulatory Shift

As inpatient demand falls, ambulatory care will rise during the 1990s. Demand for ambulatory services will grow 6–10 percent on an annual basis, and some services will grow faster. Outpatient visits in U.S. hospitals are on a record pace, reaching 80 million visits per quarter for the first time in 1990, and growing at a 6–7 percent overall rate. Hospitals are competing hard in ambulatory surgery. The number of freestanding ambulatory surgeries rose 9 percent in 1992 to 1,696 facilities, as outpatient surgeries climbed to 2.87 million, an increase of 11.1 percent. By 1995, it is estimated that nearly 4 million procedures will be performed in ambulatory centers (Henderson 1993). Healthcare Forum's panel has forecasted that one-third of hospital revenues will come from ambulatory care by 1995 (Coile 1991). Today, ambulatory care accounts for about 22 percent of total revenues in hospitals. By one prediction, ambulatory care revenues may equal inpatient dollars by the year 2005 (see Figure 2.2).

The ambulatory shift from inpatient to ambulatory care will continue in part because more than 200 procedures have been reclassified by Medicare as ambulatory from inpatient. Some 80–85 percent of all procedures that can be shifted to ambulatory care have been. Even cardiac catheterization will soon be 85 percent ambulatory.

Technology aimed directly at the ambulatory market will further stimulate demand. The new laparoscopic cholecystectomy procedure, for example, is soaring in popularity, boosting ambulatory surgery. The shift to ambulatory surgery has been encouraged by government and insurance plans. New Medicare payment policies provide favorable reimbursement to freestanding ambulatory surgery centers; more than 50 percent of all surgery by hospitals is now done on an ambulatory basis.

Postsurgical Recovery Centers (PRCs) will be the next trend in ambulatory care. These "medical motels" are located adjacent to ambulatory surgical centers. PRCs do not have to meet hospital licensure or staffing standards but

Figure 2.2 Future Growth of Ambulatory Care

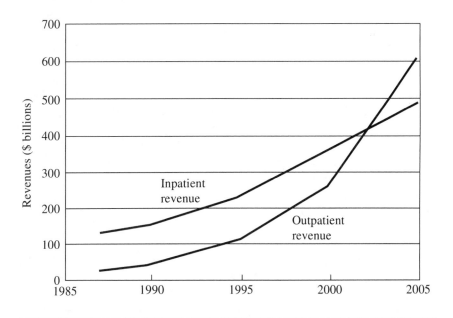

can hold patients for up to 72 hours. California is piloting a program with 14 experimental sites; only five were operational in early 1993 and two are hospital-based. The concept was developed by those who conceived of the original ambulatory surgical center. Two PRCs have already opened in Texas under hospital licensure. Freestanding PRCs will be controversial because they "cream" profitable short-stay patients from community hospitals, but they also stimulate hospital-physician competition. As evidence, physician-sponsored legislation to authorize PRCs failed in Illinois after stiff opposition from the state hospital association.

Which ambulatory services will be the winners in the 1990s? The most profitable noninpatient services will be ambulatory surgery, diagnostic centers, women's health, and industrial medicine. The losers are likely to be psychiatric and substance abuse clinics because of the tremendous pressure they face from payers, third-party review programs, and specialized managed care plans.

Trend 4: Managed Care

HMOs, PPOs, and managed indemnity plans will cover more than 50 percent of the population by 1995, predicted Healthcare Forum's national panel in a

"FutureTrack" survey (Coile 1991). Today nearly 30 percent of all Americans are members of managed care plans. HMOs are regaining momentum: enrollment in "pure" and hybrid HMOs exceeds 39.1 million as of 1 July 1992 (InterStudy 1993). HMO plans grew 6.1 percent and added 2 million new members. Mixed-model HMO plans, which include both staff-type medical groups and networks of independent physicians, are increasingly popular; their enrollment has increased by 55.8 percent, to 2.2 million. Open-ended HMO plans zoomed up by 39 percent in 1991, but slowed to 14.8 percent in 1992. Experts predict that HMO membership gains will continue, as much as 6–10 percent in the period 1992–1995 as the HMO field restabilizes and regains popularity with major employers.

Preferred provider organizations (PPOs) have now enrolled 85.4 million workers and dependents, more than double HMO enrollment. The number of PPO plans grew 19 percent, to 97 percent in 1992. Forty-nine multistate PPO chains operated in 1991, covering 67 percent of the local PPO plans (Marion Merrill Dow 1992). PPOs are profitable hospital development efforts, as well. Provider-owned PPOs enrolled 6.9 million in 1992 under 58 plans, up almost 50 percent from 1991. Hospital-sponsored PPOs can be profitable: in Seattle, two PPOs owned by Sisters of Providence earned more than $5 million in net revenues (Kenkel 1993).

Although health insurers regained financial stability in the early 1990s, profits are likely to slow through 1995. Group health insurance regained profitability in the early 1990s. CIGNA Corporation's employee life and health benefits business, for example, reported first-half income up 12.8 percent in 1992 to $108 million, from $61 million in 1989. Metropolitan Life's health care revenues rose 19.3 percent to a $105 million profit in the first six months of 1992, much improved over a $11.6 million loss in the same period of 1989. Blue Cross plans nationwide posted a $838 million gain in the first half of 1992, a 19.3 percent increase over 1991, and a complete recovery from the Blues' multimillion-dollar losses in the 1980s.

Blue Cross of California is a case in point. Its most profitable years in its history (1990–1992) came only five years after the California plan was forced to sell its HMO, land, buildings, even computers to prevent bankruptcy. The shift to managed care and increased premiums are behind the success. In 1985, the California Blue Cross portfolio was 90 percent indemnity, 10 percent HMO/PPO. In 1993, it is 90 percent HMO/PPO, 10 percent indemnity.

The fiscal stability of HMOs is expected to hold during the early 1990s. Only 9 percent of HMOs were in the red for 1992, according to Minnesota-based InterStudy (1992), compared with 1988, when only one in three HMOs were profitable. Better financial performance was due to better utilization management, reductions in physician fees, and cuts in administrative costs (Health Care Investment Analysts 1992).

This level of profitability will not last long. Earnings probably peaked in mid-1991. Business is weeding out small managed care plans, keeping only the largest and most cost-effective plans. Health insurance has become quite cyclical. Price cutting is already beginning as employers see the insurers and HMOs making large profits. More price competition among insurers and HMOs is predicted during the period 1994–1996, but prices will not fall as far or as fast because there are fewer competitors after the consolidation and market shakeout of 1987–1990.

Managed care experiments are continuing. Following the lead of Allied-Signal, Pacific Bell has entered into a rate-guaranteed contract with CIGNA to administer a managed care point-of-service network like the three-year deal with Allied-Signal. Pacific Bell just eliminated all but five of its HMOs, following a widening trend among major employers like General Motors, Bank of America, and Wells Fargo to shed all but the largest HMOs and most effective PPOs.

Every hospital in America will be affected by managed care. There will be a "learning curve," but experience is instructive. To learn, boards should invite consultants and physicians from California and Minnesota, the nation's most advanced managed care markets, where hospitals and doctors have made every possible mistake in managed care contracting.

Trend 5: Technowave

Technology will continue to be a major strategic path to success for hospitals during the 1990s. Hospitals will have to increasingly focus their capital and marketing resources on selected centers of excellence. Dominant regional medical centers and academic medical centers will create superspecialty "centers of leadership" that become the top market leaders.

The three most promising (and profitable) technologies for hospitals in the 1990s will be magnetic resonance imaging (MRI), laparoscopic cholecystectomy, and computer-aided diagnosis.

The average MRI center is only realizing 20 to 30 percent of MRI's potential (Wallace 1991). MRI manufacturers are developing upgrades and new techniques like "fast spin echo" that acquire images 16 times faster than conventional technologies. For example, MRI is now competing with ultrasound in determining the extent of prostate cancer, the second-leading form of fatal cancer in men, affecting over 100,000 each year.

Gallbladder removal surgery by "lap-choly" drastically shortens recovery time. Although some insurers still consider the procedure experimental, most are moving quickly to provide coverage. It's not the laser that's new—it's the adaptation of the laparoscope, widely used in gynecology. Hospitals don't need to add a specialized laser unit because the procedure can be done with a variety of lasers such as carbon-dioxide and argon. The laparoscope could have a dramatic effect on surgery in U.S. hospitals. By one estimate, 80 percent of abdominal surgery will be performed laparoscopically by the year 2000 (Davidson 1991). Other potential applications include bowel resections, appendectomies, hernia repairs, and diagnostic evaluations.

Using the computer to diagnose patients will be routine by the year 2000. Early applications of computer-aided diagnosis (CAD) are arriving now. The following are a few examples of over 100 current programs using computers to diagnose (Davidson 1992): "autopap" is a computerized imaging system to evaluate Pap tests for cervical cancers; CAD aids radiologists in mammographic analysis by marking suspicious areas on the film for review by clinicians; a hand-held computer will be used by cardiologists to diagnose acute myocardial infarctions (heart attacks); and computer monitoring of adverse drug reactions at the Latter-Day Saints Hospital in Salt Lake City has detected 731 incidents in monitoring 36,000 patients.

As a result, every hospital needs a strategic technology plan. Hospital trustees and medical staff leadership need to be centrally involved in planning and priority-setting for new technology investment.

Trend 6: Local Networks

Health care is a local business. Medical care and health services in the 1990s will be dominated by local networks of hospitals, medical office buildings, and ambulatory and long-term care facilities. The goal is to control the pattern of medical referrals and to be officially designated a preferred provider for managed care contracting. Better yet, the network owns its own HMO or PPO. In California, this means creating an alternative to Kaiser. This is the strategic design of UniHealth America, a multihospital system built through merger of HealthWest and the Lutheran Hospital Society. UniHealth owns PacifiCare, a 625,000-member HMO and two-thirds of a PPO with 2 million enrollees. Hospitals in UniHealth's southern California network participate on three levels of affiliation. The goal is to be the region's dominant preferred managed care provider with a distribution network extending across the Los Angeles basin. The action is at the local level. A similar strategy is being pursued by Health Dimensions in San Jose, California, Christian Hospitals in St. Louis, and Baptist Health System in Birmingham, Alabama.

What many local networks lack, however, is the medical "piece." Each hospital needs its own mini Mayo Clinic. Name-brand medical clinics will become magnets for physician referral, consumer self-referral, and managed care contracts. Hospitals will support development of hospital-based group practices through strategic planning, development capital, new medical office buildings, information systems, staff leasing, and malpractice protection. UniHealth of America, for example, has created several nonprofit medical clinic foundations to acquire major medical groups, and Loma Linda University purchased the Friendly Hills Medical Group, a 200-plus physician group practice with its own hospital, in a transaction valued at over $100 million.

The time to start networking is yesterday. The core of most of these local networks will be the best three to five hospitals in the community, in alliance with large medical groups and the best medical specialists. The core hospitals will probably be merged, and not just for administrative simplification. The strategic goal is clinical efficiency, which is where the real savings will be found.

Trend 7: Corporate Practice

For medicine, the future is corporate practice. By 1995, more than 60 percent of physicians will work for hospitals or HMOs. By 2000, it will be 75 percent. The fastest growing type of medical group today, the super group, has more than 100 physicians, many of whom work for salary and incentives. Like the law and accounting fields, only 20–30 percent of young physicians will reach partner status during the 1990s in these very large medical groups.

Like Mayo, Cleveland Clinic, Oschner, and Virginia-Mason, the biggest corporate practices will be clinics. Some will buy their own hospitals, like the Mulliken and Friendly Hills Medical Groups in southern California. Large medical groups in the 1990s will be multisite and electronically networked, with sophisticated information and management systems. Groups will set their own practice parameters and guidelines and monitor office practice. Managed care will be 50–75 percent of their business. Groups with more than 25 members will have a full-time medical director as well as an MBA-trained CEO. Strong groups will make a primary hospital affiliation and have a seat on the hospital board.

Like many corporations, hospitals will develop medical organizations "without walls." In actuality, it's a nongroup that works much like a group medical practice where physicians do not share revenues or lose control of their practices, but they do share expenses and risk-sharing contracts like a group. Independent physicians and small groups are located in the same building, on the hospital campus or across the street; hospitals provide the medical office building, information, and support systems; physicians collaborate in managed care contracting and joint ventures; staff, equipment, and facilities are shared among the physicians on an allocated-cost basis; there is one entrance and shared lobby; only participating physicians can lease space. By 1995, these nongroups will become more cohesive and may pool some or all revenues.

The trend of corporate practice boosted medical incomes 6.4 percent in 1991 over 1989 figures (Owens 1992). In 1991, the typical doctor saw a 3.2 percent jump in net practice income, as net revenues climbed $8,370 per physician. Increases in the cost of living diluted much of medical earnings during the 1980s, and physicians only gained real net income in 1982, 1984, 1986, and 1989, failing to keep pace with consumer inflation in 1990 and 1991. In response to managed care and reimbursement pressures, physicians unbundled fees and became more efficient in getting paid. This trend will continue during the 1990s. Expect physician revenues to climb by 6–7 percent in the mid-1990s, about twice the rise in consumer inflation.

A new era is emerging for hospital-physician relationships—corporation to corporation. Affiliation—not ownership—will be the primary pattern of physician participation in local health care networks. Although some hospitals will continue to buy physician practices, most will gain better results (and save their capital) by strengthening hospital-physician organizations like the independent practice association (IPA) and by contracting with large multispecialty and single-specialty medical groups sophisticated in managed care contracting.

Trend 8: Practice Guidelines

Physicians have referred to it as "cookbook medicine," but grudgingly, they are writing the recipes. Practice guidelines will dictate standards for every medical specialty, every frequently performed procedure and diagnosis. So far, the trend to practice guidelines is mostly voluntary. But eventually the appropriate medical society and the government will also approve the standards. These decision guides will become payer policy and government regulation during the nineties. The JCAHO, however, continues to pursue its agenda for change. Preliminary guidelines for monitoring the outcomes of care are being tested and will be implemented in 1995. In anticipation, Congress authorized nearly $500 million in funding for a five-year program of outcomes research. Practice guidelines will be further encouraged under national health reform.

Thus far, practice guidelines have not been linked to medical liability, but that is changing. In 1992, Maine launched an innovative five-year experiment to extend malpractice protection to doctors who provide services in accordance with the guidelines and risk-management protocols. This demonstration is voluntary and involves three of the specialties hardest hit by malpractice—anesthesiology, emergency medicine, and obstetrics and gynecology.

Quality data is the heart of practice guidelines, and as a result medical and hospital cost and outcome data will become public information. More states will follow the lead of Pennsylvania and Iowa, which already require hospitals to install a quality reporting system and publish the results. Hospital and medical data will be relatively transparent to insurers, managed care plans, government, and consumers. Major payers will demand real-time access to hospital and physician practice data as a condition of managed care contracts.

By the year 2000, it's likely that hospitals and doctors will lose control of their confidential medical data. Consequently, every hospital and health system must have an integrated financial and quality reporting system, and indicators of cost and quality must be regularly reviewed by the board. Trustees need to know how good their institutions really are, before these data become public information.

Trend 9: Rationing

Rationing is no longer in the future. First it will hit the poor. As an example, Oregon's rationing program approved by the federal government in 1993 only affects Medicaid beneficiaries. In Maryland, a $127 budget deficit compromise in 1991 was life-threatening for the state's poor and disabled. To save money, the state eliminated drug benefits for 14,000 in a three-month period, including 300 AIDS patients. More than 3,000 kidney patients will have to cover the state's 20 percent to match 80 percent federal payment for chronic dialysis services. Another 3,000 paralyzed and disabled patients will lose payments for the custodial home care that keeps them out of nursing homes. Maryland is not the only state whose Medicaid program is going broke. Hospitals have been subsidizing the poorly funded Medicaid program for a decade. In 1980, Medicaid covered 90 percent of hospital costs; by 1989 it was 78 percent. Only 12.7 percent of hospitals received Medicaid payments that covered costs (Fraser et al. 1991). Underfunding Medicaid will only worsen until national health reform addresses the Medicaid issue. Meanwhile, states will ration more services to the poor.

Insurance is no defense against rationing of care. In time, rationing will affect all patients regardless of income because insurance companies will refuse to cover advanced medical treatments even though they are no longer experimental. Human organ transplantations are a case in point where heart transplants can cost $200,000 per patient (Haubelt 1993). After losing costly lawsuits, Blue Cross plans are joining a national experiment in which the Blues will cover 600 patients for autologous bone marrow transplants to assess the cost-effectiveness of the $167,000–233,000 procedure for first-year to five-year estimated costs.

Hospital administrators believe that rationing is inevitable. In a survey by Deloitte & Touche (1992) of 1,700 hospital chief executives, 71 percent believe that health care in individual cases should be rationed because of cost. Every hospital then must develop a contingency plan for rationing. The board's ethics committee should take the lead in identifying rationing issues and in developing a strategic response.

Trend 10: Healthy Communities

The hallmark of successful hospitals in the 1990s will be healthy communities. Coupled with the environmental movement, community health awareness is a growing trend. From 1983 to 1992, the Baxter index of consumer health habits rose from 100 to 116 but is now leveling off (Baxter International 1993). The largest gains were registered in areas where healthy behaviors are mandated by law—wearing seat belts and installing smoke detectors. Not all health indicators were positive: Americans are sleeping less, eating less carefully, and exercising less frequently. *Healthy People 2000*, a plan developed by the U.S. Department of Health and Human Services (DHHS) in 1990 specified improvements in American health status to be achieved during the 1990s. The plan listed an array of 298 objectives for better health, such as: get 30 percent of Americans to exercise moderately (increase of 8 percent); reduce from 26 to 20 percent the proportion of overweight adults; nearly halve the proportion of adults who smoke, from 29 percent to 15 percent; and double the number of vehicle occupants who use automobile seat belts from 42 to 85 percent.

As an important community institution, hospitals also must participate actively in targeting lifestyle and risk factors in community health improvement projects. Heart disease is a popular focus of hospital health promotion, and hospitals should be more involved in targeting those with modifiable heart disease risk factors (percent of U.S. population)—those who have a sedentary lifestyle (63 percent), have a limit on the serum cholesterol in diet (50 percent), are overweight (81 percent), smoke (25 percent), have a limit on sodium in their diet (48 percent), and require an annual blood pressure test (15 percent) (Prevention Index 1992).

Hospitals in Alaska, Mississippi, Nevada, and West Virginia have the most to gain by increasing their community involvement. According to a ranking of states by 17 components of health grouped into five general categories, these states were the most unhealthy (Northwest National Life Insurance 1992). Minnesota and Utah are the healthiest states in the nation. Nevada also scored low on lifestyle, access, disability, disease, and mortality. Arkansas dropped in the ratings from 40th to 44th, due to an increase in infectious disease rates and a high incidence of worker disabilities.

Health truly is a community affair. As a community's largest and best organized health care resource, hospitals and health systems have a responsibility to take a leadership role in promoting community health. Hospitals must target local health problems and develop coalition approaches with employers, voluntary health agencies, and government.

Looking Forward: National Health Reform

We've entered the era of national health reform. Health care is now a top-ranked public concern, and a new national health policy is predicted to emerge before 1995. Opinion surveys indicate that nearly three or four Americans (74 percent in a 1993 *Wall Street Journal* poll) favor some form of a national health care program (Stout 1993). The Clinton health plan was introduced in September 1993, launching a national debate. Providers have developed thinly worded statements of principle, think-tanks have sent up "trial balloon" proposals, and grass-roots consumer organizations have become increasingly noisy. The future will bring continuing debate over health system reform and alternatives such as the Canadian model.

As the national policy debate heats up, more attention will be focused on Canada. According to a June 1990 study by the Health Insurance Association of America, health costs in the 1980s actually rose faster in Canada than in the United States. When general inflation in economy (as measured by the Consumer Price Index) is factored out, the average annual increase in health spending was 4.28 percent in Canada, versus 3.93 percent in the United States. The fact that Canada continues to spend proportionately less of its GNP on health care is not due to more effective cost controls, but from faster economic growth. Clearly, Canada's social programs, including health care, cost the Canadians a higher tax rate. However, recent evidence has mounted regarding the longer waiting lines Canadians face to gain access to less common high-technology equipment (Gilray 1992).

As the 1992 presidential campaign revealed, shaping national health reform is a partisan battle. The Democrats focused on two issues in the 1992 election campaign, and health care was one of them. The emphasis stemmed from the public concern to provide employer-mandated health insurance of some sort to the nation's 35–40 million medically uninsured, and the expansion of Medicare in long-term and home care, which affects millions of older Americans. However, only if an economic plan is passed by Congress that will significantly cut the federal budget deficit can Congress afford to expand Medicare, no matter the pressure from the "senior lobby."

The nation's largest employers will be forced to take a leadership role in shaping national health policy because not only do they pay about 30 percent of the nation's health expenses, but as of 1993, employers now are required to disclose future retiree health costs, which could cost billions. The Financial Accounting Standards Board (FASB) postponed implementation until 1993, but employers were still unprepared for this accounting change. General Motors, for example, charged nearly $2 billion to fund future retiree health expenses in the last quarter of 1992. Employers are frantically seeking strategies to get that unfunded liability off their books, including multiple-employer health trusts and even a federal takeover of the nation's health system.

President Clinton is organizing a coalition of employers, unions, older Americans, and consumer groups to work together on reform. Such a coalition could persuade Congress that national health reform will successfully reduce health insurance premiums to below 8–10 percent and health costs with 1–2 percent of annual inflation. A continuing recession could accelerate the reform trend. Congress may act to adopt health reform in some form before the 1994 election, but the outcome is far from certain.

Hospital trustees would be mistaken to think that fundamental change in health care delivery is impossible. Even the Canadian model cannot be discounted. However, the chance for government control may have a low probability, especially if health care providers act responsibly, moderate price increases, and keep profits modest over the next five years.

Strategies

1. **Lead by anticipating.** The changing times ahead signal a continuing need for broad environmental awareness. Intelligent leadership begins with information. Hospitals need a broadly representative group of lay trustees who are informed about the health care market and can contribute insights from their community, business. and political perspectives. Provider trustees should be active in their professional organizations and maintain awareness of national and regional trends in their field. Management should give the board its forecast of current trends, at least annually, with an assessment of local influences.

2. **Retreat in the face of change.** Every health care organization should regularly retreat in a group session to gain perspective about the changing environment and to set consensus directions for the future. Outside experts, timely articles, debates, and small-group discussions can promote an informed leadership. Additionally, consider that some hospitals and health systems prefer to call these sessions "advances."

3. **Lengthen planning cycles and shorten updates.** In times of uncertainty, the strategically minded health care organization lengthens its planning horizon five to ten years, seeking to align corporate development strategy with long-term trends. At the same time, hospitals more frequently update their short-term plans, continuously adapting to the environment with a "rolling" work program and budget of 18–24 months that is updated quarterly or at least every six months—the rapid pace of change demands it.

References

American Hospital Association. 1992a. "AHA: Adjusted Admissions Hit New High in 1991." *Hospitals* (5 November): 14–15.

American Hospital Association. 1992b. "Employment of Full-Time Staff Outpaces Part-Time Growth." *Hospitals* (5 November): 44.

American Hospital Association. 1992c. "Key Trends Through Third Quarter of 1992." *Economic Trends 8*, no. 4 (Winter): 1–8.

Baxter International. 1993. *The 1992 Baxter Survey of American Health Habits*. Deerfield, IL: Baxter.

Coile, R. C., Jr. 1991. "The 'Hospital' of the Future." *Healthcare Forum Journal* (May–June): 82–83.

Davidson, S. 1991. "Advances in Wound Management, Laparoscopy, Lasers, and Drug Therapies to Reduce Admissions and Length of Stay." *Technology Assessment* 7, no. 8 (September): 3.

———. 1992. "The Computer's Role in Diagnosis." *Technology Assessment* 8, no. 5 (June): 1–3.

Deloitte & Touche. 1992. *U.S. Hospitals and the Future of Health Care: A Continuing Opinion Survey*. Boston: Deloitte & Touche.

Fraser, I., et al. 1991. "Medicaid Shortfalls and Total Unreimbursed Hospital Care for the Poor, 1980–89." *Inquiry* (Winter).

Fries, J. F. 1993. "The Bank of America Study: Two Years' Results; A Health Promotion Program in a Retiree Population." *Journal of the American Medical Association* (May).

Gilray, B. 1992. "Standing Up for American Health Care." *Health Insurance Underwriter* (February).

Haubelt, R. H. 1993. *Cost Implications of Human Organ Transplants: An Update, 1993*. Brookfield, WI: Milliman and Robertson.

Health Care Investment Analysts. 1992. *1992 HMO Performance Almanac*. Baltimore, MD: The Analysts.

Health Insurance Association of America. 1990. *Employer-Sponsored*.

Health Insurance in America. Washington, DC: HIAA.

Henderson, J. 1993. "Hospitals Seek Bigger Cut of Outpatient Surgeries." *Modern Healthcare* (28 June): 82–85.

InterStudy. 1993. *The InterStudy Competitive Edge Data Book*. St. Paul, MN: InterStudy.

Kenkel, P. J. 1993. "Provider-Based Managed Care Plans Continue Growth Trend." *Modern Healthcare* 23, no. 19 (10 May): 26–34.

Marion Merrill Dow. 1992. *Managed Care Digest: PPO Edition, 1992*. Kansas City, MO: Marion Merrell Dow.

Medical Benefits. 1993. 10 (30 March): 6–7. Citing information of Weinschrott.

Northwest National Life Insurance. 1992. *1992 State Health Rankings*. Minneapolis, MN: NNLI.

Owens, A. 1992. "What's the Recession Done to Your Buying Power?" *Medical Economics* (7 September): 194–206.

Prevention Index. 1992. *A Report Card on the Nation's Health*. Emmaus, PA: Rodale Press.

Stout, H. 1993. "Seeking a Cure: Most Americans Pledge Sacrifice to Help Fix the Health System." *Wall Street Journal*, 12 March; See also Louis Harris, 1993, *The Public Mandate for Health Care Reform in America,"* Testimony, U.S. Congress House Committee on Aging, March 16.

Toffler, A. 1990. *PowerShift: Knowledge, Wealth and Violence at the Edge of the 21st Century*. New York: Bantam Books.

U.S. Department of Health and Human Services. 1990. *Healthy People 2000*. Washington, DC: U.S. Government Printing Office.

Waldo, D. R. 1992. "Health Spending Through 2030: Three Scenarios." *Health Affairs* (Winter).

Wallace, C. 1991. "Faster MRI on the Way." *Health Technology Trends* 3, no. 10 (October): 1, 6.

3

Managed Care: The New Era
of Health Care Reimbursement
and Market Restructuring

> Managed care: The marketplace is demanding it. There's no buyer today that
> wants anything but selective options.
>
> —Bernard R. Tresnowski, president of Blue Cross
> and Blue Shield Association (Kenkel 1993)

America's hospitals have entered a new era—the market world of managed care. The phrase still lacks widely accepted definition, but speaking
generically, it means that all health care buyers—insurance, employers,
and government—are actively managing the costs and utilization of health
services for their beneficiaries.

Managed care changes the rules of the game in important ways. Hospital boards, senior management, and medical staff need new strategies for
success to cope with this new world of discounts, risk-sharing, and third party
review of every medical decision and hospital treatment. When HMO/PPO
plans control more than 15–20 percent of a hospital's inpatients, this is
a managed care market. Add in Medicare's 40 percent of patients in the
average hospital's case mix, and suddenly a majority of patients are covered
by managed care reimbursement. Welcome to the era of managed care.

HMOs were once called alternative delivery systems, but no longer.
Now HMOs and PPOs are the dominant pattern of health care reimbursement. Traditional indemnity insurance is obsolete. Virtually all indemnity-
type health insurance plans will be "managed indemnity," with many of
the same control features and limited provider options as HMOs and PPOs.
Managed care is clearly the predominant form of health plan. Only 16 percent
of those in employer-sponsored group plans are still covered by traditional
indemnity insurance plans without utilization management, according to a

Figure 3.1   Marketshare for Employer Health Coverages (1989–1990)

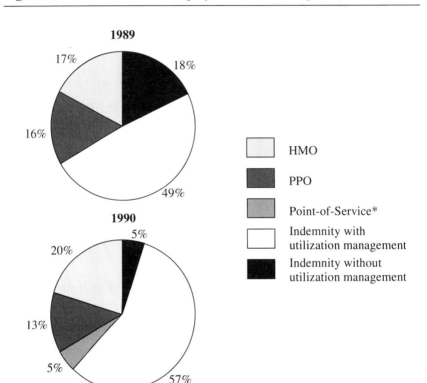

1993 study by the Wyatt Company. Figure 3.1 also exhibits this trend, per Health Insurance Association of America findings.

In the era of managed care, every U.S. hospital will need a strategy and organized capacity to respond to managed care buyers. This means physicians and hospitals together will handle discounting and risk-sharing capitation contracts. A board-level committee with business-oriented trustees, medical staff leadership, and senior management should be to develop and coordinate the managed care strategy.

In the 1990s, managed care plans will be competing vigorously for marketshare. While more than one-third (33.6 percent) of all Americans not covered by Medicare will be enrolled in an HMO or PPO, by 1995 more than one-half of the population will have joined a managed care plan, including a growing number of Medicare beneficiaries (see Table 3.1) (Coile 1992).

Table 3.1 National Forecast of Managed Care Growth (1995)

Type of Health Coverage	Number Enrolled (in millions)		Percent Population	
	1990	1995	1990	1995
HMO	38	55	15.4	21.3
PPO	38	48	15.4	18.6
Point of service	8	16	3.2	6.2
Managed indemnity	66	46	26.7	17.8
Traditional indemnity	8	4	3.2	1.6
Medicare (Non-HMO)	32	29	13.0	11.3
Medicare HMO	1	5	0.4	1.9
Medicaid	22	23	8.9	8.9
Medically uninsured	34	12	13.8	4.7
National health (HMO)	0	20	0	7.7
Totals	247	258	100.0	100.0

Sources: Data from the *InterStudy Edge* (1 January 1991), HIAA Employer Survey 1989–1990, Health Care Financing Administration, U.S. Department of Commerce, and American Association of Preferred Provider Organizations (July 1991).

The Health Forecasting Group estimate of future marketshare is based on the assumptions that:

- HMO growth from 1990–1995 occurs at the current 9 percent annual increase, outcompeting PPOs with lower prices and more comprehensive service packages.
- PPOs grow at approximately 5 percent per year between 1990 and 1995, primarily taking share away from traditional (unmanaged) indemnity plans.
- Point-of-service (POS) plans double in size by 1995 taking share away from HMOs, PPOs, and managed indemnity plans.
- Managed indemnity loses 20 million enrollees by 1995, as employers and insurers convert to HMO, PPO, and POS formats for increased cost control.
- Traditional (nonmanaged) indemnity continues to decline in availability, with membership slipping by 50 percent to 4 million.
- Medicare HMOs begin to grow strongly during the 1990s, adding 750,000 new members per year through 1995.
- Medicaid rolls grow very slowly as more states follow Michigan and cut eligibility criteria.
- National health insurance mandates for employers are passed by Congress, affecting two of three medically uninsured persons; states

are responsible for implementation, using capitation to control costs; and all of the approximately 15 million formerly uninsured are enrolled in HMO-type plans within their state.

Managed Care's Ten Trends for the 1990s

These are the key trends and driving forces that will shape the growth and development of managed care in the next three to five years.

Trend 1: The Marketshare of HMOs

In the battle for managed care marketshare, HMOs appear headed toward edging out PPOs. HMOs had a 10.5 percent enrollment gain in 1990, well above the 1989 increase of 3.9 percent, according to a report by the SMG Marketing Group (1991). The momentum has shifted to HMOs, and it's now predicted that HMO annual growth will average 9 percent through 1995.

Don't count out PPOs. Nearly 45 percent of employers offer PPO options, and their growth has been phenomenal (Hewitt Associates 1992). Since 1987, some reports say that the number of employees directly covered by PPOs increased from 12.1 to 38.1 million. Some 824 PPOs have a total of 31,004 contracts with group health insurers, third party administrators (TPAs), and self-insured employers. But PPOs must go beyond discounting to control costs and provide value to employers and enrollees. Ultimately, many PPO customers shift to HMOs for a combination of lower costs and more comprehensive services, or to open-ended HMOs, which provide more consumer choice at prices 3 to 5 percent higher than standard HMO premiums.

Long-term contracts between major employers and managed care plans is a trend still waiting to happen. The widely watched experiment between the Allied Signal Corporation and CIGNA ended in 1992 after more than three years because CIGNA lost money after guaranteeing only an 8 percent increase in year 1, and a maximum of 7 percent in years 2 and 3. Allied Signal was more than satisfied; the company saved an estimated $200 million in "cost avoidances." CIGNA has not given up on long-term contracting, but it requires employer risk-sharing. In fact, CIGNA has continued to contract with Allied Signal, adding long-term contracts with Phillip Morris, American Airlines, and Tenneco Oil, requiring employers to share the risk of rising health costs with them.

Hospitals will gain nothing in fighting the trend toward HMOs. Many hospitals and physicians prefer dealing with PPOs because they deal primarily through discounts and impose fewer outside controls on physician decision making. But PPOs are weaker players who ultimately cannot control costs and utilization. Hospitals and systems should arrange partnerships with HMOs and bargain for multiyear contracts and semiexclusive deals.

Trend 2: Large Firm Domination

The dominant managed care plans of the 1990s will be large and multistate. PPOs are leading this trend toward large regional or national firms: two-thirds of the 38 million PPO enrollees are covered by one of the 49 largest multistate plans (Marion Merrill Dow 1992). Increasingly, PPOs will be regional, not local, as nearly three in four PPOs are currently part of a multistate organization operating in more than one state. Blue Cross–Blue Shield is the largest multistate PPO with more than 4.9 million employees enrolled (see Table 3.2) (Marion Merrill Dow 1992).

The trend toward larger HMO and PPO plans will accelerate. Consolidation is occurring all across the nation: among HMOs, almost 50 plans

Table 3.2   The Ten Largest Multistate Network PPOs, by Enrollment

Multistate PPO	Number of PPOs	Number of States	Number of Employees
Blue Cross–Blue Shield (Chicago, IL)	56	40	4,966,731
Occupational–Urgent Care Health Systems (Sacramento, CA)	1	7	3,800,000
USA Healthnet (Phoenix, AZ)	35	35	3,041,787
Healthcare Compare (Sacramento, CA)	1	12	2,400,000
Pacific Health Alliance (San Mateo, CA)	1	4	1,200,000
Private Healthcare Systems (Lexington, MA)	9	24	977,000
Metropolitan Life Insurance (Westport, CN)	111	20	855,902
Preferred Care Network (Lincolnwood, IL)	4	4	645,320
Travelers Insurance (Hartford, CT)	59	33	603,402
Aetna (Hartford, CN)	105	50	565,218
Total	382		19,055,360

Reprinted with the permission of Aspen Publishing, Inc. © 1992, as it appeared in *Hospital Strategy Report*, Vol. 4, No. 4 (February).
Source: Marion Merrill Dow 1992.

were merged, sold, or acquired in 1992, and the number of consolidation transactions is expected to increase in the future under national health reform (see Figure 3.2) (Pace Group 1993).

Managed care networking must occur at local and state levels. Hospitals should participate in establishing metropolitan and statewide managed networks that would link hospitals and physician organizations into provider systems that can handle "big buyers," such as statewide employers, state government (Medicaid), and national insurance companies.

Trend 3: Consumers' Choice

Consumers want choice in their managed care options, and they're getting it. Open-ended HMOs, or point-of-service (POS) plans, allow consumers to choose their provider and are the fastest-growing form of managed care. In 1990, enrollment in open-ended plans soared by 38.8 percent, according to InterStudy (1993). Demand is still strong with 14.8 percent growth for POS plans in 1992, especially in the South where POS plans added over 100,000 new members. About 1.7 million Americans have joined open-ended HMOs since the mid-1980s (InterStudy 1993). The majority of HMOs (76 percent) now offer an open-ended plan (Palsbo 1992), and so do one-third of the nation's large employers, according to a recent study by Hay/Huggins (1992).

POS plans do create marketing opportunities for hospitals with "niching," pricing, and quality. When managed care POS consumers can seek care outside their HMO/PPO networks, then hospitals and doctors can compete on quality and value. Board leadership in strategic planning can identify

Figure 3.2   Number of U.S. HMOs Merged, Sold, or Acquired
(1989–1992)

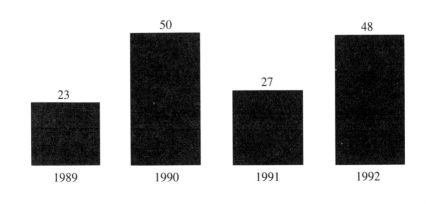

Source: Pace Group 1993.

those services and programs that will have strong appeal to POS customers to obtain services they believe are better than their HMO or PPO, such as family-oriented labor-delivery-recovery-postpartum obstetrics units.

Trend 4: Rate Wars

Much like the airline industry, health care rate wars have returned. Price competition among insurers and managed care plans will force lower pre-miums and costs. Kaiser Permanente, the nation's largest HMO with nearly 7 million members, slashed its price increases for 1992 to less than 10 percent increases in its core markets of northern and southern California. Rate cuts are overdue because employers were burdened by 20–30 percent annual increases for 1989–1991. In the same period, HMOs returned to profitability due to higher prices and "dumping" of unprofitable groups. Indemnity plans seem unable to match the cuts of HMOs (see Table 3.3). Foster Higgins & Co. (1993) reported that HMO costs per employee rose only 8.8 percent in 1992, versus a 14.2 percent increase in indemnity plan costs, leading employers to favor HMOs and point-of-service HMO-like plans, whose premiums rose only 8.4 percent in 1992. Employer interest in PPOs may slow in the future. PPO premiums hiked 10.5 percent for PPO-network plans in 1992. For the first time, more than half (51 percent) of employees who receive health benefit coverage were enrolled in managed care plans.

HMO price wars may be good national policy, but their impact on hospital and physician reimbursement will be deeper discounts and lower

Table 3.3   Health Plan Premiums for HMOs, PPOs, and Indemnity (1991)

HMO Plans	Increase (percent)	Indemnity/PPO	Increase (percent)
Blue Cross–Blue Shield	5–15	Lincoln (indemnity)	20–25
Health Net	9	Lincoln (PPO)	18
PacifiCare	10–12	Prudential (indemnity)	19–21
US Healthcare	10–15	Prudential (PPO)	17
Metropolitan HMO	10–12	Metropolitan (indemnity)	22
Metropolitan (open-end)	15	Metropolitan (PPO)	16
Kaiser Foundation	10–18	Travelers (indemnity)	20–25
Aetna	15	Travelers (PPO)	15–20
CIGNA HMO	13	CIGNA (indemnity)	20–25
CIGNA (open-end)	13–24	CIGNA (PPO)	15–19

Reprinted with the permission of Aspen Publishers, Inc. © 1992, as it appeared in *Hospital Strategy Report*, Vol. 4, No. 4 (February).
Source: Foster Higgins & Co. 1991 survey.

revenues as HMOs seek to cut their provider costs to make up for price reductions. Board policy on HMO/PPO contracting should emphasize multiyear contracts that guarantee payment levels and protect the hospitals and their physicians from price wars.

Trend 5: HMO/PPO Profits

Managed care plans made record profits in 1990–1992, and are profitable again, with 51 percent of HMOs reporting a better year in 1992. But can it last? HMO profitability dramatically improved as HMOs entered the 1990s, after barely one in three HMOs (38 percent) made money in 1987. According to an analysis of 45 plans by the Group Health Association (Palsbo 1992), HMOs regained profitability in 1989 and continued on a strong profit pace in 1990. Indeed, 1992 was the best year yet for many managed care plans as rising profits led investors to drive up prices for HMO and PPO stocks. HMO companies like FHP International, PacifiCare, Sierra Health Services, United HealthCare, and U.S. Healthcare are predicted to prosper under national health reform.

The six-year insurance cycle is entering a three-year "down" period of declining premiums and profits. Beginning in 1990, health insurance premiums have been declining. Premiums for family coverage rose only 14.6 percent in 1990–1992 (Wyatt 1993), down from an average increase of 24.4 percent in 1989 (Sullivan and Rice 1991). Insurance prices for single participants were up only 13 percent in 1990; a year before, the increase was 23.6 percent.

With managed care plans cutting prices, hospitals and doctors can guess what's next—more discounting of provider services by managed care plans and dropping of inefficient providers. As HMOs and PPOs cut prices, many plans will make up for lost revenues with steeper discounts to hospitals and physicians. Better-managed HMOs and PPOs will drop higher-cost and lower-quality providers. Hospitals and doctors can expect managed care plans to be tougher in prior approval of treatments and to continuously question and review care in process. The result will be loss of economic and clinical freedom for providers as managed care plans put the pressure on utilization. Slumping profits for HMOs is an opportunity for hospitals to partner with managed care plans. Ultimately, HMOs can only succeed if their provider partners effectively manage costs and utilization.

Trend 6: Hybrid Models

The latest philosophy at successful managed care plans is to do whatever works. Among HMOs, mixed-model HMOs are expanding rapidly, having gained 55 percent in enrollment in 1992, while staff-model HMOs are

Table 3.4 Plan Characteristics for Traditional HMOs (1992)*

Model Type	Total Members	Percent of Total	Net Change
Staff	2,232,251	6.3	−31.9
Group	9,600,346	25.8	1.4
Network	3,761,632	10.1	−7.7
IPA	15,123,259	40.7	8.2
Mixed	6,381,652	17.2	55.8
Total	37,199,140	100.0	6.1

Reprinted with the permission of InterStudy © 1992, *The InterStudy Competitive Edge* 2, no. 2 (July). (Minneapolis: 612-858-9291.)
*Study dates: 1 July 1991–1 July 1992.

losing marketshare (−39 percent) to group and IPA models (see Table 3.4) (InterStudy 1993).

Open-ended HMOs allow enrollees to chose at the point of service whether they will stay in the HMO for their care or go to an out-of-plan provider. Coverage in the plan is usually 80–90 percent, while nonplan providers are reimbursed only 50–60 percent of the HMO's fee schedule. These POS plans are increasingly popular with consumers and their employers because of the flexibility and cost controls of POS plans. Digital Equipment Corporation, for example, has just expanded its "HMO Elect" program from four HMOs to 16 plans to make the option available to its employees on a national basis. Because POS plans give consumers more choice, providers have a new opportunity to attract consumers, which facilitates hospital marketing and physician-consumer relations. Capturing "out-of-plan" utilization by dissatisfied HMO members gives hospitals and physicians another way to participate in managed care, even if they do not have a contract with the HMO/POS plan.

This is a time for innovation in managed care arrangements. Trustees should bring together members of the local business community to explore the availability of affordable health plans. These discussions may lead to direct contracting opportunities between the hospital and physicians with local employers.

Trend 7: Provider Backlash

Not all doctors and hospitals have embraced the idea of managed care. Some health care providers are mounting a legislative effort to save the physician-patient relationship and cripple the growth of managed care. Doctors and hospitals are also taking the legislative route to block the increasing intrusion of HMOs and review companies into the provider-patient relationship. During the 1991 legislative sessions, 11 states considered legislation to restrict utilization review and selective contracting practices by managed care organizations (Pace Group 1993).

Analysis by the Wyatt Company predicted a detrimental effect on managed care plans if HMO/PPO-busting legislation were enacted, such as

- Mandates that "any willing provider" be permitted to join a managed care network. The cost impact could be a 34 percent increase in PPO administrative costs, if PPOs were forced to increase from a "typical" 25 percent of the physician community to 60 percent, and if the typical 44 percent of hospitals increased to 80 percent.

- Requirements that all utilization review be performed by local providers, which could increase managed care costs by 42.5 percent if reviews were done by the 78 approved specialty and subspecialty boards of medicine and surgery in states. This legislation was pushed hard by medical societies in 1991, with 85 legislative proposals.

- Mandates that utilization review firms increase business hours from 11 to 24, which would push administrative costs up by 43.5 percent for managed care firms.

- Requirements for state-specific statistical reporting on the actions of utilization review firms, which could raise costs by $10,000–50,000 per state. Proposals such as this were included in nearly 100 pieces of legislation in 1991.

The shift to managed care cannot be avoided. Board and medical staff leadership must understand that managed care arrangements are inevitable, and they must work to create partnership arrangements that will benefit both the providers and the plans to create strong community health plans.

Trend 8: Competing on Quality

In the managed care era, quality of care will become a primary factor in selecting HMOs and PPOs, and in selecting hospitals and doctors by managed care plans. Quality will be transparent to buyers. Providers, insurers, and managed care plans will compete on quality as well as price, but the data will be public. Concern for quality will focus on both service and clinical care: In the service dimension, consumers want service and employers want a minimum number of complaints. In the clinical dimension, more sophisticated employers are demanding treatment quality and are insisting on the data from providers to prove it. HMOs will get a report card in a "buyer's guide to HMOs" designed for large employers. This *Consumer Report*–type study rated 412 HMOs in 55 markets covering about 80 percent of enrollees. Plans were compared on a basis of stability (operational and financial), control (cost and utilization), and network (structure and service) (Health Plan Management Services 1993).

Managed care plans have embraced quality improvement, and the scope of quality control programs in managed care plans is impressive (see Figure 3.3) (InterStudy 1991).

Data on provider performance will become public in the 1990s. The Joint Commission on the Accreditation of Healthcare Organizations will make its hospital certification reports public in 1995. The public release of Commission surveys could affect many hospital reputations. Between 1987 and 1989, one-third of the more than 5,000 hospitals reviewed by the Commission failed to comply with key quality standards, including safety management, monitoring the medical staff, and surgical case review (Pinkney 1992).

In Hershey, Pennsylvania, Hershey Foods has developed a network of preferred providers using hospital quality data from the Pennsylvania Health Care Cost Containment Council. The employer put the network in place, with incentives, in 1993. Hershey is a self-insured company with 15,000 covered lives in the central Pennsylvania region. A leading supporter of legislation that created the Cost Commission, Hershey is now planning to contract with selected hospitals and their centers of excellence for a dozen high-cost services such as cardiac care and cancer therapies.

Hospitals must be prepared to compete on quality, and trustees should know the leading indicators of quality care in their institutions and systems. The board must be willing to invest $250,000 or more per facility in quality

Figure 3.3   Prevalence of Quality Control Measures among HMOs

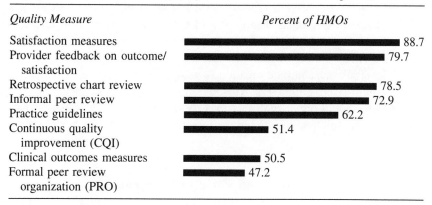

Quality Measure	Percent of HMOs
Satisfaction measures	88.7
Provider feedback on outcome/ satisfaction	79.7
Retrospective chart review	78.5
Informal peer review	72.9
Practice guidelines	62.2
Continuous quality improvement (CQI)	51.4
Clinical outcomes measures	50.5
Formal peer review organization (PRO)	47.2

Reprinted with the permission of Aspen Publishers, Inc. © 1992, as it appeared in the *Hospital Strategy Report*, Vol. 4, No. 4 (February).
Source: InterStudy's *The InterStudy Edge*, 1 January 1991.

measurement hardware and software that can track quality and compare performance with peer institutions.

Trend 9: Maintaining Health

Managed care plans and health-conscious employers are beginning to live up to the implicit promise of the health *maintenance* organization. Promoting health is a major trend for managed care plans during the 1990s. It will be the primary objective of the "third generation" of managed care plans, as predicted by Peter Boland in his latest book, *Making Managed Care Work* (1991). These "third generation" plans, he believes, will focus on optimal treatment and outcomes.

Major employers are actively promoting healthier lifestyles and punishing employees with unhealthy lifestyles. Turner Broadcasting, for instance, no longer hires smokers. Some question whether this is lifestyle discrimination or social benefit. Nevertheless, some of the health-related employer policies in existence in 1991 have been profiled (see Table 3.5).

Become a "healthy hospital" and a healthy company and lead by example. Hospitals should set board policy encouraging health promotion among hospital employees, and then work with community health agencies and local employers on health-related issues such as smoking bans.

Trend 10: Corporate Health Benefit Plans

Major employers continue to shift their employees into managed care plans. Only 62 percent of employers still offered a traditional indemnity insurance plan, according to a Hay/Huggins (1992) survey of 1,000 employers. One-third of employers offer a point-of-service plan, which combines aspects of HMO and PPO models. Employers like the cost savings from managed care plans. A traditional indemnity plan cost $158.34 per employee in 1992, while the HMO option was only $142.94.

Hospitals must initiate creation of managed care programs for small- and medium-sized employers. Hospital trustees from the local business community should organize discussions for establishing small-business purchasing coalitions that can directly contract with hospital-physician organizations.

The Shift from Price to Performance

For the five-year period 1989–1993, HMOs and managed care plans made money. They did it the easy way—by raising prices and shedding unprofitable groups. HMOs and PPOs could shadow-price indemnity insurance

Table 3.5 Lifestyle Policies: Employers Get Tough on Health

Company	Policy	Started
Baker Hughes	$10 monthly surcharge on health insurance for smokers.	1990
Exxon	Employees who have been through rehabilitation for substance abuse cannot work in "safety-sensitive" jobs. Workers in those jobs must report any arrest for drug or alcohol offenses.	1989
ICH	$15 a month off medical contributions for employees who have not smoked for 90 days and meet a weight guideline.	1991
Multi-Developers	Will not hire anyone engaging in what company views as high-risk activities such as skydiving, piloting private aircraft, mountain climbing, motorcycling.	1991
Texas Instruments	$10 monthly surcharge on health insurance for employees and dependents who smoke.	1991
Turner Broadcasting	Will not hire smokers.	1985
U-Haul	Biweekly $5 charge for health insurance for employees who smoke or chew tobacco, or whose weight exceeds guidelines.	1990

Reprinted with the permission of Aspen Publishers, Inc. © 1992, as it appeared in the *Hospital Strategy Report*, Vol. 4, No. 4 (February).
Source: *Business Week*, 26 August 1991.

plans and be competitive with prices 3–5 percentage points below the 14–17 percent increases of indemnity plans. But that will not work in the future. During the 1990s, fierce price and value competition will exist between HMOs and PPOs.

Rate wars and the insurance cycle will catch up with America's managed care plans by 1995. HMO prices rose only 10.9 percent in 1992 and 9.6 percent in 1993, well below the price hike of 16.9 percent in 1989 (Palsbo 1992). The profitability of HMOs and managed care plans will continue through 1995, but HMOs and PPOs will need to exercise more discipline to continue profitability during the 1990s by taking these more difficult steps:

- Eliminating high-cost, low-quality providers
- Installing practice guidelines for all major inpatient and ambulatory procedures
- Concentrating volume with fewer providers of proven quality

- Increasing enrollee cost-sharing for costly services such as drugs and ambulatory care
- Improving the satisfaction levels of consumers and providers
- Focusing on lifestyle changes to improve enrollee health status (and reduce health service needs)
- Pursuing relentlessly quality in clinical care and service
- Cutting further administrative overhead to get management costs below 10 percent (compared with 12.6 percent) (Palsbo 1992).

Blue Cross in the 1990s

Will the Blues be vulnerable in the 1990s, or poised for success with their national HMO network? Both perhaps. Blue Cross–Blue Shield plans have long been regarded as the steadiest in the market, so the bankruptcy of Blue Cross–Blue Shield of West Virginia in October 1990 sent shock waves across the nation. Despite earning a record $1.9 billion profit in 1990, the nation's Blue Cross–Blue Shield plans faced an uncertain future. The West Virginia plan was rescued by the Blues of Northern Ohio, but the "White Knight" had to pay $53 million in unpaid claims to West Virginia hospitals and doctors. Six more BC/BS plans were rated E (very weak) in 1992, including the BC/BS plans in Massachusetts, New Hampshire, New Jersey, and Vermont, plus the whole health insurance network of New York and the Hawaii Medical Service Association (Weiss Research 1992).

Blue Cross of California is the antithesis of its West Virginia counterpart (Blue Shield of California is a separate organization). Its turnaround during the period 1985–1993 should be instructive for other Blues as they face the future. Price wars with HMOs and "zero" premium increases left the California Blue Cross plan with few reserves and rapidly rising costs during the period 1985–1987. HMOs and PPOs were taking marketshare away. The California plan was ranked on fiscal viability last among all Blues plans in the nation when the plan's new executive, Leonard Schaefer, took over. He slashed the workforce, eliminated the Northern California regional office, sold the land and headquarters building, and leased back the corporate offices. Most importantly, Schaefer began a complete conversion to managed care, developing HMO and PPO options and rapidly increasing indemnity premiums to drive customers into the new plans. In the process, California Blue Cross moved from 10:90 (indemnity to managed care) to 90:10. The plan regained profitability in 1989 and in 1992 enjoyed the highest-profit years in the plan's history. Today, the California Blue Cross plan is the most profitable of all the Blues and ranks first among all national Blues plans in the terms of financial stability.

Managed Care Niches

As managed care becomes the dominant form of American health plan, the best opportunities for growth will be in the ten niches listed below.

1. *Workers' compensation/occupational health.* One of the fastest-growing markets for managed care is workers' compensation, and with good reason. The nation's workers' compensation programs have seen health costs soar at 20–30 percent per year since 1986. Workers' compensation HMOs take a capitated approach and provide the requisite services to injured workers for a prenegotiated monthly premium. HMO plans in workers' compensation offer substantial discounts from network providers and case management services. Adopting an HMO approach to workers' compensation cut costs by 40 percent in Florida (Sardinha 1993). Not all states allow a managed care approach to workers' compensation health care, and only 28 states allow employers to direct workers to certain providers within the first 30 days of treatment.

2. *Limited benefit plans.* These are "blue-plate special" managed care plans. By 1993, all but 11 states had enacted small employer group reforms that allow insurers to offer limited benefit plans affordable for small businesses and individuals (Pace Group 1993). Kansas, Kentucky, and Missouri are among states that have eased mandates to enable insurers and managed care plans to offer low-cost plans. These bare-bones managed care plans may provide a more limited array of services and benefits with higher levels to cost-sharing and deductibles to make them affordable. Low-cost plans should have a growing market while Congress debates national health insurance and may provide some pilot experiences for structuring a national program to cover the medically uninsured.

3. *Children and youth.* Niche plans for children and teenagers have strong appeal among working parents who must pay for dependent or family coverage. The plans are especially popular with single parents. California Blue Shield and California Blue Cross have been among the first insurers to envision this niche market as profitable.

4. *Rural HMOs.* Managed care could work in rural areas, if structural and competitive barriers are removed (National Rural Electric Cooperative Association and Metropolitan Life). What is needed are changes in state laws to encourage multiemployer trusts, to create rural exceptions for state regulation of HMOs, and to reform medical malpractice insurance in recognition of rural conditions.

5. *Long-term care.* As the American population ages, demand for nursing home, home care, and chronic illness services will increase exponentially. Payment of long-term care costs is a concern to 74 percent of Americans, according to a consumer survey conducted by the American

Association of Retired Persons (1992). Today, nursing homes and other long-term care providers have been largely ignored by managed care plans, but that will change. The nursing home industry is ripe for conversion to HMO/PPO network models with capitated enrollment, discounting and risk-sharing, and active case management. These managed long-term care programs may subcontract with HMOs, long-term care insurers, government agencies, employers, and the self-pay market.

6. *Medically uninsured.* Innovative managed care plans for small employers and the medically uninsured are being introduced in Maryland and California. Blue Cross plans in both states are launching limited benefits programs for individuals. The Maryland legislature has limited this program to those who have not been insured for at least 12 months. The California Blue Cross plan has targeted small businesses with 50 or fewer employees, many of which have been priced out of the market. The plan is sold to small groups with higher medical risks through insurance brokers, where the Blue Cross plan "balances" the risk of these small groups by selling coverage to one high-risk group for every four "normal" groups it enrolls. In only 18 months, 4,000 small groups and 200,000 individuals have become insured under the plan.

7. *Medicare HMOs.* The nation's 33 million Medicare-eligibles are the next major target market for America's managed care plans. HCFA administrator Bruce Vladeck plans to "try really hard to move Medicare patients into managed care" (*Hospitals* 1993). Officials at HCFA publicly discussed incentive programs that would encourage Medicare HMOs to expand enrollment including risk pools, reinsurance, and modified cost-based payment contracts. Medigap HMOs and PPOs have been a flourishing example of managed care's potential in the Medicare marketplace, or could have been. However, in 1991 Congress eliminated this opportunity by limiting the sales of medigap managed care products to 15 states. The limitation was the unintentional result of congressional medigap reform. In writing the reform legislation, Congress decided not to allow insurers to restrict beneficiaries' access to providers. Of course, that is the essence of managed care, dooming medigap HMOs and PPOs whose businesses are built around limited provider panels. Congress discovered its error and exempted 15 states from the provider limitation by creating test sites. But congressman Pete Stark (D-Calif.) blocked the extension of this program to other states that would have saved the medigap managed care business. The quickest way to increase Medicare HMO contracting is to increase government payment. The good news for managed care plans is that HCFA announced a 6.3 percent increase in Medicare HMO reimbursement for 1992 and is considering further increases (Kenkel 1993). In addition to increased payment, there

are a number of barriers that must be removed before Medicare risk contracting becomes a national trend.

8. *Mental health/substance abuse.* Managed mental health and substance abuse plans have a dynamic impact on health spending and hospital use for these specialized services. They're working, and employers are grateful; utilization review programs reduced hospital admissions by 12.3 percent (Bunker 1993). Length of stay dropped substantially, and the number of hospital days for these programs declined 8 percent during the study. Firms with mental health and substance abuse programs such as Campbell Soup reduced costs by 28 percent with managed care. First National Bank of Chicago cut its inpatient mental health costs from $1 million to $400,000 per year under a managed care program that now emphasizes partial hospitalization and day treatment approaches (Connors 1992).

9. *Corporate networks.* Self-insured employer buyer groups may be a major market during the 1990s. So far, the concept of employer "buy right" coalitions is still embryonic. In Florida, the Greater Tampa Chamber of Commerce created a managed care program for small employers that is expected to save its members 20–25 percent. The Tampa plan is based on the Cleveland Council of Smaller Enterprises, which has held rate increases to about 6 percent in 1990–1992, covering 175,000 employees in 11,000 small companies (Greene 1993). Similarly, Southern California Edison may become the first self-insured and self-administered company to resell its health care network to other employers. Edison covers 75 percent of its own 55,000 workers, dependents, and retirees with a company-run health plan. Several other employers, with more than 100,000 covered lives, have approached Edison to buy health services through its network of 75 hospitals and 7,500 physicians (Johnsson 1992).

10. *National networks of independent HMOs/PPOs.* New organizations are emerging to allow small, independent HMOs and PPOs access to large employers and national accounts. In February 1991, National Managed Care, Inc., announced the creation of a national network of regional independent plans that included plans from Florida (AvMed) to California (HealthNet). This is a niche market, creating regional and national alliances among HMOs and PPOs to service major buyers and multistate corporations. Managed care will be the driving force in restructuring hospital or health system market strategies and relationships during the 1990s.

Hospitals must respond to managed care entrepreneurs and their niches; examine the emerging networks for specialized services, such as transplants. High-technological services are a natural for niche strategies

—for example, a 1993 survey found that 47 percent of cardiac surgery centers plan to bundle and package open-heart surgery for insurance companies and self-insured employers (Medtronic/KPMG 1993). Creating packaged services calls for collaborative leadership between hospital trustees and medical staff leadership.

Looking Forward: Managed Care Must Control Health Inflation

The only threat to this strong outlook for managed care is public dissatisfaction with the current health system, which is still in transition from fee-for-service plans. Managed care and managed competition must work, and quickly! In *Making Managed Care Work*, Peter Boland (1991) presents this dilemma clearly:

> Managed care is now the dominant force in the healthcare industry. . . . As a result, managed care is in a race with the public's growing frustration over current healthcare programs. If managed care organizations do not make sufficient progress in addressing the healthcare needs of employers and other healthcare payers, then some form of national health insurance may appeal to a majority of the population in the 1990s.

The nineties will be the managed care era if HMOs and PPOs can satisfy consumer concerns about rising costs and the hassles of today's often-bureaucratic health systems. If managed care systems do not control health care inflation (price) and provide customer-oriented service (value) to satisfy these consumer concerns, then governmental management of the U.S. health system becomes more likely as the year 2000 approaches.

Strategies

1. **Develop a managed care strategy.** Every hospital needs a managed care strategy that elaborates the hospital's planned response regarding: (1) the physician-hospital organization, (2) pricing and discounts, (3) data systems to track costs and quality, (4) preferred managed care partners among HMOs, PPOs, and insurers, and (5) unbundling specialized services for contracting. Each hospital must analyze its managed care contracts in detail, monitoring revenues and costs to see which contracts are profitable. Beyond strategy, a senior-level manager with managed care experience is essential for contract negotiation and management.

2. **Expect eroding profits as "indemnity business" disappears.** In the transition from traditional indemnity insurance to managed care and as insurers convert to HMO and PPO models, hospitals should expect rapid shrinkage in their commercial insurance business. Hospital trustees on the

finance committee must monitor managed care contracting closely. Many hospitals have naively agreed to HMO/PPO contracts at rates that did not cover costs. There is a learning curve in the transition to managed care that outside experts can help hospitals successfully manage the learning curve of the managed care era.

3. **Know your costs and quality.** To be successful in a managed care environment, hospitals must compete on price and quality. Trustees must closely track key indicators of cost and quality. Both clinical outcomes and customer satisfaction are important. Managed care buyers are tough and sophisticated. Hospitals should put a trustee on the negotiating team to contribute business expertise and provide a link to the board in the development of these important relationships for the future.

4. **Create partnerships with physicians.** Hospitals must develop the "medical piece" of their managed care strategy, which will require new, tough-minded physician organizations. Many hospital-sponsored independent practice associations (IPAs) are too "loose" to be effective under managed care contracts. Hospitals will need physician group practices and experienced IPAs willing to provide utilization management, cost control, and risk-sharing. These physician partners deserve board seats for their strategic importance to the hospitals and health systems of the future.

References

American Association of Retired Persons. 1992. *Health Care Reform in America: Where the Public Stands.* Washington, DC: AARP.

Boland, P. 1991. *Making Managed Care Work.* Rockville, MD: Aspen Publishers.

Bunker, J. F. 1993. "Managing Behavioral Health Benefits: A COMPARE Survey Update." *Behavioral Healthcare Tomorrow* 2 (May–June): 17–19.

Coile, R. C., Jr. 1992. "Managed Care Outlook: Alternative Delivery Systems Become Dominant Health Plans." *Hospital Strategy Report* 4 (February): 1–8.

Connors, N. 1992. "Do You Need a Managed Mental Health Program?" *Business & Health* 10 (February): 48–53.

Foster Higgins & Company. 1993. *Health Care Benefits Survey: Medical Plans.* Princeton, NJ: The Company.

Greene, J. 1993. "Tampa Business Group Dives into Insurance Pool Initiatives." *Modern Healthcare* 23 (12 July): 10.

Hay/Huggins Company. 1992. *1992 Hay/Huggins Benefits Report,* Vol. 1. Philadelphia, PA: Hay/Huggins.

Health Plan Management Services. 1993. *1993 HMO Buyers Guide.* Atlanta, GA: HPMS.

Hewitt Associates. 1992. *Employer Experience in Managed Care.* Lincolnshire, IL: Hewitt Associates.

Hospitals. 1993. "The New HCFA Chief." 67 (5 July): 18–21.

InterStudy. 1993. *The InterStudy Competitive Edge DataBook.* St. Paul, MN: InterStudy.

————. 1991. *The InterStudy Edge*, 1 January.

Johnsson, J. 1992. "Direct Contracting: Employers Look to Hospital-Physician Part-
    nerships to Control Costs." *Hospitals* (20 February): 56–60.

Kenkel, P. J. 1993. "Vladeck Wants to Sweeten Medicare 'Risk.' " *Modern Health-
    care* 23 (21 June): 2.

Marion Merrill Dow. 1992. *Managed Care Digest, PPO Edition, 1992.* Kansas City,
    MO: Marion Merrill Dow.

Medtronic/KPMG. 1993. *Heart Institute Study Update 1992: Recent Developments in
    Restructuring of Cardiovascular Services.* Minneapolis, MN: Medtronic/KPMG.

Pace Group. 1993. *1993 Managed Care Regulatory Survey: Report on Status, Trends,
    Concerns.* Dallas, TX: The Group.

Palsbo, S. 1992. *1992 HMO Market Position Report.* Washington, DC: Group Health
    Association of America.

Pinkney, D. S. 1992. "More Hospitals Do Poorly on Quality Measures." *American
    Medical News* (9 March).

Sardinha, C. 1993. "HMOs Cut Workers' Comp. Costs Dramatically, New Study
    Claims." *Managed Care Outlook* 6 (18 June): 1–2.

Sullivan, C., and T. Rice. 1991. " ." *Health Affairs* (Summer): .

Weiss Research. 1992. *Ratings of Blue Cross/Blue Shield Plans.* West Palm Beach,
    FL: Weiss Research.

Wyatt Company. 1993. *Wyatt Comparison.* Chicago: The Company.

4

Technology and Ethics: High-Tech Access versus Rationing American Health Care

> Proposed changes for [government] payment and oversight of providers promise a variety of demands that will have to be satisfied before new and established technologies gain acceptance and approval.... The cumulative effect of these changes will be to restrict the use of new medical technologies to those that demonstrate the greatest differentiation or superiority in terms of: treatment results, reduction in risks or complications, decrease in hospitalization or labor resources, and cost-effectiveness.
>
> —Dennis J. Cotter (1989)

Technology will be the symbolic battleground of the cost-versus-quality policy dilemma over medical care expenditures during the 1990s. There will be nothing academic about this debate. The stakes are high—$830 billion expenditures in 1992, rising to a $1 trillion health care expense by the mid-1990s, if present medical inflation rates continue unabated. Fueled by technology, U.S. health care spending is rising through 14 percent of the GNP and rapidly heading for 15–20 percent by the year 2000.

The Costs of Technology

Americans are beguiled by the potential of medical technology. As a nation, we are technophiles, entranced by the promise of new pharmaceuticals, medical devices, implants, and life-saving systems. From network television programing to in-flight airline magazine columns, today's consumers eagerly await news of new technological marvels that will identify presymptomatic disease, cure catastrophic illnesses, and replace failing body organs. American consumers have good cause for optimism: Many of these medical marvels are in the laboratory or clinical trials and will arrive in a techno-cornucopia during the 1990s.

But there's a catch—the cost. Ethics, access, and rationing are the fallout of high-technological advances. Analyzing the ethical issues has spawned a prominent profession in health care (Friedman 1989). Substantial numbers of Americans believe their health system is too costly and requires dramatic reform. A surprising 43 percent of U.S. residents in a national survey expressed major concern with the current market-oriented health care system and professed a preference for the Canadian model (Foster Higgins & Company 1992).

Technology is a major source of the escalating costs—as much as 50 percent of health inflation is technology-driven, according to some economists (Barnum 1993). Technology is almost certainly also linked to labor intensity, which has risen dramatically in the past ten years in tandem with increased spending for new devices and medical advances. This evidence puts hospital and health system boards in a dilemma: do they continue to spend for the latest and best medical technology, or do they keep health costs below the current inflation rate as socially responsible providers?

Market trends in the economy and health care will also greatly influence the coming debate over national health reform. Hospitals and health systems should expect the following in terms of technology, ethics, and rationing (Coile 1989).

- The aging of the population means increases in the demand for inpatient services, rising inpatient admissions, longer lengths of inpatient stay for those over age 65, and increased numbers of diagnostic and therapeutic procedures.

- National health spending will creep toward $1 trillion by mid-decade, driven primarily by the aging of the population and the intensity of resources their care demands.

- Health inflation will continue at 8–10 percent (or higher) for the three years 1992–1995 for hospital and physician services.

- Medicare reimbursement for capital (technology and facilities) may fall to 75 percent of actual hospital outlays and could be eliminated by 1995.

- Managed care becomes the dominant reimbursement pattern, controlling 75–85 percent of inpatients and more than 50 percent of ambulatory care and physician office visits by 1995.

- Major payers, including employers, insurers, and government, tighten managed care approaches with extensive concurrent review, case management, exclusive provider arrangements, and specialty managed care plans such as mental health to restrain costs.

- High-tech spending in the medical "arms race" will continue unabated, as America's hospitals seek market differentiation through specialization in technology niches such as cardiac surgery.

- Home care and ambulatory care will be the major expansion zones for technology investment, as high-tech shifts away from the acute hospital setting as a result of cost-containment pressures by the payers.
- Hospital profitability will improve, with hospitals averaging 2–4 percent profit margins and regaining financial health; fewer than 50 hospitals weaken and fail each year.

Technological Breakthroughs

America's technology cup will be overflowing during the nineties. Technology will produce medical breakthroughs, but will all Americans benefit? It will be ethics versus economics. There are some tough choices ahead for patients and policymakers in the 1990s.

The emerging technological advances that will have the greatest influence on this decade and the ethical dilemmas they may bring are artificial intelligence, biosensors and implants, diagnostic imaging, genetic engineering, home health/self-diagnostics, new wave surgery, office automation, superdrugs, and transplants and implants (Coile 1988).

Medical *artificial intelligence* (AI) will produce a wide spectrum of biomedical software. New medical software will be used in a broad range of applications such as fetal monitoring, critical care management, clinical diagnosis, computer-assisted surgery, and genetic counseling. Every medical specialty will have its own software and expert systems. Early medical software will need the power of mainframe computers, but by mid-decade a number of small-scale expert systems will decentralize applications in mini- and microcomputers.

Ethical issues
1. Control: Who will endorse and control artificial intelligence in medicine? The American Medical Association? Professional clinical societies? Government?
2. Choices: Will medical software give physicians and patients choices in therapies? Or will there be a single rule or practice guideline that all must follow?

With prototypes already being tested in Japan and Europe, *biosensors* will be on the market by the middle to late 1990s, probably in tandem with *implanted* drug-dispensing devices. This will be a boon to the management of the chronically ill, eliminating drug confusion and fine-tuning dosage levels. Beneficiaries will include the millions of diabetics, hypertensives, and mentally ill on drug maintenance therapy. Biosensors with telemetry devices will replace the "lifeline" emergency response systems that now rely on the patient to push the alert button to summon emergency medical attention. Futurist Clem Bezold has envisioned the "hospital on the wrist," a biosensing device that would continuously monitor health levels and automatically summon medical help in emergencies. These medical-alert devices might be given to the chronically ill by an insurance company, managed care plan, or employer. Their cost would be easily offset by having prevented a heart attack or stroke.

Ethical issues
1. Access to biosensors: Which health plans will provide biosensors to chronically ill patients as a covered benefit? Will this monitoring technology be available only to wealthy insureds with high-option health plans? Will Medicare or Medicaid cover biosensors?
2. Cost impact: Will closer monitoring of health levels cut health costs through early intervention or increase costs by identifying more disease?

To speed the throughput of diagnosis and treatment, state-of-the-art *imaging* devices will pinpoint pathology earlier in the disease process. Medical research continues to push out the range of applications for MRI in cardiology, oncology, orthopedics, and a widening array of conditions. Lower-field strength magnets will cut the cost of MRI devices and reduce shielding and facility costs. All images, including conventional x-ray, will be digitalized and stored on optical laser disks. By the mid-1990s, optical disks will be erasable as well as available in 5 1/4-inch formats, permitting decentralized optical disk storage in smaller units. Positron emission tomography (PET) is gaining acceptance and will be installed in 100–200 major medical centers by 1996. Body-field mapping will be explored using new magnetometer devices; prototypes are being tested. Even holography may be applied in medical imaging by the year 2000, providing clinicians a three-dimension dynamic view.

Ethical issues
1. Rationing for imaging: Will state governments delete MRI or PET scans from Medicaid-covered services? Will the poor and medically uninsured have long waits, like Canadians, for high-tech imaging?
2. Payment for PET: Will insurers and the government refuse to cover costly PET scans after the technology is no longer experimental?
3. High-cost contrast agents: Will many community hospitals refuse to use higher-cost contrast agents, even though imaging quality is higher, because insurers and government will not cover the increased cost?

The first outputs of *genetic engineering* provide early evidence of the power of this technology for improved diagnosis and treatment. Genetic probes will provide doctors with clinical markers on the presence of disease, even years before symptoms appear. Recent scientific breakthroughs with rare cancers like retinoblastoma are providing new clues on cancer formation when two predisposing chromosomes are damaged. Birth defects could be reduced dramatically in the future, through a combination of genetic probes and computerized assessment of family history. Genetic therapy could alter a defective gene, turning a disease "switch" from on to off. Human experiments have already begun. tPA, the "clot-busting" drug, demonstrates the potential of genetically engineered pharmaceuticals. While tPA (tissue-type plasminogen activator) is expensive at $2,200 per dose, other drugs such as synthetic human insulin are much cheaper when the research and development costs are spread out over a larger patient population. Within the next seven years, the clinical use of single-gene therapies will be discovered in a number of major hospitals (Davidson 1993).

Ethical issues
1. Genetic gadflies: Will consumer activists slow the testing of human genetic therapies? Will gene therapy be tested in the courts as well as clinical trials?
2. Development costs: Will the high costs and risk of biogenetic research dampen the advent of new genetically engineered technologies?

The demand for *home health services* will grow at double-digit levels during the 1990s, with better reimbursement and more technology in home settings. The AIDS crisis has fueled innovation in home care. Home chemotherapy, home antibiotic therapy, infusion therapy, and home treatment of pneumonias are now safe and cost effective. International pharmaceutical companies may make substantial investments in home care, as more drug applications come to the home. The elderly are a growing market for in-home health and support services. Long-term care will be a high-visibility political issue in the health reform debate. The seniors' political clout, having repealed catastrophic benefits, will next turn to expanding long-term care and home health benefits. Indeed, the Clinton health plan calls for the gradual expansion of long-term care coverage in national health insurance (Chen 1993). Regardless, *self-diagnostic kits* will enable consumers to monitor their own health. Diagnostic kits will also be widely sold by physicians as an in-office convenience. The success of extending high-tech into the home is not dependent on technology alone; social factors will play a role. The future of home care will be determined as much by the support systems for the elderly and chronically ill in their homes.

Ethical issues
1. Home care for the homeless: Will the government provide health care for the homeless and poorly housed?

2. Home care support system: Will policymakers and elected officials recognize that the success of home care is heavily dependent on a system of
   social support services that allow patients to be treated in their homes?

   The *surgical laser* and other *minimally invasive surgery* will rev-
olutionize surgical practice in both inpatient and ambulatory procedures.
Lasers are making bloodless surgery possible, with incisions closed by
laser stitches. Hospitals are developing comprehensive laser centers with all
surgical modalities. Billboards are already proclaiming the arrival of surgical
lasers in community hospitals. In addition, arthroscopy has transformed
orthopedics, and in ophthalmology, surgeons will reshape the eyes to restore
normal vision without glasses. As the baby-boomers age, this becomes
an enormous market and societal benefit. Minimally invasive surgery has
revolutionized the treatment of gastrointestinal and gynecological disorders,
with same-day treatments where conventional surgery required five to seven–
day stays.

Ethical issues

1. Access to tools: Will public hospitals and small rural hospitals keep pace
   with technology in the 1990s if they cannot afford to acquire upgrades
   of existing technology or purchase new tools?
2. Open competition with physicians: Will hospitals experience open-market
   warfare with medical staff who build competing freestanding ambulatory
   surgery and diagnostic imaging centers?

   The "paperless" hospital is no longer a fantasy. It will become achiev-
able during the 1990s as *integrated information systems* with laser disc
storage units become the industry standard. Powerful mainframe computers
already exist. Tomorrow's health information systems will be constructed of
linked networks of mini- and microcomputers. At the microcomputer level,
Intel's 486 chip creates a new generation of micros four times the speed and
capacity of 386-based units, and a 586 chip is in development. Integration is
the key word for the future. Committees are at work to standardize hardware
and software standards for the health industry. Networks of hundreds of electronic workstations for health care's "knowledge workers" will be located
in every hospital and health facility. Bedside computing systems are demonstrating the potential to reduce nurse charting time by a half-hour to one hour
per nurse per shift. State-of-the-art hospital information systems use software
to link physician offices and channel patients in local and regional networks.
   The most sophisticated health care delivery systems, such as Inter-
Mountain, are investing $100 million in an integrated health information
network linking 25 hospitals and their physicians (Gardner 1993). Health
information system vendors are working to integrate financial with clinical management systems (Lumsden 1993). *Case management software* will

guide patient care and allocation of resources. Effective case management in the 1990s could cut as much as one day off the national inpatient length of stay, lowering U.S. health spending by $25–50 billion annually. Physicians and nurses may not be the only ones on-line as the Clinton administration hopes to improve access to cost and quality records to verify claims, switching to the UB-92 format or the more advanced ANSI 837 for speeding reimbursement electronically to providers (Gardner 1993).

Ethical issues
1. Confidentiality in networks: Will the extension of information networks to physician offices and outlying centers pose new issues of privacy and protection?
2. Employer probing: Will employers, government, and review agencies electronically "snoop" into employee medical records in the future?

Medicine's preference in the future will be for invasive therapies. A new wave of *superdrugs* will arrive on the market during the 1990s, speeded by computer-assisted design and fast-track regulatory approval by the Food and Drug Administration. Drug development time could drop to four to six years in this decade, driven by the need to find a cure for AIDS and to speed availability of promising therapies for cancer, Alzheimer's, and other high-cost diseases (Bezold 1993). Not all consumers are willing to wait: For those who cannot get into National Institutes of Health–approved clinical trials, some companies make experimental cancer drugs available on an all-cash basis. Imagine a drug that would dissolve the plaque in coronary arteries; it may be ready for public distribution by the mid to late 1990s, eliminating much of the need for coronary bypass surgery, angioplasty, and cardiac laser surgery. The AIDS epidemic is also driving the development of a widening range of vaccines for viruses and communicable diseases. Genetically engineered disease blockers could provide therapies for cancer.

Ethical issues
1. High cost of new drugs: Should drug companies be allowed to price new pharmaceuticals with high treatment costs like tPA and AZT (azidothymidine)? Should hospitals only purchase drugs they can afford under Medicare or managed care limits?
2. Fee-for-service research: Should access to experimental drugs be limited to the wealthy who can afford unlicensed drug therapies?

Transplantation is one of the most costly and controversial technologies, but it's also becoming more common. The number of human heart transplants, for example, will double and redouble by 1995. Thus far, the only limit has been the availability of human hearts, but now rationing of heart transplants is an issue (Haubelt 1993). Many health insurance plans do not cover this $200,000–250,000 procedure. This is why Oregon's state legis-lature specifically chose to reallocate Medicaid budget funds from transplants to maternal and child health (Rich 1993). There will be wireless connectivity to a new generation of microelectronic devices within the body, from drug-dispensing pumps for diabetics to miniature heart pumps that improve blood flow, and cardiac pacemakers with built-in defibrillators (McDonald 1993). The aging population is also driving demand for *implants*. Joint replace-ments of hips, knees, elbows, and digits will be especially in demand for this segment of the population. Other joint replacements will use human tissue. It's also likely that lens and cochlear implants will be installed in increasing numbers, as will pacemakers with built-in defibrillators. Research on neurological implants will advance in the 1990s, but major breakthroughs on the complex human-machine interface will probably not occur until the twenty-first century.

Ethical issues
1. Age thresholds: Should physicians set clinical guidelines that use age or other factors to discriminate which patients have access to transplantation or bionics?
2. Health plan exclusions: Will insurance companies, employers, or the gov-ernment fail to cover transplants, implants, or bionics for certain classes of consumers? Will the courts support such discriminatory exclusions?

Technology, Ethics, and Rationing: Three Scenarios for the 1990s

While the future surely holds many possibilities, three scenarios for 1990s health technology are presented for consideration.

1. Medical Breakthroughs*

This is the high-tech scenario. Two driving forces contribute to the medical breakthroughs future—sustained economic prosperity that allows a high level of investment in biomedical research and health care services, and significant medical advances in cardiac care, cancer, and AIDS. In this scenario, health spending reaches 15 percent of the GNP by the year 2000. National health levels rise and the population gains an immediate one to two years of life extension through a combination of medical technology and improved

---

*This text has been adapted from Russell C. Coile, Jr., *The New Medicine: Reshaping Medical Practice and Healthcare Management*, Aspen Publishers, 1990. pp. 373–75.

lifestyle. With major advances against several of the leading causes of death, lifespans of 100–120 years will be possible in the next century.

National economic policy identifies the health industry as a major strategic sector by 1995. Government accelerates its review of new medical devices and drugs. Medical technology is encouraged as a major U.S. export. America's medical technology leadership position makes the top U.S. hospitals a magnet in the growing global market for health services. High technology is diffused deeply across American hospitals, and quality is excellent. Regulators, employers, and insurance companies monitor quality closely and select providers for managed care contracts based on both quality and price.

High technology flourishes. Research and development spending by government and the private sector rises 10–15 percent. Key medical breakthroughs occur in cardiac care with the arrival of artificial heart pumps with implantable space-age power source. The ventricular assist device (VAD) is now permanently installed; some patients with no prior heart attacks are given a VAD as a precautionary therapy. Artificial lungs are being developed. Prototypes of artificial kidneys and livers are being tested. Artificial intelligence is widely used in medicine for diagnosis and therapy. Neurosurgery is now routinely computer-guided using robot surgeons. Genetics is opening new doors in cancer therapy. Genetic probes can identify risks for a number of types of cancers, and new pharmaceuticals are proving successful in treatment of liver, cervical, and colon cancer. An AIDS vaccine has been developed and is being administered worldwide by the turn of the century. AIDS treatments involving new drugs began to gain ground on the epidemic by the mid-1990s.

Reimbursement for physicians and hospitals is a mix of case-based and capitation, with some fee-for-service. Medicare blends hospital and physician payment in the mid–1990s, and hospitals have structured a variety of approaches to physician reimbursement with their medical staff. An innovative array of incentives reward doctors for efficiency and quality outcomes.

Health spending reaches 17–18 percent of the GNP by the year 2000. Physician incomes rise 5–8 percent as the aging of the population drives up the number of office visits and hospitalizations. Given the strong high-tech orientation of the health system, specialists continue to out-earn primary care physicians by 30–50 percent. Hospital stays are expensive. The cost of a hospital admission has doubled in the 1990s, reflecting the growing number of implants, bionics, and other high-tech treatments.

Hospitals are falling into two categories: low-tech community hospitals that provide routine medical treatment and high-tech specialized facilities. Access to capital is the critical factor. Smaller facilities that could not afford to keep pace with technology investment have drifted into a secondary status. A few have down-licensed to skilled nursing, psychiatric, or rehabilitation.

Larger hospitals with strong operating margins and capital reserves built specialized facilities for their centers of excellence. Projects costing more than $100 million are not unusual. In this scenario, academic medical centers are the most successful hospitals—magnets for patients, physician specialists, and research dollars.

Physicians are either hospital-based specialists or community-based primary care practitioners. Most (75 percent) medical specialists and subspecialists are located in a hospital or medical office building on a hospital campus. The concentration of specialists increases so that by the year 2000, half of all specialists are affiliated with academic medical centers and teaching hospitals. Research activities enhance the specialist physician's practice and referrals. Primary care physicians are essential to the system of patient referrals. Few primary care doctors admit directly to hospitals; most refer patients who need hospitalization to specialists. Only small and rural hospitals still allow primary care physicians to admit directly and to maintain responsibility for their patients. Protocols for care coordination by primary care doctors and specialists have been developed to protect both in their respective roles. Physicians control access to technology, although they share power with managed care third party reviewers who must give prior approval for major procedures.

Access/rationing of high technology is a private affair, not public policy. Most decisions are between doctor and patient. Major payers—insurance companies, HMO/PPOs, employers, and government—use health benefit policies to exclude certain high-cost procedures. Payers have created a new category of "advanced medical practices" that are routinely excluded from insurance coverage or government-paid services. This new class of procedures includes heart and liver transplants, some bone marrow cancer therapies, and most artificial organs. Technology is a discretionary purchase in the health marketplace. The rich can afford high-option health insurance covering more high-tech services. The poor receive charity care, but the middle class becomes technologically disadvantaged in this scenario.

2. Managed Competition

The United States is seeking a uniquely American "competitive" approach to managing health costs and technology as national expenditures for medical care continue at 10–12 percent of inflation. After five years of double-digit health inflation, U.S. consumers and policymakers are so discouraged that they move to limit health spending by placing a freeze on insurance premiums, drug costs, and hospital and physician prices and by temporarily controlling new investments in medical technology.

A two to three–year price freeze is intended to buy time for managed competition to work. Employers and government agencies coalign their buyers' clout in purchaser coalitions, and health care providers organize in networks. Prices are driven down in long-term (3–5 year) contracts with capitated all-inclusive prices to providers, and purchasers force providers to keep inflation close to the Consumer Price Index. Managed care becomes the mechanism of managed competition, and all consumers are given an HMO-type health plan, paid for by either their employer or government.

As a result, *health policy* reembraces competition in a return to the policies of the 1980s, but this time it works. Stung by rapidly rising health costs of 10–12 percent and more, employers rapidly organize to bargain with the U.S. health industry. Hospital use is controlled by primary care physician gatekeepers, and certificate-of-need review programs are eliminated. The market is tougher, forcing unnecessary hospitals and high-cost programs to consolidate. Some 10–15 percent of hospitals are closed by 1996 as their community care networks tighten up.

Although managed competition is uncoordinated and patchwork, it cuts health inflation to under 8 percent by 1995 and slows health spending to the Consumer Price Index rate of general inflation plus 2 or 3 percent by the year 2000.

High technology is dampened by the tightening of the market's belt. Hospitals cannot add new technology or purchase capital equipment without internal review and approval process within their community care network. High-cost equipment acquisitions and major building projects are delayed or shelved. Yet crisis often breeds opportunity: small-scale technology designed for ambulatory care environments or physicians offices flourishes; pharmaceuticals are another beneficiary of reregulation; purchasers and providers prefer medical therapies instead of high-cost surgical interventions such as cardiac bypass surgery.

Health spending is decreased, ending a five-year run of double-digit inflation. Health care may slow to only 12–13 percent of gross domestic product by the year 2000. Managed competition is only partly successful because despite the substantial buying clout of the nation's employers, health spending continues to rise at 6–8 percent annually, at least two to three points above the Consumer Price Index. Some blame the fragmented competitive approach; others point to the built-in inefficiencies of the health care market itself. The aging population contributes by driving costs up. In addition, not all reforms are complete. For example, malpractice reform is still being phased in, and some defensive medical practices continue.

Hospitals must cope with more downturns in utilization. Managed competition has no "safety net." Inpatient demand falls by another 15–25 percent during the 1990s, facing more hospital closures. Excess beds are converted to long-term care units, and few new hospitals are needed in any market. Hospitals still have freedom to invest in new facilities and new equipment, but capitation payments motivate hospitals to lower overhead costs. Hospitals that rebuilt during the eighties are now preferred network partners, with moderate capital costs and modern facilities. Those that waited for environmental stability during the early 1990s missed their window of opportunity to build or buy, and now any major capital investment has dramatic financial risk.

Physicians are a prime target of managed competition. Primary care physicians assume the role of gatekeepers, and large primary-care based medical groups control access to specialists. Some purchaser coalitions use the Medicare resource-based relative value scale (RBRVS) on physician reimbursement to create a standardized price schedule for medical services. Medicare HMOs compete for thousands of enrollees, and physicians compete to participate in them, although they may not charge Medicare patients for more than the HMO payment. Insurance companies and managed care plans adopt similar strategies, and the incomes of physician specialists fall 15–25 percent before leveling off. Cardiac surgeons, ophthalmologists, and neurosurgeons are hit particularly hard with some doctors losing 40–50 percent of their revenues before the market restabilizes. Most doctors practice in groups by the year 2000.

Access/rationing becomes universal—everyone has a health plan, paid for by employers or government. Patients and physicians continue to have access to high-tech equipment in the facilities that invested before 1995. Those that did now have a technology "franchise" since few new players are allowed by the HMOs. Rationing is a result of primary care gatekeepers and tough-minded medical directors. Public hospitals may suffer most in managed competition because there are no financial guarantees. At least the public patients, the poor and medically uninsured, now have health plans and can seek services anywhere in their networks. Innovation and new technology slow dramatically as biomedical and drug manufacturers find few clients for new diagnostic devices and therapeutics.

3. National Health System

Could the United States adopt a single-payer health system like Canada's? The Clinton reform plan would allow states to select a single-payer system. By 1995, many states opt for a Canadian-like system, and the U.S. health system is rationalized. This unprecedented policy shift is driven by rising health costs and a coalition of major employers, unions, seniors, and progressive health care providers' ability to convince Congress that America's voluntary health system is fundamentally flawed.

Health policy explicitly limits national health spending—a ceiling of 11 percent of GNP is placed on national health expenditures, with the goal of tightening to 10 percent by the year 2000 and 8 percent by the year 2010. The goal will be achieved by closing hospitals, lowering physician fees, and rigidly controlling the supply of facilities and services. (High-cost services like transplants are not covered by the national health program.) Health services are budgeted on a per capita basis and allocated through regional health authorities. Capital for new facilities and services is tightly controlled at the regional level.

High technology withers under the government's heavy hand. Biomedical device manufacturers consolidate or exit the shrinking market because suppliers are stringently limited in pricing and reimbursement. Technology and hospital equipment is purchased through the Government Services Agency (GSA). All new devices and drugs can only be approved after undergoing clinical trials. The introduction of new technology slows dramatically. On a global level, Japan and the European Community become leaders in health technology development.

Health spending slows, but downsizing the U.S. health budget takes longer than predicted. The aging of the population requires more services per capita for older Americans. Hospitals are constrained by tight budgets, but private physicians "game the system" for more reimbursement, as do many providers and suppliers.

Hospitals retain their independent ownership but now are forced to live within an annual budget set by the regional health authorities. New facilities and equipment are centrally controlled through a review process similar to certificate of need. While some adjustment is made for case mix and patient severity of illness, the system arbitrarily reduces hospital budgets across the board. For-profit hospitals argued unsuccessfully for a federal buyout and are now forced to live on limited budget allocations. Some for-profit hospital chains declare bankruptcy and exit the business. Rural hospitals fare unequally, as some regions seek to protect their small, outlying facilities while other regions rapidly move to close them.

Physicians attempt to cope with price controls by increasing volume and unbundling patient visits into more billable services, which only leads to more controls over physician services by government review organizations. Applications to medical schools drop sharply, and top medical specialists retreat into true private practice, only to see limited numbers of self-pay patients. Some physicians retire early during the transition; others gravitate toward hospitals as the centers of care in the new national system. Although physicians remain in their private offices and bill on a fee-for-service basis, their morale is low.

Access/rationing is designed to improve under a national health system, but in fact, the queues for high-tech services grow longer as the regions limit the supply of specialized services and costly procedures. Congress refuses to set explicit rationing criteria for high technology, but the regions experiment with practice guidelines that discourage high-tech procedures for the elderly and chronically ill. A small but thriving private market for specialized procedures grows in many metropolitan areas, but it is an all-cash business that poor and middle-income consumers are hard-pressed to afford. As much as 15 percent of the health care economy is private-pay under the new national health regime.

High Technology under Health Reform: What Is Likely?

Assuming a health reform future of increasing managed care while holding national health costs under control, technology will be caught in a tug-of-war of access versus costs for the remainder of the 1990s. Given the aging population, it is unlikely that the goals of improving access to technology and increasing quality can be met simultaneously. Since the number of Americans over age 65 reached 12 percent in 1990, the pressure has increased to provide those often chronically ill with the latest and best of modern medicine.

These are the potential impacts of health reform on high technology:

- Rationing of high-cost procedures such as organ transplants may be widespread; as many as 10–15 states could follow Oregon's lead to shift Medicaid funding from high technology to subsidize the medically uninsured.

- Grass-roots consumer groups like Oregon's Health Decisions will make health expenditures for technology a high-visibility public policy issue for state and local governments and fuel controversies as local hospitals propose technology investments.

- The high cost of dying will become the focus of third party expenditure control by government and insurance in the 1990s, as payers focus on the final year of life as the "last frontier of cost containment."

- Cost-benefit studies by payers of high-tech procedures will test the efficiency and efficacy of all new biomedical technologies and expensive pharmaceuticals.

- Experimental technology will take longer to be approved by payers; the competition among insurers to be the first to cover advanced medical practices and devices is over.

- Fee-for-service technology may be available only to the affluent as a discretionary purchase as managed care plans and employers limit access to high-cost procedures such as organ transplants and expensive "orphan" drugs like tPA.

- High-ticket technological procedures will be targeted for major discounts, fee-bundling, and exclusive provider arrangements by insurance companies, managed care plans, and major employers.

- Second-class medicine will be available for the poor and rural Americans only if urban medical centers have the bond ratings and operating profits to continue to acquire the latest high-cost technology.

- Hub-and-spoke referral systems will transport patients to technology from rural areas to urban technology citadels because small hospitals cannot afford to care for more complex and acutely ill patients.

- Specialty niches will distinguish the strong hospitals in a competitive marketplace as hospitals market their strengths in selected specialties, such as cardiac care and oncology.

- Medical superstars will be heavily recruited and subsidized as hospitals build high-visibility medical programs around talented physician specialists who are a magnet for physician referral and consumer self-referral.

- Community hospitals will erode the technology monopolies of regional medical centers as they selectively expand the range of high-tech services and invest in competing technologies.

- Volume thresholds, practice guidelines, and quality criteria will be imposed by government, insurance companies, and managed care plans to eliminate low-volume (and inferior quality) programs; the payers' first target will most likely be cardiac surgery programs performing less than 200 procedures per year and organ transplants with fewer than 10 patients annually.

- Design of a national health benefits package could ultimately become the most important regulator of market entry for new drugs and devices (Strongin 1993).

Looking Forward: No Quick Fixes

The technology outlook in health care will clearly be a mixed "policy stew" of managed care, cost controls, rationing, and ethical issues, with no early resolution. America's health policymakers will spend the decade sorting out the underlying issue of how much to invest in medical technology versus other social expenditures such as education, defense, or the war on drugs. None of the scenarios—medical breakthroughs, managed competition, or national health system—is dominant, nor will it emerge in a pure form. Regardless of the scenario type, hospitals should anticipate limits on technology in the future—whether market constraints or government controls. Some hospitals will take a "buy it now" attitude and make capital investments before national health reform takes effect; others will decide to defer expensive capital investments, choosing to keep their overhead costs down and to build financial reserves. Both strategies have opportunity costs and risk.

Technology will be at the center of the debate about the U.S. health system's efficiency and efficacy. America will only turn to the Canadian alternative if managed competition is unsuccessful in holding national health inflation to below 10 percent. Otherwise, more radical solutions to the issues of health technology, ethics, and rationing become increasingly possible. The decade could become one of technology-bashing by cost-pressured payers, overzealous regulators, and misguided consumer activists; they miss the point. America does need a national health policy that will raise health levels with better technology in tandem with lifestyle changes. Because America will spend more money on health during the 1990s, providers must seek the desirable social and health outcomes that may result from a rational investment in medical technology (Coile 1990).

Strategies

1. **Create a strategic technology plan.** To successfully manage technology, every hospital needs a strategic technology plan—a "bottom-up" plan that involves the entire hospital and medical staff and scans for technological innovations in the future and identifies needs and costs. The strategic technology plan is an overlay on the current strategic plan and an integral component of future plans.

2. **Seek leadership from the medical staff.** Clinical expertise is central to technology management. Lay trustees must rely on their physician partners for advice on emerging technologies. Medical staff leadership is critical in the development of strategic technology plans.

3. **Prepare for rationing.** The rationing of high-cost medical services is coming. Charge the ethics committee to take a leadership role in identifying rationing issues and developing policies and contingency strategies. Every hospital and health system should become leaders in the future debate over rationing health services.

References

Barnum, A. 1993. "Why Health Costs Soar So Steeply: Medical Technology Is Major Factor." *San Francisco Chronicle*, 22 March.

Bezold, C. 1993. "Scenarios: Setting the Stage." In *2020 Visions: Health Care Information Standards and Technology.* Rockville, MD: U.S. Pharmacopeial Convention.

Chen, E. 1993. "Clinton's Press Campaign for Health Reforms." *Los Angeles Times*, 10 August.

Coile, R. C., Jr. 1989. "Health Care 1990: Top 10 Trends for the Year Ahead." *Hospital Strategy Report* 2, no. 2 (December): 1–8.

———. 1988. "The Promise of Technology: A Technoforecast for the 1990s." *Healthcare Executive* (November–December): 22–25.

———. 1990. "Re-Visioning Health Care." *Health Management Quarterly* 11, no. 4 (Winter): 2–3.

Cotter, D. J. 1989. "Government's Impact on Medical Technologies." *Healthcare Forum Journal* (September–October): 26–29.

Davidson, S. 1993. "Medicines and Health Technology through 2020." In *2020 Visions: Health Care Information Standards and Technologies*. Rockville, MD: U.S. Pharmacopeial Convention.

Foster Higgins & Company. 1992. *Health Care Reform Survey*. Princeton, NJ: The Company.

Friedman, E. 1989. "This Thing about Machines." *Healthcare Forum Journal* (September–October): 9–11.

Gardner, E. 1993. "Computers, Networks Help Intermountain Integrate." *Modern Healthcare* 23, no. 29 (19 July): 30–31.

Haubelt, R. M. 1993. *Cost Implications of Human Transplants: An Update*. Brookfield, WI: Milliman and Robertson.

Lumsden, K. 1993. "The Clinical Connection." *Hospitals* 67 (5 May): 16–21.

McDonald, M. 1993. "Health in the Age of Telecognition." In *2020 Visions: Health Care Information Standards and Technology*. Rockville, MD: U.S. Pharmacopeial Convention.

Rich, S. 1993. "U.S. Approves Oregon Plan for Health Care Rationing." *Washington Post*, 20 March.

Strongin, R. J. 1993. *The Potential Effects of Health System Reform on Medical Technology*. Alexandria, VA: Health Care Technology Institute.

5

Business and Health: Employer Strategies to Control Health Costs

Because of rising costs, 91 percent of CEOs, presidents, and chairmen [sic] [of Fortune 1000 companies surveyed] say the health care system is in need of "complete rebuilding," and 53 percent say government intervention is needed.

—S. Findlay (1993b)

Hospitals must start paying attention to business because American business is increasingly concerned about the high cost of health care. As U.S. corporations work to lower their health benefit costs, every hospital in America will be affected. The nation's major employers are overwhelmed by the rising health costs, and hospitals are high-visibility symbols of escalating health expenses. For the largest companies, health expenses have become a costly factor affecting profits and stock prices—each Fortune 500 company pays at least $100 million per year for health costs. Health care is the nation's third largest business—total expenditures for 1992 exceeded $830 billion, more than 12 percent of the GNP. Employers bear much of these costs because 85–90 percent of all health insurance is purchased through groups.

The Toll on Hospitals and Employers

Goaded by 20–30 percent annual premium increases in the past five years, employers want fundamental health care reform; some are calling for new policy based on the Canadian model. Others are dumping their insurance company intermediaries and selecting their own providers in self-administered plans. Across the nation, American business is moving aggressively to control soaring health insurance costs and health benefits.

Corporate buyers are revolting, which will have major consequences for hospitals and the health industry. Hospital boards will be caught in the crossfire of business ire over soaring health costs because: (1) hospital trustees are often representatives of major corporations and by design serve as the channel for communication between the employer community and the hospital, but their dual role puts them in the middle. Which hat should business trustees wear when discussing hospital budgets and approving capital projects? and (2) hospitals are major employers with rising health benefit expenses themselves. Should hospital trustees participate in employer health care coalitions to reduce employee health costs? Which side are hospitals on, purchaser or supplier?

America's business and industry have good reason to be incensed about health costs—business has paid $3 for every $4 in rising health costs in the past three years, according to the 1990 poll by *Business & Health* (1991). The survey also found that 85 percent of top executives across the country ranked rising health insurance premiums as the top health care issue. Among the top five corporate health concerns were mandated benefits (69 percent), paying for catastrophic illnesses such as AIDS (64 percent), covering the costs of dependents (60 percent), and workers' compensation costs (58 percent).

A survey by The Conference Board (1992) also confirmed the concerns of 75 percent of the CEOs of 500 large U.S. employers who do not believe their companies can control health care costs in the next five years. A majority of the business leaders feel some sort of government health plan will be required to address the cost issue.

The costs of health care have been fodder for much media attention, primarily because *all* business have been so significantly affected. Small businesses have been hit even harder, experiencing one-year premium raises of as much as 60 percent. When an individually owned business in the East was quoted a health premium of $17,372 per year for its nine employees after experiencing catastrophic high costs from a critically ill infant of one employee, it's no wonder that Americans without health insurance number between 35–40 million, and growing. Small businesses cannot afford to offer health insurance benefits.

Even large employers with HMOs didn't fare much better with annual rate hikes of 13–14 percent between 1989 and 1991 but costs slowed to 10 percent in 1992 (Hewitt Associates 1992a). Some self-insured employers beat the cost push, with medical costs rising in the range of 9–15 percent. This lower rate of health cost increase was still two to three times the overall rate of inflation in the Consumer Price Index.

At one point during the mid-1980s, employers thought they had health costs under control, but then the government introduced DRGs in 1983–1984, which forced employers to crack down on their health expenditures with second opinions, preadmission controls for hospitalization, and HMO/

PPO contracting. From 1985 to 1987, they were successful: health costs abated to single-digit levels. However, double-digit health inflation returned in 1988, and continues into the 1990s as corporate health spending soared from $2,361 per employee in 1989 to $3,244 in 1992—a new record high (Hewitt Associates 1992a). In 1989, employee health expenses rose to more than $2,500 per worker.

Ten Trends For Reducing Costs

What strategies will employers use to reduce health costs in the 1990s? What will be the effects of those strategies on hospitals? As communication links the business community (purchasers) with the hospital and its medical staff (suppliers), trustees need to know how employers plan to manage health costs and the implications of those buyer strategies on their hospitals.

Trend 1: Managed Care

In 1985, 32 percent of the 5,000 largest American corporations did not offer HMOs, and 79 percent had no PPOs. By 1993, only 25 percent of major companies do not offer alternative delivery systems (Wyatt Company 1993). Managed care is clearly a national movement. The West has the highest HMO concentration, with 25.1 percent, but HMOs are catching on in the Northeast, with an HMO concentration rate of 17.4 percent; the Midwest (13.9 percent) and South (8.6 percent) still lag behind national trends (InterStudy 1993). HMO enrollment grew by 2.1 million in 1992, by 6.1 percent, reaching 39.1 million by year's end. The implications for hospitals from rising managed care enrollment are clear. By 1995–1997, the "commercial insurance" business of most hospitals will decline to less than 10 percent of their patients; the percent of managed care (including government) will rise to 75–85 percent of the average hospital's case mix. In the West, some hospitals have already reached the 95 percent level of managed care/government.

But which managed care format will be most effective in controlling employer health costs? HMO popularity is waning with some employers. Among members of the Washington Business Group on Health, 73 percent of employers offer HMOs, but only 62 percent of the companies still offer a "conventional" health plan in 1993. That is not true in the West, where 40 percent of the major corporations use HMOs, and another 40 percent are enrolled in PPOs (*Business & Health* 1992).

PPOs are gaining new respect from major U.S. corporations: nearly half (45 percent) of employers offered PPOs in 1993, and another 14 percent of companies planned to offer a PPO option (Hewitt Associates 1992a). Employers continue to rate PPOs an effective means for cutting costs. Some

51 percent of employers rated PPOs cost-effective, versus a 47 percent rating for HMOs (Harris 1992). Today, PPO enrollment tops HMO membership. Almost 40 million Americans are now covered by a PPO. California by far leads in PPO penetration, with 13 million PPO eligibles. Only New York and Florida have more than 2 million PPO-covered residents, followed by Colorado (1.9 million), Illinois (1.8), Washington (1.5), and Pennsylvania (1.2).

Some employers have shifted their managed care strategy from an HMO to PPO emphasis. American Express has achieved more than $4 million in savings since initiating efforts to move employees out of HMOs into more cost-effective PPOs. In 1987, American Express hired a consulting firm to analyze its HMO and PPO providers, and a three-year strategy was developed that would force HMOs to become more competitive by encouraging employees to shift to lower-cost PPOs. By establishing itself as a proactive health care buyer, American Express was unyielding in negotiations with providers, eliminating inefficient providers and achieving better prices for hospital and medical services. From the HMOs, American Express shifted from community to experience ratings, and HMOs and PPOs were consolidated along geographic lines. Health care vendors are now forced to compete for American Express's business based on both cost and quality. As a result, the company hopes that it can create long-lasting relationships with health care providers and managed care plans.

The most important strategic decisions hospitals will make in the 1990s is which HMO and PPO contracts to sign. Failure to sign a managed care contract with a major plan could mean the loss of substantial patient volume. On the other hand, signing with a young, high-growth HMO may build both volume and marketshare for the hospital. Hospitals need (1) a managed care contracting plan that identifies preferred HMOs and PPOs, (2) a knowledge of their costs when negotiating per diem rates with HMOs/PPOs, and (3) an experienced negotiator or lawyer to negotiate, monitor, and manage the HMO/PPO contracts.

Trend 2: Self-Administration

A growing number of companies are taking control of their own health care delivery—a signal that employer-provided health care has returned as a trend. Not since the days of the mining and railroad companies have so many employers provided their own medical care. Self-administration is a logical extension of employer self-insurance. Virtually all large companies self-fund their health benefits.

Southern California Edison is one of the most advanced companies in terms of self-administered health plans. It has a long history of corporate health care, dating to the turn of the century. Southern California Edison moved to self-administration in 1987 after health costs rose 23 percent.

The company health plan was redesigned to eliminate first-dollar coverage and emphasize primary care and prevention. Three of four employees are enrolled in the company health plan. Basically, Edison's corporate health plan is a PPO with 7,500 physicians and other professionals and a network of 85 hospitals. The utility company has eight primary care clinics, two first-aid stations, and what may be the largest corporate pharmacy in the United States, handling 300,000 prescriptions each year by mail. The Edison plan works because it's lower in cost than competing HMOs and employees must pay more to enroll in HMOs, which then compete for Edison business. Negotiated discounts and mandatory utilization review saved the utility some $7.9 million in 1989. Another important reason for Edison's cost-savings is that health promotion receives more than lip-service. Edison's "Good Health Rebate" provides employees and enrolled spouses with a cash incentive of up to $120 per person for achieving and/or maintaining high personal health. A preventive health account provides a credit of up $100 for preventive services and programs not otherwise covered. In addition, Southern California Edison has achieved an estimated $120 million in savings through a combination of managed care, HMO pricing competition, and retiree health plan changes. For the five-year period 1988–1992, total savings were estimated at $150 million (Sokolov 1993).

Edison shifted its strategy in 1992 to reduce the burden of managing its own health plan and hired Aetna to administer its health program; in return, Aetna guaranteed prices in a multiyear contract. Inspired by these cost-savings, other major employers are following Edison's example by creating corporate PPOs or working with private third-party administrators. Hospitals and medical groups may have opportunities for negotiating exclusive provider arrangements with self-administered health plans in the next three to five years. Once self-administered employers select a hospital or medical group, they may be willing to sign a two or three–year contract to reduce the costs of provider relations.

Trend 3: Employer Purchasing Coalitions

Employer health cost coalitions will become purchasing groups during the 1990s, using their buyers' clout to control costs and obtain preferred status in the health care marketplace. Few of the more than 150 regional health care coalitions have moved this far, but the potential for group purchasing is substantial. As many as 10–15 percent of employer health coalitions may pursue group purchasing strategies before 1995. In the managed competition model, purchaser coalitions will be a major mechanism for health care reform.

Consider the example of Buyers Health Cooperative, started in 1988 by six major employers in Nashville, Tennessee, to negotiate hospital contracts directly on behalf of its members. By 1992, the Cooperative had grown to 400 employers with 380,000 employees in Roanoke and Richmond, Virginia, as well as Nashville. Using sophisticated software, the Buyers Health Cooperative analyzes and compares hospital charges. Armed with this data, the Cooperative works with three local employer coalitions to negotiate health benefits, and then shares in the savings negotiated. For example in Richmond, when the Cooperative's data identified one hospital as a very high-cost facility, it steered its employers to other lower-cost facilities (Frieden 1992).

In 1983, members of the Florida Gulf Coast Health Coalition were reeling from 30–300 percent increases in their health insurance premiums. As reported in a recent issue of *Managed Care Outlook*, the employers decided to pursue group purchase actions. Their first step was to compile a comparative data base of health claims among the Gulf Coast employers. The database study showed that 92 percent of employees and dependents were receiving care from 25 of the 50 hospitals in the local six-county area. Based on utilization and case-mix adjusted charge data, 12 of the 25 hospitals were selected to become PPO providers. The coalition selected a PPO administrator, the Florida Health Network, to administer its preferred provider organization. After fine-tuning its incentives program for employees to enroll in the employer's PPO, the new plan generated 14–15 percent savings to its corporate sponsors. The PPO network has grown from 4,900 to 22,000 employees in its brief three-year history.

If employer coalitions do purchase hospital and medical services through competitive contracting, it's an opportunity for hospitals, and a threat. Hospitals gain the opportunity to become preferred providers, or have an exclusive arrangement with local employers. On the other hand, hospitals may find themselves condemned by employers who have selected other hospitals and are channeling employees to competitor facilities. This loss of insured business could be a real factor in hospital profitability.

Trend 4: Reduced HMO Options

Major employers are rebelling at the glut of HMO options they administer. Changes in the federal HMO law no longer mandate that employers must offer all federally qualified HMOs in their area. As a result, employers are hiring consultants to review HMO performance and reduce the number of HMOs offered in favor of the most cost-effective plans.

For a demonstration of the concept of managed competition, look at California's Public Employee Retirement System (CALPERS). In place since the 1960s, CALPERS has 874,000 beneficiaries through 19 HMOs and seven health plans. Purchasing clout works. In 1992, CALPERS held its health costs to 6.2 percent, barely half the national increase in health spending. By citing the weakened condition of the California economy, CALPERS was able to negotiate HMO prices to increases of 3.2 percent in 1992 and –0.5 percent in 1993. Because it has two self-funded health plans, CALPERS warned the HMOs that some plans could be eliminated if rates were not frozen. CALPERS demonstrates the market power of a large, sophisticated purchaser (*State Health Notes* 1993).

In northern California, Chevron dropped all but two of its health plans, keeping only two HMOs and creating a new point-of-service plan out of the "company health plan" (Sardinha 1993). Chevron's health plan consolidation follows similar moves by several other large California firms, including Pacific Bell, Wells Fargo, and Bank America Corporation. Chevron hopes to save $500 per employee by reducing its health plans to two, Kaiser and HealthNet.

A hospital's success will be linked to its HMO/PPO relations. As major purchasers—statewide employers, Fortune 500 companies, and government—reduce their HMO and PPO options, the impact of hospitals and physicians contracting with those plans could be substantial. Surviving HMOs and PPOs will have greater marketshare, and so will their provider network. The HMO/PPO losers will negatively influence their contracted providers.

Trend 5: Quality Monitoring

At a Los Angeles conference on future health delivery sponsored by Women in Health Administration, a Blue Cross executive bluntly told hospital administrators, "We now know more about your business than you do, and this gives Blue Cross a tremendous advantage in negotiation" (Gertner 1990). Insurance companies, managed care plans, and employers are gathering and analyzing provider data. Buyers are monitoring quality to weed out inefficient providers and identify preferred providers for HMO and PPO networks. More than 300 utilization review (UR) companies and quality consulting firms assist employers and insurers to screen providers for quality as well as cost.

Employers want to control costs, but ultimately they want quality providers. A three-year, $6 million initiative in Cleveland, Ohio, may be a model for health insurance purchasing cooperatives (HPICs) under national health reform. The Cleveland Health Quality Choice (CHQC) released its first report 28 April 1993, which profiled 29 hospitals in the greater Cleveland area. Now, employers can compare the performances of area hospitals on disease- and procedure-specific bases. Major employers such as the Parker-Hannafin Corporation, which has 1,600 employees, consult the data to identify hospitals with the best track records in certain types of surgery. It uses the centers of excellence approach to contract with hospitals that have the best outcomes (Findlay 1993a).

Quality will increasingly become the focus of outside review companies during the 1990s. Some insurance companies require all contracting hospitals to install quality assessment (QA) data systems like MedisGroup, developed by MediQual Systems of Westborough, Massachusetts. Pennsylvania and Iowa now require all licensed hospitals to record and disseminate quality data; the reports are public information. Managed care plans, insurance companies, and major employers will use the quality data to select preferred providers in the future, using both efficiency (cost) and effectiveness (quality) criteria. Hospitals should expect that more state legislatures will require hospitals to purchase quality data systems like MedisGroup or Iameter and to report data publicly. Major purchasers—insurance companies, managed care plans, employers, and government—will compare hospitals and their physicians on the basis of private and public data on quality.

Trend 6: Health Promotion

As the body of research demonstrating the cost-effectiveness of prevention programs grows, more employers are promoting good health. In Control Data's study of its "Staywell" program, health care costs averaged $87 per year greater for a 35-year-old male at high risk on six lifestyle factors (exercise, weight, smoking, hypertension, cholesterol, and seat belt use). The cost differential increases with age, too, as a 65-year-old male at high risk on all six factors averages $798 more per year in health expenses than his low-risk counterpart (Jose 1990). Health care costs for a 35-year-old woman at high risk on all six factors averages $103 more than her low-risk counterpart. At age 65, the cost difference is $330 between high- and low-risk women. Another study of risk reduction in retirees of the Bank of America showed that investing $30 in a health promotion program reduced health costs by $164 per year (Fries 1993).

Not surprisingly, smoking is potentially the highest cost employee health hazard. Persons who smoke one or more packs of cigarettes per day experienced 18 percent higher health costs. Those who do not wear seat belts have 54 percent more hospital days than those who do. Hypertensives are 68 percent more likely to have medical claims of more than $5,000 (Brink 1993). Employers cannot afford to ignore the implications of this data; they have had to participate in wellness programs. In 1990, executives ranked the seven top wellness programs (*Business & Health* 1991) (see Table 5.1).

Many companies are recognizing that as much as 55 percent of health care costs may be associated with lifestyle-related illnesses (Hewitt Associates 1992b). The Coors Brewing Company, for example, has experienced a savings of $5.50 for every $1.00 invested in health promotion. The Baker

Table 5.1 Executives Rank the Effectiveness of Wellness Programs

Service	Currently Offer (percent)
Mammography	40
Employee assistance programs	9
Weight loss	43
On-site health screening	34
Health risk assessment	31
Smoking cessation	64
In-house employee gym	22
Stress reduction programs	30

Hughes Company in Houston, Texas, has had similar results, saving $3 million in 1992 due to lower absenteeism, reduced claims and costs, and better rates from insurance plans (Naas 1992).

Hospitals are assisting employers interested in health promotion. In 1992, the number of outpatient occupational health facilities rose to 417, from 329 in 1991, according to *Modern Healthcare's* annual survey of multiunit providers (Burns 1993). Hospitals may contract with employers to identify employees who have high-risk lifestyles or chronic health conditions because these employees will likely experience higher levels of health costs. Once identified, these employees, dependents, and retirees can be counseled about their lifestyle and treated for their chronic health problems on an ambulatory basis to prevent costly hospital episodes for heart attacks, strokes, or other cardiovascular maladies.

As business accepts the cost/benefit of health promotion and occupational medicine, there will be opportunities for hospitals to provide employers with a variety of employee health enhancement programs, including health-risk appraisal, smoking and weight reduction, stress management, rehabilitation, and employee screening such as drug testing.

Trend 7: Direct Contracting Arrangements

This is a minitrend—a small but growing number of employers are contracting directly with selected hospitals and medical groups. An alliance of nine health care institutions in Dallas, Texas, is using outcomes data to position the hospitals as preferred providers with local employers. The Dallas Medical Resource is a network of hospitals and physicians that has contracts with six major employers ranging in size from 10,000 to 120,000 covered lives. The hospitals use quality as their primary selling point. Cardiovascular mortality, for example, is under 2 percent, some 60 percent lower than the national average. The hospitals collect and share quality data, but each facility contracts independently with employers to avoid antitrust issues (Darby 1992).

Employers and insurers are negotiating exclusive agreements with centers of excellence. Provident Life and Insurance contracts with ten medical centers to provide organ transplants at discounted rates. More insurers and employers are taking an exclusive contracting strategy for specialized services such as transplant surgery, bypass grafts, and lithotripsy (Sardinha 1992). Hospitals respond with deep discounts to volume purchasers on high-cost procedures. The volume-discount price of bypass surgery at some well-known medical centers is $15,000–16,500, only half the cost at many hospitals. In such agreements, bundling "global fee" arrangements are typical and include the hospital, surgeon, and anesthesiologist, plus all related services. Employers and insurers will make increased use of their buyers' clout in the managed competition approach to negotiate exclusive arrangements to preferred medical centers. Hospitals cannot say "no" when asked to bid for local employers' business, or they risk being left out of negotiations, according to Allan Fine, director of managed care of Quorum Resources (Harris 1993).

Any hospital that receives more than 1 percent of its patients from a local employer should try to strike a special deal. Ground rules for exclusive provider arrangements include assuring reasonable access and choice for employees; transferring risk to providers; managing utilization with stipulated data from providers; bargaining for price but not going "strictly by the numbers"; using experienced negotiators; inserting a "bullet-proof" indemnity clause; and guaranteeing payment to providers.

Hospitals must initiate marketing of their services to local self-insured employers on an exclusive basis. Large employers with 500–1,000 employees have the purchasing power and volume to make discounts of hospital charges and physician fees worthwhile. Hospitals should not neglect mid-size and smaller employers. Use local insurance brokers and third-party administrators to create a preferred provider network that includes the hospital and its medical staff. Small employers (under 25 employees) can be added through a "multiple employer trust" insurance plan.

Trend 8: Cost-Shifting

One of the most effective corporate quick-fixes for rising medical costs is to raise employee and retiree copayments and deductibles. For companies that decide on employee cost-sharing, a percentage of salary or defined contribution are the most frequent options. More companies are indexing copayments and deductibles to the inflation rate. Even HMOs are moving toward use of larger copayments as another way to discourage overuse of ambulatory benefits.

With health care costs rising at alarming levels, many companies are increasing the employer share of health benefits—cost-shifting. During 1989–1991, 75 percent of increased medical costs were shouldered by the companies, but looking ahead to 1995, 82 percent of CEOs predicted more employee cost-sharing (*Business & Health* 1991). A company's bottom line often dictates which way the firm will move on cost-sharing. If business is expanding, cost-sharing is less necessary, whereas in a declining market, employers are more likely to share health costs with employees.

In the 1990s, expect major employers to increase plan users' out-of-pocket limits to make employees even more cost sensitive. High out-of-pocket costs have been demonstrated in research projects to dampen health care use. Critics of high deductibles and copayments are concerned about underutilization and deferral of needed care. There may be employee resistance to higher out-of-pocket limits. Raising deductibles to $250 or $500 may hurt lower-paid employees. Health insurance deductibles may become hospital bad debts if consumers cannot pay. Where employees may have to pay 10–30 percent of their own health costs, not all may have the cash to pay the hospital first. Deductibles can become bad debts if the hospital is not paid promptly. This may be a growing problem, as more employers shift a percentage of health expenses to their employees, dependents, and retirees.

Trend 9: Specialty Managed Care Plans/Case Management

Specialty managed care plans are gaining popularity with business. These "carve-outs" occur when a set of benefits are carved out of a health insurance plan and managed by a specialized firm. Managed mental health care holds promise. Some 25–35 percent of employers use or plan to use them, depending on region, according to the *Business & Health* (1991) survey.

Managed mental health and substance abuse (MHSA) plans have achieved considerable success since the concept emerged in the early 1980s. Some 200 managed MHSA plans now compete across the country. The specialty plans carve out the mental health and substance benefits from a company or insurer's health plan. These capitated (HMO) plans often take most or all of the financial risk, using case management and a limited provider network to control costs. Specialized MHSA PPOs arrange for provider discounts, limit consumer choice, encourage ambulatory and noninpatient alternatives, and offer savings of 15–30 percent for employers and insurers.

This is only the beginning for specialty managed care plans. The nation's first cardiac PPO was launched in 1990 by the Borgess Medical Center in Kalamazoo, Michigan. As its name suggests, CardiacPath covers five cardiac DRGs, 104–107 and 112, that include bypass surgery, valve repair, and balloon dilation. Savings range from 17 percent on radiology to 77 percent for monitoring. The hospital is marketing the PPO directly to employers who would carve cardiac care out of their existing health plans. Many hospital-based heart institutes are planning to develop a "global pricing" structure that includes both hospital and physician services. Almost half (47 percent) of hospitals in a 1993 survey planned to market aggressively cardiac packages to employers, insurance plans, and HMOs (Medtronic/KMPG Peat Marwick 1993).

In terms of case management, it was ranked most highly among the top five of all cost management strategies by employers in a *Business & Health* (1991) survey. Thirty-five percent of firms using case management consider it highly effective. Some firms are using their employee assistance programs (EAPs) as the locus of case management systems, taking the role of gatekeeper and integrator of employee assistance, mental health, and health promotion. Companies like McDonnell Douglas and Bergen Brunswick have cut their costs 25–33 percent with integrated case management (Bryant 1991).

The one out of three American hospitals with inpatient mental health or chemical dependency units should be prepared for major downturns in these services lines. As the specialty plans become more prevalent, rates of admission and length of inpatient stay are plunging. Some hospitals have lost 35–50 percent of their acute psychiatric/substance inpatient admissions and patient days in the past two years.

Trend 10: National Health Insurance

National health insurance is high among business' public policy concerns. The report of the Pepper Commission, headed by Senator Jay Rockefeller (D-W.V.), was split on its recommendations for universal access to health insurance. Almost 50 proposals were floated in Washington during 1992, from think-tanks, congressional offices, and providers. Now the timing for national health reform is here, and employers are urging Congress and the Clinton administration to expand access but with built-in cost controls (Findlay 1993b).

The National Leadership Coalition on Health Care Reform has offered its business perspective to the debate. The coalition is led by AT&T, Ameritech, Dupont, Ford, 3M, and Lockheed, with union participation by the United Steelworkers, Service Employees International Union, Electrical Workers, and other national labor organizations. Eventually, all large companies will become involved. The varying opinions on the subject do not help: in 1990, 45 percent opposed national health insurance, 30 percent favored, and 25 percent neither opposed nor favored; in 1990, 30 percent thought national health insurance would be instituted in five years, 47 percent thought ten years, 12 percent thought more than ten years, and 11 percent thought never (*Business & Health* 1991). Fortune 500 executives polled were more negative on national health insurance: most (52 percent) of the CEOs preferred an expansion of managed care, as opposed to a new form of federally sponsored insurance, with a primary reliance on improved private-sector efforts to contain health care costs with only the current level of government regulation (Buck Consultants 1993).

The Canadian model. As previously stated, there is a small but growing number of major employers, the Chrysler Corporation among them, who have recently called for fundamental structural reform of the U.S. health system, holding Canada as a potential model. Why? First, as noted, businesses' inability to control their health expenditures is a bonafide frustration. The impact on corporate profitability has been substantial: employer health costs totaled over $300 billion in 1992, or 40 percent of the nation's multibillion-dollar health total. Three in five Americans receive their health protection from their employer. The United States is the only major industrialized nation to cover health expenditures through the workplace. America also spends more on health per capita than other major countries (see Table 5.2) (Scheiber, Poullier, and Greenwald 1992).

In addition to what's shown in Table 5.2, there are other admirable features about Canada's health system, in particular the government's interest in health promotion. For routine services, the Canadian system works

Table 5.2 U.S.–International Health Expenditure Comparison (1990)

Country	Health Percent GNP	Per Capita	Length of Stay	Bed Days per Capita	Infant Mortality
Australia	8.2	$1,304	—	—	0.82
Austria	8.4	1,393	11.9	3.0	0.78
Canada	9.3	1,770	—	2.0	0.68
France	8.8	1,532	12.4	2.9	0.72
Germany	8.1	1,486	—	3.4	—
Japan	6.5	1,171	50.5	4.1	0.46
Sweden	8.6	1,451	18.0	3.5	0.60
United States	12.1	2,566	9.1	1.2	0.91

Adapted and reprinted with permission from G. J. Schieber, J. P. Poullier, and L. M. Greenwald's "U.S. Health Expenditure Performance: An International Comparison and Data Update," *Health Care Financing Review* 13, no. 4: 1–87, Summer, 1992.

well and is more cost-effective. But for advanced technology and specialized procedures such as hip fractures and cardiac surgery, Canadian medicine is not as effective in managing complex care.

The cost of care may make this debate of U.S. versus Canadian models academic. American corporations are smart enough to know that they would pay for any conversion to a nationalized health system on the Canadian model (Faltermayer 1993). In an era of $200–300 billion federal budget deficits, there is no public surplus to fund a national health scheme. Companies would pay through taxes, probably an earmarked "head tax" like Social Security to subsidize the extra costs for covering the 37 million medically uninsured. The additional costs to business and the public would be *at least* the $65 billion estimated by the Pepper Commission, and very likely higher—between $100–150 billion over the current health spending level. In any transition to national health, Congress is likely to set a relatively "rich" benefits package to make it politically acceptable to the middle class who would sacrifice their company-provided health protection. Unless Americans are willing to settle for fewer services and longer waits, costs will go up, not down, in a conversion to a national health program such as Canada's.

Limits on Medicare Cost-Shifting

Employers will have to act aggressively to control providers who seek to subsidize their Medicare losses with higher prices and more billings to employers and insurance companies. Medicare cost-shifting has reached epidemic proportions among providers seeking to compensate for the loss of income with the introduction of DRGs. Private insurers and major employers were the primary targets of increased prices by hospitals and doctors, and Medicare's RBRVS payment scheme for physicians may make this problem worse. Benefits consultants warn employers that health costs will rise in the three to five years after Medicare's physician payment reform goes into effect 1 January 1992. Physicians facing a significant loss of Medicare income under Harvard's RBRVS may increase rates for their non-Medicare patients as compensation when Medicare's physician payment plan goes into effect. An analysis by Foster Higgins and Co. (1992) showed that for each dollar decrease in Medicare spending, the private sector can expect a compensatory increase of two to three dollars by non-Medicare patients. However, managed care is holding down medical inflation. Employer health costs rose only 10.1 percent in 1992 (Faltermayer 1993).

To control cost-shifting by providers, major employers will increase the percent of employees and retirees enrolled in HMO capitated plans, request favored status to receive hospitals' best prices, increase company overseeing of HMOs and PPOs, use third party review companies to review PPO and indemnity claims, target high-volume ambulatory care procedures for discounts and select provider contracting, and place stricter controls over discretionary health services such as mental health and substance abuse.

Unresolved Issues

High technology may be in trouble in the 1990s. Fewer insurers and employers will compete to offer the latest treatments if they are too expensive. In *Paras v. Blue Shield of Virginia* (1990), Blue Shield lost its case to deny payment for a treatment it considered experimental. At issue was a $150,000 treatment involving near-fatal doses of chemotherapy combined with a bone marrow transplant. The U.S. District Court of Virginia acknowledged that Blue Shield had acted within the limits of the terms of benefit coverage in denying reimbursement for the treatment, but the court held that the policy itself was flawed because it "required plan members to wait until somebody chooses to provide statistical proof that would satisfy all the experts that a treatment would work." No wonder the insurer resisted paying this bill—the population at risk is 150,000 women who get breast cancer each year. There may be more cases like this if insurers decide not to provide reimbursement for costly new technologies and treatments. Employers and insurance plans are expected to add specific exclusions to coverage for the highest cost of new therapies, even if they are approved by the Food and Drug Administration and beyond experimental (Anderson 1992).

The two other major unresolved issues for employer health cost management during the 1990s will be retiree health and the FASB (Federal Accounting Standards Board) rule that companies must account for future costs of retiree health benefits. Retiree health costs are rising even more rapidly than employee wage costs, and generous wage settlements and labor agreements in the 1970s have burdened major corporations with substantial costs for retiree health benefits, picking up whatever Medicare does not cover under the retiree's former health benefit program.

Managed care could help constrain costs, but few employers have more than 10–15 percent of the retirees in HMOs or PPOs. Some employers are restricting retiree health benefits for future retirees ("two-tier" retiree health benefit policies); others are experimenting with a lump-sum payoff of $15,000–25,000 to the employee at retirement in lieu of future health protection. A small but growing number of companies are simply reneging on their promise of retiree health benefits, leaving pre-Medicare retirees on their own.

A new rule, FASB 106, threatens further complications for employers and retirees. FASB requires that all companies fund the liability for retiree health benefits beginning January 1993, just as the companies prefund pension liability. The estimated cost of this now unfunded liability has been projected between $200 and $400 billion, or higher. Companies can write off all the costs at once or phase in over a 20-year period. Writeoffs cost Pepsi Co. $125 million, Ford $7.5 billion, and General Motors a staggering $20.8 billion (Mandelker 1993). FASB 106 will accelerate corporate attention to health costs and reform in the 1990s.

To combat FASB 106, some companies are increasing the cost-sharing by retirees, and a few, like McDonnell-Douglas, are paying off the medical benefit obligation with a lump-sum payment. As a result, hospitals must anticipate a growing community need—pre-Medicare retirees abandoned by their companies and now without health coverage. Creative solutions will be needed to help these new medically uninsured to find interim health coverage until Medicare, or national health reform, addresses the problem.

Looking Forward: Strategic Health Benefits Plans

The Manufacturers' Alliance for Productivity and Innovation surveyed 160 corporate executives from large industrial and service firms. Most (79.7 percent) of the CEOs rated their cost-containment efforts as "only somewhat effective" in reducing corporate health costs. Among other results of that survey: only 22 companies (14 percent) ranked their efforts to contain health costs "very successful"; second opinions, the most widely employed cost strategy (by more than 80 percent of companies), was rated "not effective"; and most companies were cutting benefits (46.1 percent), increasing copayments (88.3 percent), or eliminating "first-dollar" coverage (74.7 percent) to constrain rising costs. These results underscore the challenge major companies face in controlling their health costs during the 1990s. They lack the information, constraints, and expertise to confront health expenditures. Providers are constantly "gaming the system" of corporate health benefits to subsidize inadequate government health reimbursement. The health cost problem will only worsen for employers in this decade given the aging population and technology that have resisted most corporate efforts for improvement. And, despite runaway health inflation, many employers are still reactive, not proactive. They must create a strategic health benefit plan to control health costs and promote employee and retiree health. Self-insured corporations like Southern California Edison have set precedents in this area by developing an internal health management capacity, shedding ineffective HMOs and PPOs, targeting high-volume and high-cost procedures for discounting select provider contracting, and tightly monitoring their providers.

During the 1990s, savvy employers will move from a strategy of health benefits management to health *care* management and assume a more direct role in controlling provider behavior. Companies will hire experienced health care managers, develop comparative data bases on costs and quality, implement strong utilization and quality review programs, and become leaders in provider selection and employee health promotion. Far-sighted companies are already aware of the problem of retiree health costs and are moving retired workers into managed care plans and working to promote their health. In the long run, corporate investments in health promotion will pay off with lower health expenses for workers and retirees.

In one vision of employer-provider relations during the 1990s companies would develop long-term relationships with their insurance companies, managed care plans, and providers; long-term agreements of at least three years would replace the annual "shoot-out" over price and performance; hospitals and physicians would offer long-term price protection; and companies would provide volume guarantees and take an active role in worksite health promotion. In this ideal relationship, both health care providers and corporations would recognize their mutual interest in maintaining a healthy workforce for today and healthy retirees for the future. This is the potential of the managed competition concept. Japanese firms have these types of relationships with their suppliers—it's a model worth emulating and expanding in the U.S. health care industry.

Strategies

1. **Foster business-to-business relationships.** Send a trustee instead of the administrator to represent the hospital with the local employer health coalition. This is a business-to-business strategy. Select a hospital trustee from a large company or organization who understands health cost issues from the employer's perspective.

2. **Ask trustees to assist in contracting.** Put a hospital trustee on the negotiating team in developing contracts with local employers. Select a trustee familiar with negotiation, and use that individual's experience in developing contractual relationships with local employers. Trustee participation can raise the level of negotiation from purchaser-supplier, dealing only in dollars and cents. Hospitals need support from their local business community. Trustee involvement is a continuous reminder that the nonprofit hospital is a community institution, not just another vendor.

3. **Prepare for business backlash.** Trustees should be prepared to explain the rising costs of health care to unhappy employers. The hospital board should explain its position on cost-effectiveness and community service. Use local organizations to relate the hospital's programs in cost management and quality/productivity improvement. Local media coverage of technology acquisitions can emphasize the contribution to cost efficiency and improved quality. Trustees should take leading roles as hospital spokespeople with both local organizations and the media.

References

Anderson, K. 1992. "Do You Know What Treatments Your Health Plan Covers?" *Business & Health* 10, no. 13 (November): 34–40.

Brink, S. D. 1993. *Health Risk and Behavior: The Impact on Medical Costs*. New York: Milliman & Robertson.

Bryant, M. 1991. "Testing EAPs for Coordination." *Business & Health* 9, no. 8 (August): 20–24.

Buck Consultants. 1993. *National Health Care Reform Panel Survey Results*. New York: Buck Consultants.

Burns, J. 1993. "Outpatient Providers Notch Another Year of Robust Growth." *Modern Healthcare* 23, no. 21 (24 May): 176–80.

Business & Health. 1992. "Datawatch: 1992 Health Benefits in Review." (February): 14–15.

———. 1991. "The 1991 National Executive Poll on Health Care Costs and Benefits." (September): 61–70.

Chen, E. 1993. "Clintons Press Campaign for Health Reforms." *Los Angeles Times*, 10 August.

The Conference Board. 1992. "Business and the Health Cost Crisis." *Chief Executive Opinion* (June). Darby, M. 1992. "Provider Alliance in Dallas Uses Outcomes to Woo Clients." *Managed Care Outlook* 5 (23 October): 6–7.

Faltermayer, E. 1993. "A Health Plan that Can Work." *Fortune* 127 (14 June): 88–96.

Findlay, S. 1993a. "Cleveland Health Quality Initiative Bears its First Fruit." *Business & Health* 11 (June): 30–36.

———. 1993b. "Employers to Clinton: Proceed Cautiously on Reform." *Business & Health* 11 (July): 20–24.

Foster Higgins. 1992. *Health Care Reform Survey*. Princeton, NJ: A. Foster Higgins.

Frieden, J. 1992. "Employers Negotiate with Hospital Group." *Business & Health* 10 (September): 57–59.

Fries, J. F. 1993. "A Health Promotion Program in a Retiree Population." *American Journal of Medicine* (May).

Gertner, W. 1990. Presentation at Women in Health Administration Conference. Pasadena, California, 20 September.

Harris, N. 1992. "1992 National Executive Poll." *Business & Health* (July): 13–14.

———. 1993. "Navigating the Direct Contracting Maze." *Business & Health* 11 (May): 36–42.

Hewitt Associates. 1992a. *Employer Experience in Managed Care*. Lincolnshire, IL: Hewitt.

———. 1992b. *Managed Health Promotion Initiatives*. Lincolnshire, IL: Hewitt.

InterStudy. 1993. *The InterStudy Competitive Edge Data Book*. St. Paul, MN: Inter-Study.

Jose, William S. III. 1990. "The Cost of Unhealthy Workers." *Wellness Management* (Winter–Spring).

Lumsden, K. 1993. "The Clinical Connection: Hospitals Work to Design Information Systems that Physicians Will Use." *Hospitals* 67 (5 May): 16–26.

Mandelker, J. 1993. "Facing Deadline: Businesses Are Shifting More Costs to Retirees." *Business & Health* 11 (March): 18–24.

Medtronic/KMPG Peat Marwick. 1993. *Recent Developments in the Restructuring of Cardiovascular Services.* Chicago: Medtronic/KMPG.

Naas, R. 1992. "Health Promotion Programs Yield Long-Term Savings." *Business & Health* 10 (November): 41–47.

Sardinha, C. 1993. "Chevron Following Trends Drops All HMOs But Kaiser Health-Net." *Managed Care Outlook* (7 May): 1–2.

———. 1992. "Provident Signs 10 Facilities as Transplant Centers of Excellence." *Managed Care Outlook* 5 (6 November): 9.

Scheiber, G. J., J. P. Poullier, and L. M. Greenwald. 1992. "U.S. Health Expenditure Performance: An International Comparison and Data Update." *Health Care Financing Review* 13 (Summer): 1–87.

Sokolov, J. J. 1993. "Third-Generation Managed Care Plans." Unpublished ms.

State Health Notes. 1993. Cited in *Medical Benefits* 10 (15 March): 4.

Wyatt Company. 1993. "Coordinated Care Is Transforming Medical Benefits." *Wyatt Comparison* (February):

6

National Health Reform: Politics, Pluralism, and National Health Policy

I think we have crossed the divide and we're no longer debating whether or not we'll have universal health-care coverage, but what kind.

—Senator Paul Wellstone (D-Minn.) (Keen 1993)

The American health system will undergo fundamental reform within the next three to five years. A comprehensive plan for universal coverage and health reform could be enacted by Congress as soon as November 1994. Yet it is far from clear what kind of changes are likely. Dozens of reform proposals have been offered in the past three years by think-tanks, health industry associations, and politicians. After seven months of secret deliberations and at least three false starts, the long-awaited debate on U.S. health care reform began on 11 September 1993—12 days ahead of schedule, with the leaked release of a 246-page draft of the Clintons' plan for restructuring the nation's health care system (Wyman and Downing 1993).

The era of national health reform arrived with the President's speech to Congress on 22 September 1993, which outlined a plan for the fundamental restructuring of American health care. If the Clintons succeed, they stand a good chance of being reelected in 1996. This is risky. When the Clinton proposal was released, a three-tier headline in the *New York Times* read: "Clinton Offering Health Plan with Guarantee of Coverage and Curb on Private Spending." The subhead predicted the difficulties of enacting the Clintons' bold health reform initiative: "Clinton's Roll of the Dice; If It Passes, He's Bold, If Not, He's Reckless" (Clymer 1993a).

But if partisan rivalry, Democratic infighting, and gridlock persist, Clinton risks losing all chance at a second term. A Clinton stumble could be fatal for passage of health reform. If the president's proposal fails to win congressional approval in the next two years, the momentum will be lost. The failure of the Clinton-led movement for health reform now could mean postponing real change in the U.S. health industry until after the year 2000.

The Time for Reform Is Now

There will be no more waiting for health reform. The public cautiously believes by a 2 to 1 majority (67 percent) that the Clintons can successfully reform health care, according to a September *Time*/CNN poll (Barrett and Thompson 1993). In another poll, a majority of American consumers (55 percent) predicted that the Clinton plan would help the nation (Seib 1993). More important, many in Congress—Democrats and Republicans alike— extend optimism that a compromise can be reached and express the belief that the time for health reform has arrived. As the health reform debate begins in Congress, here are five predictions:

- The Clinton plan will be substantially modified by Congress before enactment of universal coverage and insurance reform, probably before the elections in November 1994.
- Health reform will not be financed from savings, and Medicare and Medicaid will not be cut substantially (more than $50–100 billion), due to opposition from seniors and liberal Democrats.
- Financing of universal health coverage is likely to come from a combination of employer mandate, "sin taxes" on tobacco and alcohol, payroll taxes of 1 to 2 percent, and/or a 1 to 2 percent tax on insurance premiums.
- Small business insurance reform will provide portability of health plans, community rating of premiums, prohibition on exclusion from coverage due to a prior health condition, and the Employee Retirement Income Security Act of 1974 (ERISA) reforms to allow groups of small employers to purchase health coverage and services like large self-insured employers.
- Managed competition may be adopted, but with flexibility for states to regulate the market between purchasing groups and provider networks.

The American Health Security Act presented by President Clinton to Congress and the American public on 22 September 1993 reads more like a consultant report than a legislative proposal. The plan contains a set of principles that should guide the formulation of a health reform program, but one that is often vague on just the areas that will be most controversial, such as funding. The public version of the Clinton health plan will have to be drafted into legislation and sponsors will have to be found for submission, not expected until the return of Congress in January 1994 (*New York Times*

1993). In the meantime, a wide number of congressional committees will hold hearings on the plan, and the Clintons will campaign for enactment in the Congress and among voters to urge congressional approval.

The White House plan for health reform is being skillfully guided by Hillary Rodham Clinton. Early congressional response to testimony from the nation's first lady was very positive, with her hearings ending in rarely heard applause from committee members (Clymer 1993b). Not everyone is supportive of health reform or the Clinton plan. One Washington observer calls the Clinton proposal a "new middle-class entitlement that puts another 14 percent of the economy under the sway of government and thus of politicians (Gigot 1993). A Texas surgeon protests the takeover by HMOs, fearing that gatekeepers threaten to destroy the advocacy of doctors for their patients (Freudenheim 1993b). Physicians fear that the Clinton plan's reliance on managed care will force doctors to follow orders from gatekeepers located hundreds or thousands of miles away who have little or no knowledge of the patient or problems involved.

Big Buyers and Big Sellers

Restructuring the health care marketplace under national health reform should be simple: big buyers contract with big sellers in a wholesale market for medical care. Health care purchasers, represented by regional purchasing alliances, contract with providers to serve hundreds of thousands of enrollees. They agree on a price (capitation), and buyers use their market clout to get good deals from providers. Of course nothing government does is ever that simple. The basic scheme is called managed competition by Stanford economist Alain Enthoven.

But market reformers like Enthoven are concerned that purchasing alliances may become too bureaucratic, losing the market-driven incentives encouraged by managed competition. Under the Clinton reform proposal, the purchasing alliances of employers become government agencies, established by states to be the sole purchaser of care for metropolitan areas or even entire states. Health insurers, hospitals, and doctors form "accountable health plans" that would contract with purchasing alliances to provide all services specified in the minimum health benefit plan. Consumers would choose among competing plans.

More regulation is likely if the Clinton plan is enacted as proposed by the White House task force. Health services prices could be determined by a global budget set for U.S. health spending by a National Health Board, which would then allocate expenditure targets to states. Purchasing alliances would be limited in their pricing discretion by the budget caps. All this is making providers uneasy, as well as congressional moderates like Rep. Jim Cooper (D-Tenn.), who has introduced a bill closer to the market philosophy of managed competition.

Universal Coverage by Employer Mandate

Congress is expected to act by 1994, or 1995 by the latest, to guarantee universal health coverage by the federal government, but it may not be fully phased in until the year 2000. Employers will pay most of the costs, under a mandate that all firms (or most, if the Clinton plan is compromised) must provide a health plan for their workers. Employers would cover their part-time employees on a pro-rated basis, with government subsidizing the rest. Health premiums for employers (not "taxes") for government-required health plans are estimated at $1,800 per individual and $4,200 for family coverage, about the cost of a limited-option (PPO-type) Blue Cross–Blue Shield plan.

Large companies with more than 5,000 employees could continue to self-fund and manage their own health plans, but the larger companies could lose much of the freedom they now enjoy under ERISA to negotiate better prices from insurers and managed care plans. Although the Clinton proposal would give state governments the authority to apply state taxes and regulate the health plans of large employers by state insurance commissioners, this is not likely to occur. The loss of ERISA protection will be vigorously opposed by large corporations and congressional Republicans, and will likely be compromised or dropped before enactment.

The employer mandate is likely to be implemented progressively over a five to seven–year period, despite the president's hope to have universal coverage fully in place by 1997 (Stout and Rogers 1993). As a concession to small employers, Congress is likely to stretch implementation over a longer period, beginning with the largest firms (more than 5,000 employees) and delaying the mandate for the smallest employers (five or fewer employees) until 1999 or 2000.

Every consumer will receive a "health security card," guaranteeing access to the nationally defined set of comprehensive health benefits through the consumer's chosen health plan. Consumers will have choices among competing local plans, and they will pay 20 percent of individual or family coverage. Medicaid will be disbanded. Under-65 Medicaid recipients on Aid to Families with Dependent Children (AFDC) and supplemental security income (SSI) will be folded into the program, with their care purchased through the regional health alliances.

Not everyone will be covered by national health reform. Specific exemptions are provided for everyone already covered by Medicare, the Veterans Administration, Department of Defense, or the health service for Native Americans. Undocumented aliens are not eligible for government coverage, but employers must provide a health plan to all workers, even the undocumented. Residents of territories like Puerto Rico will not be affected; they will continue to receive health benefits through the existing health systems. States are instructed to address the health needs of migrant workers, but there is no specific provision or federal funding for their health coverage. Students who are not dependents can enroll in the local alliances where their schools are located, and prisoners remain the responsibility of the various prison systems.

Paying for Health Reform

President Clinton is still having trouble convincing Americans that health reform can be funded without major new taxes. Despite Perot-type charts prepared for the Clintons that show dollars flowing in and out to pay for universal coverage, skeptics charge that the health package "fails the math test" (Risen 1993). The bill would be funded through massive cuts ($238 billion) from Medicare and Medicaid between 1996 and 2000, and $105 billion in new revenues from a "sin tax" on cigarettes. Critics call the financing scheme "smoke and mirrors," and question whether Medicare and Medicaid, now growing at 13 percent per year, can be slowed to 5 percent growth in spending (Thomas 1993).

The Clinton plan proposes new benefits for the elderly, including limited nursing home coverage and drug benefits, which would cost $152 billion. White House reformers believe that federal workers, veterans, and military personnel can be moved into HMOs, saving $47 billion. Business savings from lower health premiums will be plowed back into wages, creating a windfall of $51 billion in additional income taxes. Not convinced the numbers all add up? Neither are lawmakers, but they may pass health reform before the 1994 elections anyway. Recall the Medicare experience in 1965: President Lyndon Johnson told Congress that the cost to taxpayers would be only $8 billion by 1990; the actual cost was $90 billion. Today, if Washington policymakers actually knew what health reform would truly cost, they probably would not pass it.

Debating the Cost Estimates of Reform

Taxpayers and elected officials may never get a good answer to the one question that may really determine the outcome of the national health care debate: *How much will it cost?* America currently draws on a number of sources to fund the nation's health care (see Table 6.1).

All the cost estimates will be in billions as politicians vie to present their plans as low cost but comprehensive. Any tinkering with America's more than $800 billion health care expenditures will surely require billions more. Estimates for implementing play or pay proposals are ranging from $65 to 120 billion in increased employer expenses. Medicaid reform could easily cost $25 to 40 billion to bring all states up to some national standard of

Table 6.1 Estimated Sources of Financing for U.S. Health Care
Expenditures: Fiscal Year 1992

Sources of U.S. Health Expenditures	Costs (Billions)	Percent of Total Expenditures
Private health insurance, employer share	$149	19
Private health insurance, employee share	57	7
Private out-of-pocket	151	20
Other private funds	21	3
Medicaid	109	14
Medicare	128	17
Federal tax subsidies	63	8
State tax subsidies	12	2
Other public sources	78	10

Source: *Hospitals* (5 January 1992), from information provided by C. Eugene Steuerle of the Urban Institute, Washington, DC. Presentation at a conference sponsored by the American Enterprise Institute, October 1991.

benefits. Insuring all medically uninsured children would cost $10 billion, according to the Children's Defense Fund of Washington, DC (Families USA. 1991). A single-payer national health system (like the Canadian model) could cut $58 billion—or add $7 billion—according to a report by the U.S. Congressional Budget Office (CBO) (1991). The CBO predicted that a system applying Medicare rates to all payers could save $17.3 billion—or cost another $30 billion. One last note about estimates: they are almost always preliminary and almost as invariably lower than actual. Political analysts—to your pencils (and calculators)!

Republican and Democrat Proposals for Reform

The Clinton health reform plan will compete with proposals from all shades of political opinion, from progressive Democrats who prefer a Canadian-style single payer approach to Republican alternatives that emphasize the responsibility of the individual—not the employer—to achieve the goal of universal access to health care.

1. *Universal access (Reps. Cooper and Grandy)*—A new coalition of conservative Democrats and moderate Republicans, led by Representatives
   Jim Cooper (D-Tenn.) and Fred Grandy (R-Iowa), have submitted a
   proposal they describe as "squarely in the middle" of the reform debate
   (Tumulty and Cimons 1993). Supporters from both parties backing the
   Cooper-Grandy proposal contend that the president's goal of "universal
   coverage" is economically unattainable. Their suggested substitute is the
   more modest aim of universal access to medical care by making health

insurance more affordable to small employers, with subsidies to the poor, but no employer mandate for small firms.

One of the underlying disagreements is whose proposal is closer to the original concept of managed competition. Cooper contends that his bill is more like the market-oriented reform strategy of the Jackson Hole Group, headed by Paul Ellwood, M.D., of Minnesota-based InterStudy and co-authored by Alain Enthoven. From Cooper's perspective, the Democratic proposal developed by Hillary Rodham Clinton "went to the left" and is now too government-dominated, while the Republican proposal that puts the mandate for health coverage on individuals "went to the right." Under Cooper's proposal, businesses with fewer than 100 workers would be required to join purchasing cooperatives but not mandated to buy health plans for the employees. Workers would not be required to purchase health insurance but would have access to reasonably priced plans through the purchasing groups.

2. *Republican alternative (Sens. Chafee and Dole)*—Leading Republicans have embraced the goals of national health reform but reject cost controls and employer mandates as the means to achieve them. This plan, headed by John H. Chafee (R-R.I.), calls for individuals, not employers, to be responsible for purchasing health insurance in the same manner that most states require motorists to carry auto insurance. The Chafee-Dole plan will establish a uniform set of health benefits and simplify handling health claims to reduce administrative costs. Purchasing health plans through regional alliances would be optional, not mandatory. Like the Clinton plan, the GOP alternative would also be funded in part through a $200 billion cutback in Medicare/Medicaid spending. Alternative proposals from the GOP side include those of Senators Phil Gramm (D-Texas) and Robert Michel (D-Me.), which would go further in malpractice controls and exempting small employers from mandatory coverage (Clymer 1993c).

3. *Single-payer (McDermott)*—Almost 90 House Democrats are in support of a plan to reform American health care on the single-payer (Canadian) model. Their plan, led by the Democrat from Washington, would simplify health care payments through a government-controlled approach. Government would set prices for physician and hospital services, and insurance companies would be eliminated. Benefits would be established by a health security board, which would also set pricing standards. Substantial payroll taxes would be imposed on employers, replacing insurance premiums most employers now pay. Individuals would pay nothing, but the total tax bill could exceed $300–400 billion (Clymer 1993c).

4. *Federal Employee Health Benefits Program*—Conservative Stuart Butler (1993) of the Heritage Foundation asks: "Why invent a new health plan when Washington already has a health insurance program that works?" He is referring to the Federal Employee Health Benefits Program, which

covers 10 million government workers, dependents, and retirees. Butler, director of domestic studies for the Heritage Foundation, calls the Clinton strategy a "Rube Goldberg–style system based on something that has never worked, price controls" (Butler 1993).

Butler advocates the federal workers program as a proven method for purchasing health care recommended by the Heritage Foundation as a low-cost alternative to the Clinton reform proposal. The federal employee health system, in existence since 1960, is a government system in name only. Federal employees choose from one of a dozen or more local health plans. Plans compete to attract and retain government enrollees, and competition works. The U.S. Office of Personnel Management announced in September 1993 that costs would increase only 3 percent in 1994 and that some enrollees would actually see their premiums drop. Why did the Clinton health task force ignore a health plan that already works? Butler (1993) notes that every full-time government employee is covered by the program, from presidential health reform advisor Ira Magaziner to the clerks who distributed the president's 239-page health proposal.

Controlling Costs with Caps

The gravest danger to the Clinton plan for health reform is that passing out millions of health security cards to the medically uninsured could trigger a $100 billion boom in annual health spending. To prevent costs from rocketing out of control, the president's plan calls for caps on health insurance premiums to ensure that medical prices are held in check. But what if the caps do not work?

Critics of the Clinton plan say that caps will not work and that health expenditures may lead to a huge federal budget deficit to pay for the Clinton promises of health benefits for all Americans (Stout 1993). The government has never attempted to impose a ceiling on private health spending. Suppose that insurance companies and HMOs find they cannot provide all services guaranteed in the minimum health benefit coverage for the standard health insurance premium, estimated at $1,800 per person? If costs exceed the premium, insurers and managed care plans have three choices: (1) convince government to ease the price limits and increase premiums, (2) cut services to beneficiaries, or (3) scale back reimbursement to physicians and hospitals. Ira Magaziner, chief architect of the Clinton plan, prefers the third option where providers and insurers would be squeezed.

Global Budgets and the States

The first task of the National Health Board will be easy—setting a national target for health spending. Establishing such a global budget for the United

States may be simple compared with allocating a similar spending target to each state. New data from the federal government show wide variation in state health costs and per capita spending (Pear 1993). The impact of a budget cap would vary widely by state and could frustrate government budget-setters as Washington attempts to put a lid on health expenditures that is fair from state to state.

Where is health spending the highest? Topping the expenditure list is the state of Massachusetts, with per capita spending of $2,402, consuming 10.5 percent of per capita income. Idaho is the lowest, spending only $1,234 per person or 8 percent of personal income. Other high-cost states are Connecticut, Florida, New York, North Dakota, and Pennsylvania. California, a state with a reputation for high health care costs, was not in the top ten, with per capita spending of $1,914 consuming 9.1 percent of consumer income. The national average spent on medical care is $1,877 per person—about the price of the president's proposed health benefit plan—which consumes 11 percent of per capita income.

Any effort to put a lid on national health care spending must confront the reality that expenditure patterns have wide disparities without any obvious explanation. Two states, California and New York, account for one-fifth of all U.S. expenditures on hospitals, physicians, and prescriptions in 1991. These two states also are home to about 20 percent of the population. Other states show markedly different spending patterns. From 1980 to 1991, health costs rose fastest in New Hampshire, most slowly in Illinois. On average, residents of New England spend more for their health care than those in the Rocky Mountain states, but the statistics "wash" when compared on per capita basis, with both regions at 9 percent of per capita income spent on health. If the Clinton plan relies on national or regional spending averages as a guide to setting local prices for health plans, the process could overwhelm a platoon of actuaries and accountants. Providers know what comes next—reimbursement levels that have no basis in actual costs for provision of care.

Conflict and Compromise

There are a number of key areas in which the Clintons will be forced to compromise elements of the president's proposal:

1. Small employers—To get Republican approval for universal coverage, the Clintons may be forced to compromise in forcing the smallest employers to pay for health insurance. The economic impact on small firms could be eased by phasing in the program over time, starting with the biggest companies. But opposition from small businesses may force a compromise that would exclude the smallest

firms (fewer than ten employees, or fewer than five workers) from the employer mandate. Inclusion of the remaining small firms could occur in future legislation, after health reform had demonstrated that real savings to employers will come from restructuring the health system.

2. Funding—While the president continues to try a "shell game" with financing options for health reform, ultimately the Clintons must compromise either the goal of universal coverage or find more tax funding. More taxes will probably be needed under any scenario, with likely sources sin taxes on cigarettes and alcohol, a tax on excess benefits paid by employers over the federal minimum, taxes on employer payrolls, and taxes on insurance premiums. Even taxes on hospital and physician revenues are possible.

3. Malpractice reform—The Clinton proposal may be strengthened by Republican initiatives to impose tougher controls over attorney fees and to impose limits on damage awards for "pain and suffering."

4. Purchasing alliances—The Clintons may compromise with GOP proposals to make regional purchasing alliances an option. As proposed by the White House task force, state governments would establish only one purchasing alliance per region—a new form of government bureaucracy. The compromise would be to make regional purchasing alliances optional, in expectation that large self-insured employers would continue to purchase their own plans. Small employers could use the state-designated alliances as an option to find lower-cost health coverage.

The President's Political Risk

Political observers are already calculating the risks that the president runs in proposing such a sweeping health reform package. No president in recent memory has bet so much on a single issue (Clymer 1993b). By defining health care as the most important issue of his presidency, Clinton makes health reform a crucial test of his leadership ability.

The health reform debate places the issue squarely with Congress. Congress has been unable to break through intra-party gridlock during the past five years to enact any significant reform program to address the problems of a nation mired in economic stagnation, a banking crisis, and unmet social issues such as education, crime, and drug abuse. Will Congress rise to the test of health reform, putting partisanship aside? Washington observers are skeptical. Health care has been called the "third rail of electoral politics" by David Durgan (1992), the White House media strategist. Government meddling in private health insurance has been staunchly resisted by a wide array of opponents, including major employers, insurance companies, doctors, hospitals, unions, the elderly, and consumer groups. The opponents had different reasons for blocking reform, but fundamentally no group wants to give up anything in order to fund health coverage for those 35 to 40 uninsured Americans.

In the past 40 years, Congress has blocked the presidential efforts of Harry Truman and Richard Nixon to enact national health insurance. Only Lyndon Johnson, the master of congressional politics, was able to initiate fundamental new health programs with Medicare and Medicaid in 1965.

So far, congressional response to the Clinton proposal has been generally positive, but the reform debate is just beginning. With few exceptions, Republicans have been following the advice of Senator Bob Dole (R-Kans.) to "keep their powder dry" so that they can compromise and legislate in good faith (Clymer 1993b). Republicans are likely to support at least one principle of the Clinton reform proposal—relying on the marketplace through managed competition to limit inflation of insurance premiums.

Surprisingly, even the Democrats are far from united on health reform. Some 88 congressional Democrats are cosponsors of health reform legislation favoring a Canadian-type single-payer system where government would set health care prices and regulate service delivery. Abortion coverage in the government-guaranteed plan is sure to draw fire from both Democrats and Republicans. The Clinton plan attempts to side-step the issue, using the phrase pregnancy-related services.

It is not yet clear that the Democrats have the votes for passage of health reform in 1994. House Speaker Tom Foley (D-Wash.) predicts approval before the current Congress adjourns for elections in November 1994. But Congressman Dan Rostenkowski (D-Ill.), chair of the powerful House Ways and Means Committee, cautions the Clintons about the enthusiasm of House Democrats for reform: "They [the Clintons] are very enthusiastic, [but] I don't see it among the members" (Clymer 1993b).

Early public and congressional response has been favorable to Bill Clinton's September 22 speech and Hillary Rodham Clinton's appearances before Congress in the following week. "Health care shows both the Clintons at their best," observed Geoffrey Garin, a Democratic political consultant (Dowd 1993). "Mrs. Clinton looks good in terms of a mastery of a very complicated matter, and President Clinton looks good in terms of his compassion and willingness to take on hard issues of change" (Dowd 1993). It is far too early to predict whether the Clintons' hold on the health care debate will continue, but they are off to a promising start in managing the process and the publicity.

Five factors may ultimately determine the outcome of national health reform in the Congress:

- Being willing to compromise to gain support from Republicans
- Stifling the criticism of progressive Democrats who would really prefer the Canadian single-payer model
- Reducing Medicare and Medicaid cuts from $250 million to $100 to 125 million
- Reducing the scope of benefits and the cost of a minimum package from $1,800 to $1,200 per individual ($100 per month)
- Finding additional sources of real funding for the program, such as an insurance premium tax or provider revenues tax.

Winners and Losers under National Health Reform

There are sleepless nights ahead for physicians, hospitals, drugmakers, and America's health care industry as they worry whether they will be "winners" or "losers" under national health reform (Freudenheim 1993a). The Clinton American Health Security Plan means insecurity for providers and suppliers. Doctors fear that a plague of health alliance purchasing bureaucrats will swarm over their practices, cutting fees and digging into patient records to monitor quality. Consumers are uneasy about the prospect of being herded into a few large HMOs. Hospitals and physicians are anxious they may be excluded from provider networks because their practice profiles do not fit the computer model. Pharmaceutical and device manufacturers expect to be hit with government price regulation and heavy discounting from big HMOs and purchasing groups.

This could happen. There are threats from health reform for the medical profession, patients, hospitals, insurers, suppliers, and almost everyone working in the nation's $900 billion medical industry. Not all of the forecasts are gloomy. There will be a silver lining to health reform, as many real benefits will come to the health industry in the proposed restructuring of the nation's $900 billion health/medical field. The upside forecast: national health reform could be the "provider full-employment act," as 37 million uninsured consumers (about one in six Americans is uninsured) get a medical credit card.

The Winners under Reform

At this point, the likely winners under national health reform will be (Coile 1993):

- *Physicians and their waiting rooms.* When America's medically uninsured get their health security cards, they will flood the waiting rooms of physicians and medical groups across the nation. The plus in this is that if

Medicaid patients are folded into the program, millions more patients can choose mainstream health plans and HMOs. The minus is that the phase-in of the employer mandate will mean that small employers may not be required to pay health benefits for three to five years from enactment.

- *Primary care providers.* All health plans and HMOs will rely on primary care medical groups as the front lines of health care delivery. Primary care physicians will be capitated. Many will take on "gatekeeper" roles. Salary levels for primary care doctors will jump, as every health plan competes with HMOs to hire them out of residency and active practice. Medicare reimbursement will continue to reward primary care doctors and cut payments to specialists.

- *Mental health providers.* If mental health services are part of the minimum benefit plan approved by Congress, hundreds of thousands of Americans may call their therapists. A caution: HMOs and health plans are likely to channel patients away from $200 per hour psychiatrists toward lower-cost psychologists and group therapy.

- *Specialists in large groups/networks.* Provider networks with a strong primary care base will prefer to contract with large single-specialty medical group practices that can handle subcapitation and can bundle prices for specialized services.

- *HMOs.* National health reform could also be titled the National HMO Enrollment Act. The Clinton plan gives a competitive advantage to HMOs as "accountable health plans." Regional purchasing alliances are likely to prefer HMOs, which integrate financing and delivery in a comprehensive package. The purchasers will prefer HMOs knowing that HMO administrative costs are often 50 percent lower than traditional health plans, and 25 percent better than PPOs. Surviving HMOs will have to be large enough to match the purchasing clout of alliances. HMO mergers and consolidation have already started in California, including Health Net/Qual-Med.

- *Long-term care.* Nusing homes may benefit under health reform, mostly from expanded use of skilled nursing beds by cost-conscious HMOs that use the lower-cost beds for post-surgical care and rehabilitation. The Clinton plan also calls for expansion of Medicare to cover some skilled nursing home costs for the disabled, which senior advocacy groups like the American Association for Retired Persons (AARP) hope may be the opening wedge in the creation of Medicare Part C, which could be enacted in 1997–1998 once universal access is in place.

- *Information systems.* Health care information systems will be big winners. The Clinton reform strategy will create an informed marketplace where purchasing alliances and consumers can select among competing health plans using a "report card" of 50 indicators of cost and quality. Regional data bases of clinical and financial data will be used extensively to manage the costs of care under capitation. Information system integration will be capital-intensive, with multimillion dollar investments to integrate and standardize data systems across provider-insurer networks.

- *Physician executives.* Make room for physicians in the executive suite. The chief medical officer may be the most critical position in the hospital and health system. A doctor to manage doctors is needed. The control of clinical costs will be the make/break factor for providers under capitation.

- *Attorneys and consultants.* Health reform is also a full-employment program for attorneys and consultants. Everyone will need expert advice in forming new organizations like physician-hospital organizations (PHOs) and regional health networks. Doctors selling their practices and the hospitals and medical groups who buy them will all need platoons of accountants and attorneys.

The Losers under Reform

At this point, the likely losers under reform are (Coile 1993):

- *Solo physicians.* Physicians in solo practice are like "sushi"—the smallest and most vulnerable fish in the food chain of capitation and managed competition. As big purchasers prefer to contract with organized groups of physicians, solo doctors will lose contracts and see managed care patients channelled to groups. Independent physicians must join groups quickly, or lose out in this game of musical chairs.

- *RAPs, hospital-based specialists.* Hospital-based specialists like radiologists, anesthesiologists, and pathologists (RAPs) will quickly find that they are a cost, not a revenue, to their hospitals under managed care and managed competition. Many hospitals are moving to employ these RAP physicians, or contract with them for steep discounts. The RAP specialists must form multihospital groups to gain market leverage and become cost-management partners with the hospital to reduce ancillary costs.

- *Single-specialty groups.* Physicians in small single-specialty practices will be disadvantaged under managed care and managed competition. They are vulnerable to deep discounting by HMOs and health plans because they are too small to have any market clout. Single-specialty groups must expand rapidly to multisite networks with broad geographic coverage and the capacity to subcapitate and bundle prices for frequently performed procedures. Medical specialists can be the base for development of multispecialty groups, especially if they can add primary care physicians to their physician mix.

- *Emergency room groups.* Emergency room physicians may lose patients as the medically uninsured gain access to private physicians, paying with their health security cards. Emergency room physicians had better cut deals now with HMOs to subcapitate emergency services or be vulnerable to discounting by HMOs and health plans. Emergency physicians are likely to diversify into primary care and intensive care to offset their lost income in the emergency room.

- *Hospitals.* Although hospitals stand to benefit if millions of uninsured obtain hospital and medical coverage, America's hospitals will be losers if deep Medicare cuts are used to finance health reform. Hospitals will welcome the increase in revenues from the uninsured and hope their uncompensated care burden will ease. But hospitals cannot afford further losses from Medicare reimbursement. In California, for example, more than 50 percent of hospitals are losing money. Another discouraging factor is that illegal aliens would not be covered by the national plan and the proposed $1 billion in federal aid would be grossly inadequate to cover hospital losses for care of illegal residents in Arizona, California, New York, and Texas.

- *Inpatient mental health.* The mentally ill had better not need much inpatient care. Inpatient benefits would be limited to 30 days per year, according to the Clinton plan, with an emphasis on ambulatory care.

- *Drug companies.* Pharmaceutical firms will get price controls under health reform, although the proposed new drug benefit under Medicare could expand demand for pharmaceuticals. The Clinton health plan gives the Secretary of the U.S. Department of Health and Human Services new powers over drug prices, including the authority to obtain rebates from drug manufacturers where suppliers are not giving government their best price, even comparing prices with companies and other countries. The drug industry's offer to voluntarily hold prices to the rate of the Consumer Price Index was slapped down by the Justice Department in October, as a potential violation of anti-trust if the drug firms cooperated industrywide (Fritz 1993). Expect consolidation among the drug firms, and vertical integration strategies such as Merck's purchase of Medco, the national mail-order pharmaceutical distributor.

- *Insurers.* Health insurance profitability will fall as insurers lose experience-rating and the right to screen out unhealthy enrollees. The good news for health insurers is that at least they are still in the game under the Clinton plan, providing services to regional health networks as they contract with purchaser health alliances. Insurers are scrambling to abandon indemnity insurance plans and to rapidly convert enrollees into HMOs, PPOs, and POS managed care programs to prepare for managed competition.

- *IPAs.* Hospital sponsored IPAs are too weak and undisciplined to survive under managed competition. Physicians must migrate into stronger economic organizations where doctors are chosen based on their cost-efficient practices and willingness to be team players under capitation. Today's open-membership IPAs must make the transition to smaller, more select closed-panel physician organizations.

This chaotic picture of winners and losers will change rapidly over the next 12 months, as Democrats and Republicans fight and compromise over health reform. But it would be a mistake for hospitals and physicians to wait for the dust to settle. The next two years will determine the fate of health care for a decade. Physicians must act now to promote and protect their future under national health reform, or they will be the "little fish" in the food chain of managed competition.

Three Scenarios for U.S. Health System

The year is 2000, and the dust is settling after a major restructuring of America's health system during the mid-1990s. What happened? The future is a plethora of possibilities. Futurists use scenarios to sketch possible futures. Three health care reform scenarios for hospitals and local health systems, as projected by the Health Forecasting Group, are managed competition (managed care scenario), community care networks (public-private model), or all-payer system (government regulation).

Managed Competition

For a preview of managed competition, visit California, the seedbed of one future for American health care. This scenario envisions large regionally integrated health care organizations contracting for services with large buyers (major employers, HMOs/PPOs, insurance plans, and government). Everybody is enrolled in a managed care plan—group employees, the self-insured, and Medicare and Medicaid beneficiaries with even a safety-net HMO to cover those between jobs and health plans. All plans are community-rated and accept their share of consumers with prior medical conditions.

To date, managed competition is still more theory than proof. The success of the California Personnel Employees Retirement System (CALPERS), which purchases coverage for more than 800,000 state government workers, by holding its health costs to only 1.5 percent inflation, was an early signal of the potential of managed competition. In its 1993 contracts with 19 HMOs, CALPERS sought to keep prices flat, and in a slumping California marketplace, the HMOs went along with a zero percent rate increase from CALPERS. It is this kind of market clout that managed competition will bring (Findlay 1993).

Managed competition is an effective cost-containment strategy. Price competition among managed care plans would moderate health plan inflation to 7–10 percent annually. Case management, prior authorization, and continuous utilization and quality review hold hospital use rates well below 400 inpatient days per 1,000 enrollees (non-Medicare) and 1,250–1,500 days per 1,000 Medicare enrollees. All provider rates are negotiated prospectively. Providers are at financial risk in capitated agreements. Inefficient and ineffective providers are computer-monitored, and the worst and most costly providers simply do not have their contracts renewed.

This future may be right around the corner. In California, hospital systems are consolidating with large physician groups to form regional delivery systems contracting with large managed care buyers. California is a managed care marketplace—more than 70 percent of its non-Medicare population is enrolled in a managed care plan (Morse 1992). Some 4 million Californians belong to the same health plan, Kaiser Permanente, the nation's largest HMO (Taravella 1992). Other providers and managed care plans are trying to create new health care organizations that can compete with Kaiser (DeLafuente 1993). Consolidation into regional and statewide networks is proceeding rapidly among insurance plans, HMOs, PPOs, and self-insured employers, leading major employers like Bank of America, Wells Fargo, IBM, and the State of California to drop small HMO/PPOs in favor of plans with regional or statewide coverage.

California hospitals and multihospital systems are creating the "medical piece" of their strategy to become regionally integrated health care organizations. UniHealth, an 11-hospital multihealth system, has created UniMed, a medical subsidiary, to acquire large physician practices. UniMed will create nonprofit medical clinic foundations for the medical group affiliations to avoid California's ban against the corporate practice. Loma Linda University has acquired the Friendly Hills Medical Group in a $100 million deal, which included a 200-bed hospital owned by the doctors. To secure a base of community referrals, Stanford University signed an affiliation with the San Jose Medical Group. Merger discussions between the Sutter Health System and the Palo Alto Medical Group concluded with acquisition. In Sacramento, the Sutter Health System acquired the Sac-Sierra Medical Group, an innovative "medical group practice without walls." Sac-Sierra will give Sutter a mechanism to build group practices at its Northern California hospitals (DeLafuente 1993).

But managed competition is not just a California phenomenon; it is emerging strongly in a number of metropolitan areas—Portland, Oregon; Minneapolis, Minnesota; Dallas, Texas; Norfolk, Virginia; Boston, Massachusetts; Albuquerque, New Mexico; Knoxville, Tennessee; and Phoenix, Arizona. The State of Massachusetts, in fact, has initiated plans to close four state mental hospitals and place its 22,000 non-Medicaid eligibles into managed care plans (Mandelker 1993). Managed competition has powerful momentum to replace America's enterprise-oriented fee-for-service system and preserve the voluntary model of health care in the United States.

Community Care Networks

America's health system may emerge as a checkerboard of local and regional health delivery systems that contract with government (Medicare/Medicaid) and major purchasers (employers, self-insured groups, and government). The inspiration of community care networks is the German model, in which workers join a regional health plan when they enter the labor force and stay with that plan for life, regardless of who employs them or whether they are employed; if unemployed, the government pays.

The AHA in particular has encouraged development of community care networks. Ideally, these networks would be capitated arrangements among hospitals, physicians, and other providers who assume responsibility for defined community populations. Community care networks are self-insured or affiliated with an insurance plan with enrollment premiums shared (75/25 or 50/50) between employers and workers. The unemployed, the aged, and the poor would be subsidized by government in extensions of Medicare and Medicaid. National Medicaid reform would eliminate the Medicaid gap that covers all nonworking consumers and brings all state Medicaid programs to the same level of uniform national benefits. Federalizing Medicaid programs could occur through enrolling the poor in Medicare (Anderson 1992).

To be successful, community care networks require a public-private partnership between government and private insurance/managed care/self-insured employers. Network designation by Medicare and Medicaid is a key element in this strategy. Competitive bidding and contracting would be the catalyst, as hospitals and physicians organized into local and regional community care networks to compete for Medicare and Medicaid business. Federal/state contracts could be exclusive or semiexclusive, allowing Medicare and Medicaid beneficiaries a choice of three or four competing community care networks in each local region that met government standards for service availability, price, and quality. Private insurance companies, self-insured employers, and managed care plans would "piggyback" on government contracts, developing exclusive or semiexclusive arrangements with the community care networks. It's possible that Medicare and private insurance would contract jointly (for example, medicare HMO/PPO) and designate the same community care networks.

This scenario facilitates a more orderly pattern of stable relationships for America's voluntary health system, eliminating excess capacity in the health system through self-disciplined management of the local networks and programming service availability within the networks. Community care networks would be self-organized, but all providers would have to select one network as their primary affiliation. Long-term contracts of three to five years would bind provider members of the networks, whose responsibility would include utilization management and quality assurance. Variations of this model are possible—for instance, networks could contract with large buyers on a single or multiyear basis and compete on price, or prices could be set akin to an all-payer system.

All-Payer System

Proposals for an all-payer system for American health care often use the Canadian system as the archetype. In this scenario, Congress would eliminate private health insurance and become the sole payer. Health plan premiums would be replaced with a withholding tax on wages as well as a health services tax on employers to fund the health services program. The public monies would fund a global budget allocated to states based on population, and just as Canada relies on provincial governments to set local provider budgets, each state would administer its program.

The allocation of public funds to health care is centrally controlled. Congress would set a target level of health spending—such as 10 percent of the gross domestic product—and the monies would then flow out to the states for local allocation according to formula. Local health systems and hospitals have budgets for operations and capital investment. Technology acquisition would be controlled by state and regional health authorities, with new technology budgeted only after proven cost-effective in national clinical trials.

In addition, states would have flexibility to vary health benefits within national guidelines. Under the all-payer plan, health care is accessible to all. Through income-indexed withholding of wages, the employed help pay while the poor and unemployed receive health services free. Access is universal and independent of financial qualification. However, some services are not covered: elective procedures primarily, such as cosmetic surgery, are self-paid. Rationing of services would occur most often through limiting supply and consumer waits for service (queuing) rather than by arbitrary guidelines (for example, "no cardiac bypass surgery on those over age 75").

Physician spending under the all-payer scenario would be through an allocated budget on a regional basis, with preset physician fees. Medicare's RBRVS system could be used universally for all physician payment. Although physicians would still charge on a fee-for-service basis, payments would be scaled back proportionately if physician expenditures exceed the budgeted ceiling.

To hold health costs down, the all-payer system model adopts five strategies employed by the Canadian system: lower administrative costs, emphasis on primary care, cooperation among hospitals, tight control over technology, and tort reform to control malpractice awards and costs.

Through this plan, administrative costs are reduced 2–3 percent of the national health care budget, a savings of $34–67 billion of administrative costs that inflate today's national health expenditures (Goodman and Musgrave 1991). Also, malpractice reform would implement medical tort claims into an administrative system with defined limits on awards. Tort reform would both reduce direct costs of litigations and awards, while easing the long shadow of defensive medicine, estimated to add 5–15 percent to current U.S. health expenditures. These savings will help hold national health spending to a congressional target of 10 percent of GDP in the future.

Hospitals in states with mandatory rate review systems recognize this scenario. Though still organized voluntarily, these hospitals and medical groups have aligned for efficiency rather than competition. Under the all-payer system, there is no preferential treatment or reimbursement to multi-institutional systems or medical group practices, except that hospitals and doctors can stretch their budgets further through efficiency if their costs are lower than regionally set budgets. Voluntary cooperation among local hospitals would allow shared capital budgets for high technology and new facilities.

The all-payer system would truly alter American health care. Hospitals would operate with spartan efficiency under global budgets, and it would be more difficult for providers to be innovative although quality is generally good in this scenario. Staffing levels are lower, but employees' morale is improved. This is a very different system than Americans have known, but the free care and improved accessibility make the scenario more than possible.

Hospitals Unprepared for Reform

America's hospitals are not well organized to manage in a post-reform environment, according to a national survey of 402 health care CEOs and chief financial officers (Cerne 1993). The key issues are: development of physician-hospital organizations; a lack of primary care physicians; a struggle with controls such as practice guidelines; increased demand but decline in reimbursement; and cutbacks in Medicare payments.

Global budgets and insurance caps will mean tough financial years once health reform is enacted. CEOs like Gerald Mungerson, president of Illinois Masonic Hospital in Chicago, fear that inadequate hospital reimbursement will only worsen as federal and state budget deficits continue to rise: "I think we were entitled by legislation to two times the rate of increase that we've received under PPS, and I think that shows where the federal government is coming from" (Cerne 1993).

Hospitals suspect who will be providing major financing for health reform—providers. Hospitals fear reimbursement cuts or even taxes on hospital revenues, such as enacted in state initiatives by Minnesota and Washington. Bipartisan proposals by President Clinton (Democrat) and Senator Chaffee (Republican) for cuts of $200–300 billion in Medicare and Medicaid payments over five years to finance universal access only add to administrators' and trustees' unease about fiscal prospects in the post-reform environment.

The worst nightmare of America's health executives and trustees is more patients and less money. Health reform will create significant new demands for services that hospitals will have to provide with a lower level of reimbursement due to budget cuts or payment freezes. Some hospitals will close or merge. Fewer than half (48.6 percent) of surveyed administrators expect their hospital or health system to stay the same, while one in four (26.4 percent) expect to merge with another institution or to acquire another hospital (21.6 percent) (Cerne 1993).

In this environment, nothing will be sacred. Religious hospitals will merge with non-religious institutions or systems, and vice versa. For-profit hospitals will buy nonprofits and be acquired by nonprofits as well. Hospitals and physicians must scramble to form regional integrated delivery systems that can contract for 250,000–500,000 or a million covered lives with a comprehensive services package.

The era of national health reform is front-page news across the country, affecting millions of Americans. Implementation of a reform plan will be phased over a five to seven–year period, even beyond the year 2000. Unfortunately, too many hospitals and health organizations may be watching when they should be responding with a proactive stance and calculated strategies to the market changes that national health reform will bring.

Strategies

1. **Foster hospital-physician integration.** Every hospital needs an on-campus multispecialty medical group and a well-organized physician practice association for managed care contracting. Hospitals and physicians must organize now for the day when Medicare and managed care plans will pay them one global fee for an ambulatory visit, procedure, or stay. Effective management of costs and quality needs a high level of physician involvement in administration and governance.

2. **Establish networks.** Now is the time to establish new business and clinical relationships among hospitals and physicians. The goal is to

create regional distribution systems that can take responsibility for thousands of community residents under a managed competition or all-payer scenario.

3. **Organize for managed care.** Accommodating a future of managed competition requires building new organizations, relationships, and support systems to allow providers to live within prenegotiated payments and external utilization controls.

4. **Manage costs management/improve clinical efficiency.** Building support systems for a managed care future begins with true-cost accounting systems that provide fiscal and clinical managers with cost information—per patient, case, procedure, and stay. Data must be cumulatively available in "real time" for continuous management. Doctors must manage doctors, with expanded responsibility for medical directors and clinical department chiefs. Physicians must be much more actively involved in managing the clinical costs of care.

5. **Implement continuous quality improvement standards.** The new bottom line under whichever national reform system is enacted will be more than costs—new national standards for clinical outcomes and customer satisfaction will be established. Mandatory data systems will continuously monitor quality, with public reporting likely in any future scenario. Hospitals and health systems need to know their own quality and manage the outcomes of their care.

References

Anderson, H. J. 1992. "Hospitals Seek New Ways to Integrate Care." *Hospitals* 66 (5 April): 26–36.

Barrett, L. I., and D. Thompson. 1993. "Ready to Operate: Clinton's Health Plan Would Cover Everyone." *Time* 142 (20 September): 54–58.

Birnbaum, J. H. 1993. "Clinton Health Package Has a Little Something for Just Enough Factions to Splinter Opposition." *Wall Street Journal*, 23 September.

Butler, S. M. 1993. "Rube Goldberg: Call Your Office." *New York Times*, 28 September.

Cerne, F. 1993. "Prepared for Uncertainty?" *Hospitals and Health Networks* 67 (20 August): 22–25.

Clift, E. 1993. "The Second Blooming of Hillary." *Newsweek* (20 September): 37.

Clymer, A. 1993a. "Clinton's Roll of the Dice." *New York Times*, 11 September.

———. 1993b. "Hillary Clinton on Capital Hill Wins Raves, If Not a Health Plan." *New York Times*, 29 September.

———. 1993c. "Many Health Plans, One Political Goal." *New York Times*, 17 October.

Coile, R. C. 1992. "National Health Reform: Three Scenarios for American Hospitals." *Hospital Strategy Report* 4 (March): 1–8.

———. 1993. "Winners and Losers Under National Health Reform." *Northern California Physician* (November): 34.

DeLafuente, D. 1993. "California Groups Join for Survival." *Modern Healthcare* 23 (21 June): 24–28.

Dowd, M. 1993. "Witness Works Panels, Ending Era on the Hill." *New York Times*, 29 September.

Durgan, D. 1992. Remarks to the American College of Cardiology. National Health Policy Forum. Washington, DC. 21 February.

Families USA. 1991. *Health Spending: The Growing Threat to the Family Budget.*

Findlay, S. 1993. "CALPERS: A Model for Health Care Reform?" *Business & Health* 11 (June): 45–54.

Freudenheim, M. 1993a. "Changing Fortunes of the Medical Business." *New York Times*, 19 September.

———. "Many Patients Unhappy with HMOs." *New York Times*, 18 August.

Fritz, S. 1993. "Drug and Insurance Firms Cry Foul." *Los Angeles Times*, 11 October.

Gigot, P. A. 1993. "Potomac Watch: How the Clintons Hope to Snare the Middle Class." *Wall Street Journal*, 24 September.

Goodman, J. C., and G. L. Musgrave. 1991. *Twenty Myths about National Health Insurance.* Dallas, TX: National Center for Policy Analysis.

Keen, J. 1993. "Health Reform: Not If, But 'What Kind.'" *USA Today*, 30 September.

Mandelker, J. 1993. "Government Purchasers See Value in Managed Care." *Business & Health* 11 (July): 40–44.

Morse, L. 1992. *1991–1992 Hospital Fact Book*, 16th ed. Sacramento: California Association of Hospitals and Health Systems.

New York Times. 1993. "Excerpts from Final Draft of Health Care Overhaul Proposal." 11 September.

Pear, R. 1993. "Health Care Spending Is Found to Vary Greatly State by State." *New York Times*, 7 October.

Risen, J. 1993. "Health Package Fails the Math Test, Critics Charge." *Los Angeles Times*, 12 September.

Seib, G. F. 1993. "Hurdles Await Clintons in Selling Health Plan." *Wall Street Journal*, 15 September.

Stout, H. 1993. "Insurance Premium Caps Sound Good, But Will Clinton Plan Keep Costs Down?" *Wall Street Journal*, 30 September.

Stout, H., and D. Rogers. 1993. "Health Debate: Outline of Compromise Is Dimly Discernible as Clinton Offers Plan." *Wall Street Journal*, 23 September.

Taravella, S. 1992. "Keeping an Eye on Kaiser the Giant." *Modern Healthcare* 22 (27 April): 30–36.

Thomas, R. 1993. "Back to Smoke and Mirrors: What the Plan and Reaganomics Have in Common." *Newsweek* (20 September): 36–37.

Tumulty, K., and M. Cimons. 1993. "Bipartisan Group Offers Health Plan in the 'Middle.'" *Los Angeles Times*, 7 October.

U.S. Congressional Budget Office. 1991. *Selected Options for Expanding Health Insurance Coverage.* Washington, DC: U.S. Government Printing Office.

Wyman, I., and L. Downing. 1993. "The Clinton Solution." *Newsweek* (20 September): 31–35.

7

Integrated Health Systems: The Building Blocks of Community Care Networks

What it means to be a hospital and what it means to practice medicine are being reinvented in response to new economic, technological, and societal forces.

—Stephen Shortell (1991b)

The transformation of American hospitals into systems will occur during the 1990s. To join or not to join, that is the question hospital trustees will ask as their hospitals review options to participate in tomorrow's integrated health systems. These options will include becoming a systems organizer and center of a "hub-and-spoke" network; merging and fully integrating with a system; becoming a managed care partner sharing capitation contracts; contracting for external management with an administrator from the system; or affiliating in a local network for group purchasing, technology sharing, and regional clinical programs, such as cardiac care.

The future vertically integrated delivery systems will favor that can offer a full continuum of care for a fixed price and be responsible for a defined population (Hudson 1993a). Systems will be local, not national, and constructed on a regional basis by local hospitals, physicians, and trustees. In the era of health reform and managed competition, the coordinating force in health will have to be the integrated health care system. When the dust settles in the year 2000, more than 80 percent of all U.S. hospitals will be part of local and regional health systems, vertically organized across a medical market to provide a range of services to a defined and enrolled population. Physicians will be part of these regional delivery systems, as "medical firms" of doctors collaborate in business partnerships or merge with hospital systems, like the Fallon Health Care Organization, which merged a multispecialty clinic, an HMO, and a hospital to develop a fully integrated system for Worcester, Massachusetts (Hudson 1993b).

Hospital trustees must understand that it is time to choose. Few hospitals can go it alone in a systems-dominated market. They may salvage their independence (avoiding merger), but they cannot survive without partnering in managed care networks. It is no longer a question of whether to affiliate or not, but which emerging integrated health system to join.

Thinking System: The Challenges and Possibilities

Integrated health care systems will be the dominant pattern for the provision of a continuum-of-care services to all Americans. Whichever health reform system is adopted, each scenario will rely on local and regional health care systems to organize and deliver services. How widespread is the interest in systems? In late 1991, the Healthcare Forum convened a conference titled "The Future of Integrated Healthcare Systems" that was attended by more than 500 health care executives representing 80 systems, who were advised to "ask where you want to be right now, and then plan backward" toward their vision of tomorrow's health system (Flower 1992). The conference featured the stories of multihospital systems—Innova Health Systems (Fairfax, Virginia), UniHealth America (Burbank, California), Sutter Health (Sacramento, California), Henry Ford Health System (Detroit, Michigan), Presbyterian Healthcare Services (Albuquerque, New Mexico), and Kaiser Permanente Medical Care Program (Oakland, California)—presented in case-study format. The attraction was learning what works and what elicits physician commitment, the biggest challenges facing hospital systems.

Toward this end, Stephen Shortell of Northwestern University has directed the Health Systems Integration Study (HSIS), which researched some of the best-known of America's multi-institutional health systems, from all regions of the country. (Peat Marwick assisted in the data-gathering and analysis.) The goal of the three-year study was to determine which strategies, functions, and system activities were the most successful, where "success" is defined as "adding value to patients." This self-funded study was undertaken because Shortell's prior research had raised a number of questions about the benefits of developing large multihospital systems. In fact, the research revealed just how far America's multihospital organizations are from being called integrated systems. Shortell has defined "system integration" as the extent to which functions and activities are appropriately coordinated across operating units so as to maximize the value of services delivered to patients. The ten multihospital systems in the HSIS study created a research consortium to collaboratively study their own system integration. When Shortell presented a preliminary baseline report on the perceived levels of integration by the ten system sponsors at the 1991 Healthcare

Forum conference, the results were that participants had rated their systems 2.96 on a scale of 1 to 5 (1 = low, 5 = high) in year 1 of the survey, which assessed management's perspective of the current level of systemness in strategy, management, and clinical coordination (see Figure 7.1) (Shortell 1991a). The final results of the HSIS will surely offer critical information for governing and implementing systems.

Can Systems Manage the Imperatives of the 1990s?

The core assumptions on which health systems were established in the 1970s and 1980s are undergoing rapid change. Pioneering systems that developed 15–20 years ago included Samaritan Health Services (Arizona), Presbyterian Southwest (New Mexico), InterMountain (Utah), and Innova (formerly the Fairfax Hospital System) in Fairfax, Virginia. Early rationale for systems development included: access to capital, economies of scale such as joint purchasing, quality improvement such as new facilities, efficiencies of operation such as shared information systems, and corporate management.

But there are new imperatives for the 1990s that Shortell (1991a) believes will drive system development away from horizontal "bigness" (number of hospitals, total revenues) toward vertical integration on a local basis with a regional distribution system that can contract as a system with managed care buyers. These imperatives are: being accountable for the health status of defined populations; establishing global budgets/targets; creating

Figure 7.1 Baseline Level of System Integration of Ten Multihospital Organizations (Managerial Responses)

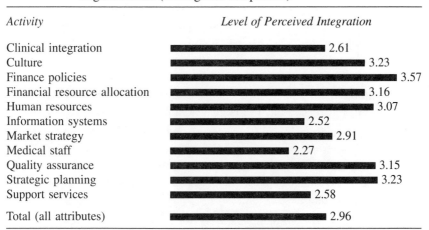

Activity	*Level of Perceived Integration*
Clinical integration	2.61
Culture	3.23
Finance policies	3.57
Financial resource allocation	3.16
Human resources	3.07
Information systems	2.52
Market strategy	2.91
Medical staff	2.27
Quality assurance	3.15
Strategic planning	3.23
Support services	2.58
Total (all attributes)	2.96

Reprinted with the permission of Stephen M. Shortell from his presentation "The Current State of Integration in Health Care," at the Future of Integrated Health Systems conference, 6 November 1991.

incentives to actively manage clinical care, to provide a coordinated continuum of care, and to implement continuous quality improvement standards; and demanding value. Hospital trustees must recognize that integrated health systems are still experimental. Shortell's study is proving that decentralized, loosely coordinated systems do not work. Systems have made progress in integrating financing and human resources, but the more difficult challenges will be clinical integration and medical staff collaboration. Only through clinical integration can health systems achieve real payoff by operating as one company.

Lessons from the System Builders

As Shortell stated in 1988, most hospital systems are still "unfulfilled promises." They were formed as a defense against an increasingly hostile environment, but many have not produced according to the high expectations of lowering costs, improving profitability, and creating capital. What lessons can today's hospitals learn from the first 20 years of multihospital systems (Shortell 1988)?

- Economies of scale. Except for bulk purchasing, there is no evidence to support economies of scale.
- System efficiency. No consistent evidence exists that system hospitals operate at a lower cost per adjusted admission than nonsystem facilities, although Shortell's (1988) research on proprietary systems suggests that chain-owned hospitals' costs were somewhat lower than hospitals in not-for-profit systems.
- Financial status. At least for-profit hospitals improved their finances under proprietary system management, due to cost-cutting and higher prices.
- Profitability. No significant difference in profitability between system and nonsystem hospitals can be found in research comparisons, although investor-owned chains managed to achieve higher profit-margin levels in the 1980s than nonprofit hospitals generally.
- Capital access. While investor-owned hospitals made more use of debt as a source of capital than nonprofit hospitals, there is no evidence to support system affiliation improving capital access, once the basic financial strength of the hospitals is factored out of the comparison.
- Services. System membership is not a factor in the range of services offered by hospitals; there is no evidence that system hospitals offer more inpatient or ambulatory services to the community than do nonsystem hospitals.

- Charity care. Although nonprofit hospitals do provide more uncompensated care than hospitals of investor-owned systems, there is no evidence that system-affiliated hospitals perform more charity care than other community hospitals.
- Quality. Some evidence indicates that hospitals acquired by investor-owned systems did upgrade their plants and equipment, which raised quality at least in the units of production.
- Patient outcomes. Health services research did not find any significant differences in patient care outcomes between system hospitals and nonsystem facilities, regardless of ownership.

Consequently, health systems of the 1990s will have to be smaller, more local, and vertically organized. Partnering in these small-market matchups will exist between hospitals that share mission compatibility, geographic linkage, and the opportunity to gain bargaining leverage with managed care buyers. Systems will be organized to serve a medical service area. Most systems will be regional, some statewide. To be successful in this emerging future, the two most critical functions are managed care strategy and physician relations (see Table 7.1). For example, three major hospital groups in Minneapolis–St. Paul are exploring the creation of a provider network with managed care payers and employers under the State's "Minnesota Care" health reform plan (Greene 1993).

Handling managed care is one of the most pivotal roles for the vertically integrated health system of the future. Key factors for success

Table 7.1 System Profiles: Managed Care and Physician Affairs

System Function	*Number of Systems with Function*									
	1	2	3	4	5	6	7	8	9	10
Managed care										
Ownership interest (HMO/PPO)									X	
Centralization of managed care contracting							X			
Use system leverage in negotiating contracts					X					
Physician affairs										
System VP for medical affairs				X						
Designated function or office for medical affairs						X				
Acquire physician practices						X				
Physician on systemwide board								X		

Reprinted with the permission of Stephen M. Shortell from his presentation "The Current State of Integration in Health Care," at the Future of Integrated Health Systems conference, 6 November 1991.

include: market power of a regional hospital netw rk, consolidation of medical groups, primary care distribution network, direct contracting with large employers, management information systems, insurance expertise, clinical care protocols, compensation incentives to reward productivity, and strong utilization review. Trustees from facilities within the community together must create a network of local hospitals, physicians, and related services for managed care buyers. Managed care is the driving force. So if hospitals do not organize their own system and package-price their services directly to employers or other large buyers, they will become the vendors and be treated like commodities.

Creating an integrated continuum of care will require focused diversification into areas such as ambulatory care, home care, subacute care, and specialized rehabilitation services. Market strategies will emphasize continuous differentiation of services based on price, quality, and service. Customers must see the system as both different and better than alternatives. The true challenge is *behaving* like a system. To achieve that synergy, systems will have to tackle the painful task of rationalizing (consolidating, merging, downsizing, strengthening) redundant programs and facilities. Effective hospital-physician relationships are fundamental to system success. New organizations, support activities, and shared clinical and financial relationships must be created to bring physicians into the system as strong partners. Achieving integration will require better-functioning information networks that connect hospitals, doctors, and all system components.

Shortell's (1991a) bottom-line for the successful vertically integrated health system of the future is simple—value-added in the provision of services and satisfying customers. Integrated health systems must add value to internal customers (hospitals and component facilities, physicians and caregivers, boards and volunteers) and external customers (patients and families, managed care enrollees, employers and purchasers, government as purchaser and regulator, and the community).

Perhaps the most elusive dimension of system-building is leadership development. At the senior and middle-management levels, leaders must be adept at negotiating and managing change, networks of people and projects, markets with competitive differentiation strategies, and quality of clinical care and customer service. Hospital trustees must select and reward CEOs who can work in a system environment. Go-it-alone mavericks are obsolete in the hospital field; hospital CEOs must be team players who can collaborate with other hospitals and their own medical staff.

A System-Dominated Future

In Shortell's (1988) vision of the future, locally integrated health systems become the dominant regional delivery systems with several competing systems in each metropolitan area or small state (Anderson 1992). Large, national systems will dissolve during the 1990s, positioning their hospitals into regional organizations where there is compatibility of mission and corporate culture. Eventually, more than 80 percent of all U.S. hospitals will belong to integrated systems, as the "last wave" of system affiliation occurs near the end of the 1990s. In large part, these smaller and outlying hospitals will join existing systems rather than create new ones. By the twenty-first century, Shortell (1988) predicts that partnering will have run its course, with the nonaligned hospitals filling niches in service or location. System development in the 1990s will result in a new geology for the U.S. hospital industry (see Figure 7.2) (Shortell 1988).

Figure 7.2   The Hospital Industry as Organizational Strata

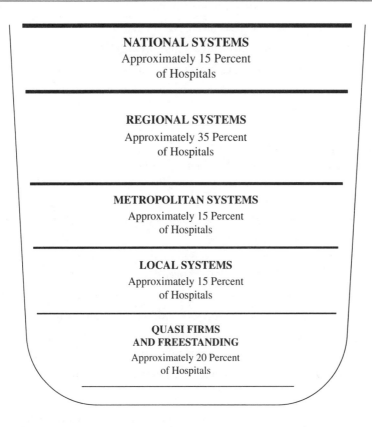

NATIONAL SYSTEMS
Approximately 15 Percent
of Hospitals

REGIONAL SYSTEMS
Approximately 35 Percent
of Hospitals

METROPOLITAN SYSTEMS
Approximately 15 Percent
of Hospitals

LOCAL SYSTEMS
Approximately 15 Percent
of Hospitals

QUASI FIRMS
AND FREESTANDING
Approximately 20 Percent
of Hospitals

The changing industry will alter how people are managed and production is organized. As evidence, the Hay Group has developed a data base on the management strategies and human resources performance of 30 health care management companies (integrated health systems) and has found that the most successful of the integrated health care systems operate differently than most hospitals or multihospital systems (Williams 1992). Features of these systems include

- Simple top management structures and rather complex middle-management structures (product-line managers, dual reporting relationships, very unique/specialized jobs)
- A reliance on management processes (for example, task forces, planning, budgeting) rather than on a formal organizational structure
- Functions decentralized to directly relate to patient care in a restructured patient care delivery system/unit
- Staff functions that are centralized, standardized, and/or consolidated
- Management with fewer layers and broader spans of control
- Staff specialists who are business partners with line managers
- Staff functions measured for value-added investment, not as overhead cost
- Spending more time/money in staff functions since managing vertical integration is more complex
- Integration of total quality management/continuous quality improvement (TQM/CQI) standards into the ongoing operational management process, rather than as a separate process
- Streamlining of the time and preparation for conduct of board meetings throughout the system
- Minimized a limitation on the number of boards for subsidiaries and clarification of roles of local boards with the system
- Human resources function links to the system's business strategy
- An emphasis on teamwork and building of strong teams
- Greater use of incentives and experiments with nontraditional compensation programs such as gain-sharing
- Recruitment and selection of key personnel with competencies in managing in a systems context.

Integrated health care systems cannot exist without integrated health care information systems, which are easier to describe than to build. Inter-Mountain Health Care (IHC) may be the most advanced health system in developing a state-of-the-art information network. InterMountain manages 24 hospitals and health care facilities spread across the Rocky Mountain states. Its goal is to transform this "confederacy" of facilities into an integrated continuum of care (Gardner 1993). InterMountain has created clusters of its facilities in the urban valleys, with linkages to its often remote rural facilities. More recent, InterMountain has introduced physicians to the system and promoted its managed care and health insurance products. Across all facilities and medical practices, InterMountain seeks excellence in clinical and customer service quality.

To be successful across the states, IHC has built one of America's most highly developed health care information systems, with some $65 million invested. With its internally developed software, financial data is centralized and integrated, although some local functions such as printing of bills are distributed. IHC's HELP (Health Evaluation through Logical Processing) system software was jointly developed with 3M, which purchased Inter-Mountain's information systems/software subsidiary. Clinical systems is a new development but will be fully operational at all urban IHC facilities. Laboratory services are supported by a centralized lab computer systems interfaced to HELP. The clinical system applications currently in place include admit/discharge/transfer, order communications, results review, pharmacy, radiology, nursing (bedside), ICU, respiratory care/blood gas, and infectious disease monitoring.

Telecommunications are a major integrating function across IHC's widespread system. IHC operates a private, internally managed telecommunications network that provides phone service to all IHC facilities except a few very rural locations. This digital network provides an electronic highway to link financial and clinical computers among sites. IHC operates an 800 number patient information/physician referral service that averages 26,000 calls per month where access to health information is the number-one requested service; "Ask-A-Nurse" alone generates more than 1,200 referrals to IHC physicians each month.

Information integration supports system integration. To encourage resource-sharing, nurses are scheduled and systems are staffed on a multihospital basis, job openings are electronically "posted" companywide, and inventory control involves all facilities. Although InterMountain is not quite paperless, electronic mail (E-mail) is a primary format for communication.

Physician offices are also on-line to IHC's information system, enhancing InterMountain's managed care and insurance products. Doctors can easily track their inpatients and access clinical data from office or home. A comprehensive clinical decision support system permits the physicians to be involved in protocol development, research studies, and quality management, regardless of their location across the system.

Managing costs and quality may ultimately be the most compelling reason to support a highly elaborated information system. Providing computerized expert-system capacities assists IHC's managers and clinical caregivers to optimize quality and resource management. At IHC, patient care management teams are being implemented to manage each patient's care from admission to discharge. For IHC, continuous quality improvement is based on two principles: *Eliminate inappropriate variation,* and *document continuous improvement.* InterMountain's studies focus on two areas where increasing quality can lead to significantly lower costs: (1) quality waste, where resources have been wasted by a quality failure, or the output was discarded; and low productivity, which occurs because two health care processes produce the same desired outcome but one process requires more resources. QUE (Quality/Utilization/Efficiency) studies compare and contrast physician utilization and hospital efficiency to identify and eliminate inappropriate utilization. InterMountain believes that effective information systems are essential to facilitate and monitor integration of their systemwide business strategy (Kralovec 1990).

Hospital trustees must prepare to make million-dollar investments in information systems during the 1990s. Managing costs and quality through integrated information systems is a critical success factor. In a managed care marketplace, hospitals and their doctors will be evaluated on clinical and cost performance.

A Case Study in Systems Integration: UniHealth America

At UniHealth America, "thinking big" comes with the territory. The company is competing in southern California, the largest health care market in the United States, and the most competitive. Trends start quickly in southern California, a region with 250 hospitals known for its entrepreneurship and for-profit competitiveness (Weber 1992). UniHealth believes an integrated system discipline can create a sustained competitive advantage over less-integrated competitors. In the managed care fixed-price marketplace of southern California, UniHealth has recognized that redundant service capacity within its system only adds costs. In its business strategy, UniHealth is one of the most highly evolved of America's multihospital systems. This system has actively shifted paradigms from the assumptions that drove multihospital systems during the 1970s and 1980s to a new vision of the essentials for a successful health care organization in the 1990s and beyond (see Figure 7.3) (Strum 1992).

Conceptually, UniHealth has turned the corner from being a multihospital system to an integrated health system. According to Dennis Strum, senior vice president of corporate development, "The UniHealth America vision is to develop a capacity within our organization to manage the health of a known population over time" (Weber 1992). It is making the transition from a hospital system to a health constellation. Key components of that vision include: regionally integrated premier health network of hospitals and ambulatory care settings with multiple locations and access points; organized physician components aligned with the regional network characterized by pluralistic practice models and multisite locations within the region; quality and value in corporate culture and clinical practice; centers of excellence regionally distributed for cost-efficient health care services; integrated managed care merging with financing and care delivery; unique multihealth continuum; and organizational infrastructure with an emphasis on cross-governance, physician participation, and team performance.

As a "hospital company," UniHealth America operates 12 medical centers in two major markets, but predominantly in southern California. UniHealth also owns a behavioral medicine company with a network of care centers, a dialysis service in eight locations, and a senior health membership plan.

As a "managed care company," UniHealth operates an HMO (PacifiCare) in four states—California, Oklahoma, Oregon, and Texas. PacifiCare's Secure Horizons plan is one of the nation's most successful Medicare risk-sharing HMOs. CareAmerica, a second managed care plan, has 160,000 enrollees, including a popular Medi-Gap plan. UniHealth's PPO Alliance covers 500,000 lives in Southern California.

Merging care and financing is one of the key strategic initiatives in UniHealth's vision for the future. UniHealth is merging with Blue Shield of

Figure 7.3 A Systematic Change Process

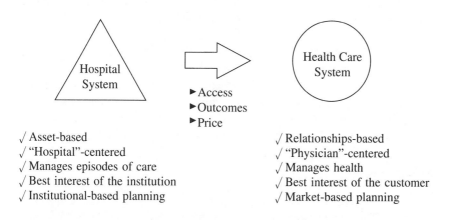

Reprinted with the permission of Dennis W. Strum of UniHealth America. Data adapted from a model of Stephen M. Shortell's.

California, which would have established a $6.5 billion company covering 3 million enrollees (DeLafuente 1993) before merger talks broke off. In a system that includes both managed care plans and delivery systems, Uni-Health is building its capacity to manage the health of a known (enrolled) population over time. With its managed care plans and regional integration, UniHealth aims to gain competitive advantage and differentiate itself in the intensely competitive California marketplace.

UniHealth operates its integrated health system on a seven-point management philosophy: (1) alignment of system and physician interests, (2) QUEST program for total quality management, (3) managed care market leadership, (4) case management, (5) regional service lines, (6) integrated information systems, and (7) HealthCity health care campuses.

A critical dimension of becoming a vertically integrated health system is the medical component. Creating a physician organization is essential for success in tomorrow's managed care marketplace. UniMed is UniHealth America's medical division. UniMed has purchased two major medical groups under the umbrella of nonprofit clinic foundations (Roberts 1993). Ultimately, each UniHealth hospital will have an exclusively affiliated medical group on each campus. The medical groups will be magnets for physician referral and managed care contracts.

Is UniHealth's integrated strategy working? Early results say yes: PacifiCare is a proven winner; the HMO's publicly traded stock hit $60 per share in early 1992 before splitting; more than 75 percent of UniHealth's net profitability comes from its managed care plans; UniHealth is adding hospital affiliates that are likely to become fully merged members of its regional delivery system for southern California in the future. As a market leader, however, UniHealth faces risks. Physician-associated risks include alienating medical staff physicians through acquisition of competing medical group practices and/or affiliating with the wrong medical groups. System risks include losing major purchasers (other competing managed care plans) as UniHealth's PacifiCare, CareAmerica, PPO Alliance, and VertiHealth plans become their competition; a failure to balance sometimes competing goals of the system versus an individual entity (hospital or managed care plan); the complexity of managing a pluralistic product; and the loss of credibility among external publics (patients, consumers) and internal publics (employees, medical staff) if integration is not achieved.

Strategies

1. **Join a system.** By some predictions, 75–80 percent of all U.S. hospitals will be part of systems by the year 2000. This new wave of systems-building is not a repeat of the"acquisitions fever" that built multihospital chains during the 1970s and 1980s. Now the emphasis is on developing local vertically integrated systems. Depending on the size of the local

market, systems will need three to five hospitals to provide multiple access points as the minihubs of a regional delivery system.

2. **Establish trustee-to-trustee negotiations.** Partnering is too important to leave to the lawyers, and the CEOs should not carry the burden of negotiation system formation. With their jobs at stake, senior staff may not have the unbiased ability to manage networking and mergers. Rely on savvy trustees for leadership in sensitive system-building negotiations.

3. **Encourage physician involvement.** Their support is critical to systems development and integration. In the 1980s, a number of proposed mergers failed due to medical staff opposition. Building tomorrow's integrated health systems must recognize the complexity of creating new medical organizations as integral building blocks of the system. Systems negotiation committees should be composed of 35–50 percent physician leadership.

4. **Build community care networks.** Trustees should ensure that systems-building efforts put the community first. In the debate over national health reform, the AHA has recommended development of community care networks that will assume responsibility for community populations. The AHA's emphasis on the community is appropriate. As tomorrow's health systems are constructed in the 1990s, community benefit, not institutional welfare, must drive the integration efforts. This is the essence of stewardship for hospital and health system trustees.

References

Anderson, H. J. 1992. "Hospitals Seek New Ways to Integrate Health Care." *Hospitals* 66 (5 April): 26–36.

DeLafuente, D. 1993. "California Blue Shield, UniHealth Unveil Proposal to Merge." *Modern Healthcare* 23 (5 July): 4.

Flower, J. 1992. "New Tools, New Thinking: A Conversation with Russell Ackoff." *Healthcare Forum Journal* 35 (March–April): 62–67.

Gardner, E. 1993. "Computers, Networks Help Intermountain Integrate." *Modern Healthcare* 23 (19 July): 30–31.

Greene, J. 1993. "3 Minnesota Hospital Groups Seek Closer Ties." *Modern Healthcare* 23 (19 July): 9.

Hudson, T. 1993a. "The Race to Integrate: Who Will Be the Leaders?" *Hospitals & Health Networks* 67 (5 June): 25–27.

———. 1993b. "Flexibility and Teamwork Are Keys to Success in Worcester System." *Hospitals & Health Networks* 67 (5 June): 29–32.

Johnsson, J. 1992. "Direct Contracting: Employers Look to Hospital-Physician Partnerships to Control Costs." *Hospitals* (20 February): 56–60.

Kralovec, O. J. 1990. "Clinical Quality in Provenant." *Healthcare Forum Journal* 33 (July–August): 33–34.

Roberts, A. W. 1993. "IRS Endorses Facey IDS." *Health Care Competition Week* 10 (30 April): 1–3.

Shortell, S. M. 1991a. "The Current State of Integration in Health Care." Presented at "The Future of Integrated Health Systems" conference, 6 November.

————. 1991b. *Effective Hospital-Physician Relationships*. Ann Arbor, MI: Health Administration Press.

————. 1988. "The Evolution of Hospital Systems: Unfulfilled Promises and Self-Fulfilling Prophesies." *Medical Care Review* 46 (Fall): 177–214.

Weber, D. O. 1992. "Case Study: UniHealth America: Moving to Assume Risk and Eliminate Intermediaries." *Healthcare Forum Journal* 35 (March–April): 49–50.

Williams, J. B. 1992. "Guidelines for Managing Integration." *Healthcare Forum Journal* 35 (March–April): 39–47.

8

Hospital-Board-Physician Relationships: Creating a Partnership Model of Governance

> Embarking on the path of creating an integrated healthcare organization from a matrix of private practice is a little like driving a truck loaded with nitroglycerin along a bumpy road. Leaders without the political skills to see the bumps in the road will never know what hit them.
>
> —Jeff Goldsmith (1993)

American hospitals need a new model of integrated management. The successful hospital boards of the 1990s will construct a new relationship with their physicians that is built on the strengths of the corporate model. Key elements of this new model as it evolves in the 1990s will be the physician-hospital organization, a vice president for medical care, physicians who govern, clinical management, and integrated information systems.

Relationships between the hospital and physicians will be reconstructed to establish an integrated physician-hospital organization (PHO) that can jointly contract with managed care plans as a hospitalwide organization. In a completely integrated model, all members of the active medical staff will join together in a professional corporation covering all clinical departments, an arrangement sometimes referred to as the Kaiser model, from the relationship between the Kaiser Foundation Health Plan (hospitals) and the Kaiser Permanente Medical Group (physicians). Regardless of details of national health reform, the health care market will demand regional delivery systems of hospitals and physicians who can contract with managed care and insurance plans and self-insured employers to carry out patient care, quality assurance, and cost management activities.

A doctor should be in charge of the doctors. The vice president for medical care will have full authority and responsibility for the medical care provided in the hospital and should be a voting member ("inside director") of the board of trustees. As a chief engineer in a manufacturing organization or chief scientist in a high-tech firm, the vice president for medical care will plan, organize, direct, and control medical care in the hospital. By reporting to the vice president for medical care, chiefs of clinical services and medical directors of programs will have direct-line responsibility for medical care provided within their departments.

The hospital's board of directors should include substantial physician representation—between one-third (33 percent) and one-half (49 percent). Physicians should regularly chair major committees such as finance and planning and rotate as chairs of the board of trustees. The clinical expertise and input provided by physicians will be critical for board success in the 1990s. Physicians must be an integral part of the management and governance of the hospital and health system at every level.

The secret of a successful hospital in the 1990s will be clinical efficiency and effectiveness with the goal top-quality service at the lowest feasible cost per case, stay, and procedure. Financial success in the era of health reform is critically dependent on fine-tuning clinical management that controls costs for every patient and service. The medical management challenge will need to coordinate case management, utilization review, quality assurance, and traditional clinical aspects with cost control, staffing, and support services. Understanding and managing the "core business" of clinical care demands that tomorrow's hospital boards have substantial physician participation on the board.

Hospitals in the 1990s will "live and die" by the quality of their data systems. Physician and nurse case managers must have the ability to manage their patients in "real time." Financial and clinical data must be timely and accurate, and computerized workstations should be networked and universally accessible across the hospital, ambulatory settings, and physician offices. Consider the savings generated by cutting the hospital's length of stay by one day: Fine-tuning clinical management could save the average hospital at least one-half to one full patient day. Quicker, more accurate diagnoses and more efficient use of resources during the stay or procedure may add 3–5 percent to the hospital's bottom line. The board should regularly review a set of key medical performance indicators on the hospital's clinical cost-efficiency and quality. Like their American business counterparts, hospitals in the Information Age must strengthen their board composition with expertise in information systems.

A Culture of Cooperation

The most important finding from a study of the hospital-physician relationship is the importance of a culture that emphasizes board and management collaborating with physicians in pursuing the institution's mission and objectives. *Effective Hospital-Physician Relationships* by Stephen M. Shortell is based on an in-depth study of ten hospitals, which was supported by the Estes Park Institute and American Hospital Association. As was noted at the outset of the study, "There is nothing more important to the successful operation of a hospital than a medical staff that works in harmony with the hospital. And there is nothing more difficult to attain and maintain" (Shortell et al. 1993). Through this research and extensive case studies, Shortell developed a "stage model" (Shortell 1991) of hospital-physician relationships that outlines the evolution of a culture of trust and collaboration (see Figure 8.1).

This culture of physician-hospital collaboration is required by environmental changes "yet if it is trivial, it is meaningless" (Sheldon 1979). Significant physician-hospital cooperative effort requires paradigm-breaking effort, which is why collaboration has proven to be so difficult and poorly handled. During the mid-1980s, most hospital executives recognized the need

Figure 8.1 A Stage Model of Hospital-Physician Relationships

Stages	Characteristics	Requirements for Effectiveness
Stage I Early (Infancy)	Low experience Low capabilities Low confidence	Strong culture Strong board Extensive education Develop relationship fundamentals High outside consultation Some early successes
Stage II Middle (Adolescence)	Some experience Some capabilities Moderate confidence (sometimes misplaced)	Understanding board Patient administration Willingness to experiment Ability to accept failure Learn from mistakes Continued education Some trust builders
Stage III Late (Maturity)	High experience High capabilities High confidence	Facilitating board Shared management and governance Build on successes Seek new opportunities Continued education Avoid complacency Some failures

Reprinted with the permission of the Hospital Research and Educational Trust © 1991, as it appeared in Stephen M. Shortell's *Effective Hospital-Physician Relationships*, p. 262.

for significant physician involvement, which led to a new era of "conjoint" physician-hospital effort (Shortell 1985).

The successes of the ten hospitals and health systems profiled in Shortell's (1991) study is inspiring. But it would be a mistake to ignore the impediments and failures that often occurred. Trust between and among board, administration, and the medical staff was a critical success factor. Often this trust had been built on long-standing personal relationships among the board, senior management, and medical staff leadership. Most of the CEOs in the study hospitals had five to ten years of experience in the facility, with strong board continuity. The ten-hospital study searched for and found cross-cutting strategies that promoted a climate of trust for hospital-physician collaboration. To achieve successful hospital-physician relations, hospitals must effectively manage six key issues (Shortell 1991): hospital-physician competition, managed care, joint ventures, cost containment, nurse-physician relationships, and quality improvement.

As hospital boards and their medical staff face the future, a process for shared decision making and governance between hospitals and their physicians is demanded. From a process perspective, the secrets of effective hospital-physician relationships are open decision-making and managerial style, extensive physician involvement, continuous communication, mutual trust, conflict-resolution procedures, and a willingness to change. The lesson for board, medical staff, and administration is to establish continuity in physician leadership on the board by encouraging them to make a two-term (or six-year) commitment to board service.

Causes of Medical Staff-Administration Breakdown

Hospital-physician relationships are among the most important make/break factors in a hospital's success, and in CEO survival. Creating a partnership for governance of tomorrow's integrated health systems will not be easy, as Jeff Goldsmith (1993) cautions: "Both sides of the bizarre, sadomasochistic relationship between medical practice and management bring baggage to the 'arranged marriage' of the integrated health care system."

Generations of physician leaders have sought to preserve clinical autonomy and entrepreneurship when the emerging marketplace of managed care and integrated systems encourages sharing of power and collegiality. Remember that doctors have been trained to be independent decision makers. Consequently, physicians may require additional assistance and training in group decision making (Goldsmith 1993). Physician-hospital collegiality must be based on mutual tolerance and shared professional values. In troubled and turbulent times, the trust relationship between management and medical staff undergoes greater stress. A national survey by Deloitte & Touche (1992) found that hospital-physician relationships were not as compatible in 1992 as they were four years prior: only 31 percent of hospital CEOs characterized their relationships with physicians as "excellent" in 1992, down from 37 percent in a prior survey.

Both sides are at fault, as demonstrated by the five reasons why health care executives get in trouble with their medical staffs.

1. They withhold strategic information. Often this is labeled a "communication" problem. Actually what the doctors mean is that top administration prefers to operate from an information advantage, and key information is either late or incomplete when it is presented to the medical staff.

2. Hospital and physicians compete. As hospitals expand their ambulatory care activities, they begin to compete very directly with the two-thirds of the medical staff who are office-based practitioners. Equipment wars are a variation on the theme of competition when the hospital acquires technology such as magnetic resonance imaging (MRI) that competes with physician-owned equipment.

3. A "bonding backlash" occurs. When hospitals employ a variety of incentives to strengthen their ties with key admitters, other physicians are likely to feel neglected or threatened. Their paranoia is real and often justified.

4. Medical staff leadership is weak (or hostile). Failure of medical staff leaders to lead or communicate are frequent causes of the disintegration of trust between medical staff and administration. Worse yet, some immature medical staffs deliberately choose a weak physician or antagonistic doctor to represent them.

5. Incentives are not shared. The lack of shared incentives between doctors and the hospital is problematic because hospitals are still paid primarily by case or stay while doctors are reimbursed on a fee-for-service basis. Only in risk-sharing arrangements with managed care plans do physicians and management share economic incentives for efficiency. Until this problem is solved, hospitals and their doctors will only cooperate based on goodwill and a concern for quality patient care.

Physician Leadership

The physician culture is fundamentally different from the cultural values shared by board and management (Merry 1993). The concept of leadership held by board and management includes vision, strategy, communications, and consensus-building. But doctors do not share this concept. In the physician culture, Merry (1993) suggests leaders should be clinically competent; carry out certain bylaw provisions relating to accreditation and facilitate a peer-review process to ensure quality; advise administration on technology and other practice needs; and represent physicians' interests to administration and the board. Possibly greatest among these is their felt need for personal autonomy unencumbered by the bureaucratic rules that seem to govern most institutions.

Physicians who are admired as leaders by their colleagues are those who first and foremost are clinically excellent. Strong physician leaders do not build consensus—they build excellent clinical programs. Physician leaders do not build support for institutional vision because they risk being considered "administrative stooges" for promoting the hospital's agenda. The physician culture does not build team players because the independent thinking so essential for physician clinical decision making is generally at odds with an organizational culture of group decisions and teamwork.

Merry (1993) predicts that two types of physician leaders will emerge —those who make the full transition to true health care executives, and the "bridge" leaders who divide their time between patient care and administrative duties. These part-time physician leaders will be critical to physician-hospital integration in this transitional period, while hospitals and systems "grow" the medically trained health care executives for the future.

Building trust and sharing values *are* the preconditions to the ability to cooperate and successfully manage the economic risk of managed care contracts. It is the cultural transition, not creating new organizational forms like PHOs or medical foundations that is the true leadership challenge of the 1990s for hospitals and health systems.

Physician-hospital cooperation is a path littered with the debris of failed projects and fired executives. Too often, the problem has been the "rank and file" physicians who did not subscribe to proposals agreed upon by the medical leadership. Managing an integrated health care organization requires widespread physician participation in decision making at all levels of the organization. Without broad support from practicing physicians, new physician-hospital initiatives will be vulnerable to apathy, slow implementation, and even sabotage from the medical staff. Weak or isolated medical leadership is often the actual culprit. According to one physician leader: "You have to understand that we are really three groups—the management and board, the medical staff leadership, and the rank and file. For the most part, we [the medical staff leadership] are much closer to management and the board than we are to the rank and file" (Shortell 1991).

Shortell (1991) has discussed how younger medical staff members have expressed general suspicion of the hospital as an institution, a wariness of medical staff leadership, and a "show-me" attitude. Apathy often prevailed unless these alienated physicians could see the direct relevance of a hospital decision on their own practices. One hospital's attempt to establish a medical director position was frustrated when the medical staff voted 67–59 to censure the medical staff executive committee for proposing the position. The "no" vote shocked the medical leadership, who had polled the 150 physicians on the medical staff earlier on the issue of recruiting a medical director, and found two-thirds in favor (Shortell 1991). A key lesson then in hospital-physician relationships is the need to work with younger members on the medical staff to create a sense of interdependence and shared responsibility. A sense of involvement and commitment by these physicians can be promoted by effective communication, a collaborative managerial decision making and style, and strong physician leadership.

Partnering Strategies for the 1990s

In the next few years, a hospital can "make its market" by partnering with its physicians, or lose marketshare and referrals to a more proactive competitor. The hospital board needs to take an active posture in hospital-physician relations. Five promising approaches to developing a strong, committed relationship between a hospital and its key physicians are presented.

Direct Contracting/Risk Sharing

Eliminating the intermediary (insurer) is not easy. If successful, hospitals and cooperating physicians can lock in employer or managed care plan loyalty for multiyear contracts. But failures can be costly, if volumes are low, costs are high or discounts too deep to cover expenses. Physician partnerships are essential: "Purchasers buy health care from organized medical groups—not hospitals" (Glatstein 1993).

Managed competition envisions many direct contracting relationships between employer purchasing groups and physician-hospital networks. Most direct contracting arrangements involve discounts from normal billed charges for physicians and negotiated per diem reimbursement for hospitals. Some direct contracts are based on anticipated revenues or admissions, and a few utilize DRG-based payment schemes. Single-service contracting is growing, particularly obstetrics and cardiac care; here hospital and physician agree to accept a single fee for the service and share the financial risk if costs exceed the all-inclusive price. According to one CEO: "We have a very strong partnership between systems, hospitals and most important, between physicians. Hospitals can't effect much change in case management, utilization, and cost without a strong partnership with the practicing physicians" (Johnsson 1992).

A managed competition strategy for national health reform will strongly encourage the development of direct contracting with employer purchasing groups. Southern California Edison is an example of direct purchasing of health care by a large employer. By constructing its own network of hospitals and physicians, Edison saved $100 million in five years, some 20 percent below what it would have otherwise spent (Sokolov 1993).

Boards beware: direct contracting is not for all hospitals or physicians. This future opportunity will be limited. Perhaps 5–10 percent of the largest firms have the buying power and sophistication to engage in direct provider contracting. Hospitals often lack specific data on costs and quality to price their bids, and hospital information systems are often inadequate to provide the detailed reporting employers will want. But the coat-tail effect of contracting with a high-visibility employer can enhance the hospital's status in managed care contracting with other major employers and insurance companies.

Hub-and-Spoke Networks

Think hub-and-spoke in constructing tomorrow's regional delivery systems to contract with managed care buyers. Dominant regional medical centers will develop affiliations with primary care hospitals and physicians that channel patients to the hub tertiary care facility for specialized services. Community hospitals and primary care/multispecialty medical groups will be the spokes. For the 1990s, the network provides a regional delivery system for managed care contracting. Networks that include the area's best hospitals and top-quality physicians will be preferred providers by HMOs, PPOs, and insurance companies. Ideally, the network will include a hospital/physician-owned HMO and/or PPO, and then it will be a fully integrated health care system. Networks will be linked by business and clinical relationships, with shared ownership and control. Sharing financial risk in capitation contracts will be the glue that keeps the network model together. But the networks must share patients and revenues fairly—not just as suppliers to the regional hub. Only where these relationships are perceived to provide mutual value to all participants can alliances thrive. Today their primary value is referral patients for the tertiary center and services/subsidies for the outlying facilities. In this decade, the primary benefits will be managed care contracts that protect marketshare for all hospitals and doctors, and the economies of operation from a fully integrated delivery system.

The alliance can be a model for the regional delivery system of the 1990s. Milwaukee's Horizon Healthcare is a "non-ownership alliance" of three area hospitals launched in 1989. Executives and board members came together to collaborate on managed care initiatives and clinical programs. Governance is shared equally, with each partner having an equal voice in voting, representation, and decision making. The alliance-based system works, according to one CEO of an alliance hospital: "We didn't see a need (for a merger) because the way Horizon is structured certainly meets all the criteria of an integrated system without the consolidation of assets. I don't think it would have been possible to bring together three very strong independent organizations and boards" (Anderson 1992). A network can be an independent hospital's response to the Super-Meds prediction that all hospitals would be owned by very large national systems, which never happened. In 1993, a slim majority (51 percent) of the nation's 7,000 hospitals belonged to multihospital systems, according to the AHA (Hagland and Cerne 1993). Rather than becoming part of a national system, hospitals have adopted the network or consortia model and have begun building systems through voluntary affiliation and alliance. The network model will be the dominant pattern of hospital-physician relations during the 1990s.

The primary foundation for building a successful network is locally specific mutual benefit. Affiliations and alliances are constructed around specific local needs. Most networks give small hospitals access to group purchasing contracts, which can provide savings of 10–40 percent on supplies and equipment. Some networks also make group purchasing available to the hospital's physicians. Other services include management contracting, clinical department contracting, physician education, staff recruitment, accounting and information systems, quality assurance, licensing and certification compliance, marketing and planning, and shared advertising. Even a new CEO or CFO can be part of the package. Some networks provide loaned executives on a short- or long-term basis.

In return for patient referrals, hub medical centers can provide capital, facilities, and equipment to the smaller network hospitals. One hub is building medical office buildings on the campuses of affiliated hospitals, which will include support services such as radiology, laboratory, diagnostic services, corporate health, psychology, and pharmacy. Many networks support group practice development; some also manage small medical groups, and a few networks have purchased medical practices. The goal is to create an integrated regional service distribution system that will outcompete other local hospitals for insurance and managed care contracts.

The network concept is appealing—it is relatively simple to construct and requires little capital. But the affiliation concept has a serious weakness, in its reliance on voluntary cooperation. Basically a network is a confederacy and commitment by local hospitals to cooperate with the decisions and directions of the network is completely voluntary. This is where the network model could break down. If every decision is open to challenge and every managed care contract must be validated by all network members, then the network's cohesion could rapidly fall apart. Strong leadership from the network's leadership council of trustees and a spirit of trust by local hospital members is essential to continued success. The hub hospital cannot dominate the network, and all network members must believe there is mutual benefit in the alliance. The integrated regional network model is very much still experimental (Philbin 1993).

Multihospital networks will need a new form of governance that is consistent with the alliance model of voluntary affiliation. Networks will be governed by mutual cooperation at the trustee level, a "council of allies." Participating hospitals will send delegates to the network's regional council, and strategic decisions will be collaborative. But ultimately, the majority must rule and partners must commit to the network decision. If voluntary networks fail, more integrated models, including a government takeover, may follow.

Centers of Excellence/Clinical Networks

The centerpieces of American hospital market strategy today are medical centers of excellence—cardiac care, oncology, obstetrics, and other specialized services. The market pull of these magnet services must be reinforced by the creation of clinical networks that reach out to referring hospitals and physicians.

Clinical networks formalize and give structure to traditionally informal patterns of medical referral. There are benefits to all parties: Tertiary hospitals provide specialized physician services to outlying hospitals, allowing local patients to receive consulting services at home and stay in the community. Some specialized clinical networks develop written protocols for patient referral and transfer, specifying the communication, privileges and guarantees of patient return to reassure local physicians.

For example, two hospitals and their physicians are collaborating to provide state-of-the-art cardiac care without duplication of effort in Boston (Johnsson 1992). The Beth-Israel Hospital, a 504-bed Boston facility, has developed a clinical alliance with 285-bed Framingham Union Hospital. Together, cardiologists from the two institutions have formed the MetroWest Cardiac Center, with a 12-bed coronary unit that will give the suburban Framingham hospital access to tertiary-level services and backup. Framingham's coronary unit is essentially a satellite cardiology program. Beth-Israel provides cardiac surgery and angioplasty as needed and protects its lines of clinical referral. The cardiology programs of both facilities are headed by the same doctor. The regional network provides the outlying hospital access to the latest in medical practice and technology without the capital investment. The collaboration eliminates unnecessary duplication of skills and technology.

Clinical networks are "bridge" strategies to more extensive alliances and partnering. Engaging in clinical networking among hospitals and physicians is an excellent training ground for collaboration. Successful clinical partnerships can build a basis of trust for managed care networking and even merger.

Primary Care Network

The front line of tomorrow's health delivery will be primary care. Networks of primary care providers—both physicians and hospitals—are being organized. To serve its market of the northern and western suburbs of Chicago, the Lutheran General Health Care System (Park Ridge, Illinois) is building a primary care base for managed care and health reform. Building blocks of the network include (Johnsson 1992):

- The Health Practice Organization (HPO), which is a for-profit venture between the Lutheran General System and Greater Northwest Independent Practice Associates, a 400-doctor IPA that includes more than 50 percent of the physicians with staff privileges at Lutheran General Hospital.
- The Lutheran General Medical Group, which is an on-campus multispecialty group practice with 160 physicians.
- The Parkside Health Management Corporation, which is an 85,000-member PPO that is now jointly ventured with neighboring EHS Health System.

The concept of a primary care network is equally valid in rural areas like New Ulm, Minnesota, where 85-bed Sioux Valley Hospital is developing a partnership with the New Ulm Clinic. The hospital and clinic share goals of recruiting physicians, sharing support services, and creating a more efficient community health system. This minisystem is growing: the clinic has added six physicians, and the hospital built a new medical office building on campus to house the clinic (Johnsson 1992).

To succeed in tomorrow's managed care/managed competition marketplace, every hospital and system will need a primary care base. Hospital boards must fundamentally rethink their capital investment strategy, redirecting capital into physician acquisition, group practice development, and ambulatory care facilities both on and off-campus for primary care. The future begins with primary care.

Managing Quality

Involving lay and physician hospital trustees in the quality management process is a critical success factor for the future. The board's responsibility for managing quality begins with its legal liability, established by *Darling* v. *Charleston Community Memorial Hospital* (1965), where the hospital as well as its medical staff were jointly found liable in a case of malpractice. There are four principle reasons why boards are responsible for quality are: ethical and moral obligation, legal accountability, legislative and regulatory requirements, and fiduciary responsibility (Orlikoff 1993). The board may place day-to-day responsibility for assuring quality on the medical staff, but it must actively monitor quality on an ongoing basis.

Far-sighted physicians have seen the need for managing hospital quality. As far back as 1916, E.A. Codman, M.D., said that to improve, hospitals must:

- Find out what their results are
- Analyze their results to find their strong and weak points
- Compare their results with those of other hospitals
- Care for the cases they can care for well, and avoid attempting to care for cases they are not qualified to care for well
- Welcome publicity not only for their successes, but for their errors, so that the public may give them their help when it is needed
- Promote members of the medical staff on the basis that gives due consideration to what they can and do accomplish for their patients (Orlikoff 1993).

Quality is a critical success factor in a marketplace where purchasers have detailed clinical data on the outcomes of hospital and physician performance. Lay and physician trustees must collaboratively review quality performance using a set of key clinical indicators, such as these suggested by Orlikoff (1993): mortality rates (for example, overall hospitalwide mortality rate, neonatal and maternal mortality rate, surgical mortality rate); nosocomial infection rates (for example, overall hospitalwide nosocomial infection rate, post-operative infection rate); adverse drug reactions or interactions; unplanned returns to surgery; unplanned transfers to surgery, isolation, intensive care units, or cardiac care units; unplanned transfers to other acute care facilities; hospital-incurred traumas; discharges against medical advice; returns to the emergency room with 72 hours of being treated there; readmissions to the hospital within one month of discharge; unplanned admissions to the hospital following outpatient procedures; and cesarean-section rates.

Physician-hospital "economic organizations" such as IPAs, not the organized medical staff, may ultimately take responsibility for credentialing physicians and managing physician quality. Daniel A. Lang, M.D., medical director for Valley Presbyterian Hospital of Van Nuys, California, predicts that peer review will increasingly be affected by external requirements and that the organized medical staff may no longer be the locus of peer review (Ewell 1993), and that economic organizations, including the PHO and IPA, will decide that physicians will be part of the medical group that shares managed care contracts with the hospital.

Hospitals, doctors, and health systems must be prepared to compete on quality. Sophisticated purchasers, insurance plans, self-insured employers, and government will all have detailed data on quality performance. First, hospital boards need to know how the quality of care at their institution compares with peer institutions. Hospital boards need to partner with their medical staff to develop a comprehensive on-going system for auditing quality. At that point, hospitals can use their quality improvement processes to systematically improve quality, both clinical care and customer satisfaction.

Hospital-Physician Links

Health care, high technology, computers, and medicine—is there a more natural combination for hospitals in the Information Age? A growing number of hospitals are experimenting with physician computer linkages, but the results are mixed. The promise of physician computer linkages is the rapid transmission of data between the hospital and the physician office. The goal is to reinforce the symbolic linkage between a hospital and its key admitters and enhance quality patient care through expedited data transmission. Some systems have been in place in dozens of hospitals for more than five years. This is because computer-link systems work and data is flowing. A survey of 901 medical group practices found that only 14.4 percent have external systems linked to hospitals (Bergman 1993). The most popular services were lab results, radiology results, and insurance/billing. Pharmacy results, census information, and admissions data were frequently offered. Preadmission, radiology, and pharmacy order entry were newer services some hospitals were adding to their systems.

However, there is widespread disappointment with the systems' limited applications and technological bugs. Physician acceptance has been slow. The *Modern Healthcare* survey (1989) revealed that 60 percent of the hospitals with physician-link systems were dissatisfied; some 25 percent of the hospitals said the system had not been marketed properly, while physicians had not accepted it in another 18 percent of computer-linked hospitals (Gardner and Perry 1989). Only 38 percent of these hospitals said physicians used it regularly, most frequently to check lab or census data. The cost of network linkages is coming down. For example, a 300-bed hospital with 250 physicians on a shared network would now cost $190,000 (Bergman 1993).

It is too early for systems to deliver the full potential of linking a physician office with a hospital's information system. Hospitals should not expect dramatic results from their linkage systems in terms of increased admissions and incremental revenues—these will come as hardware becomes less expensive, software more user-friendly, and available information expands. It's expected that by 1997, more than 50 percent of all hospitals with over 200 beds will have installed computer linkages in the offices of their key physicians and medical groups. If that's true, doctors and hospitals will be symbiotically linked in the future, through computer linkage systems. Therefore, physician computer linkage systems are an investment in the future. The hospital that installs its computer terminal in the office of its key admitters will gain a sustained competitive advantage over competing hospitals who try to bring in a second computer.

One *Modern Healthcare* magazine cover (Burda 1993) on the hospital-physician relationship was titled "Provider Self-Interest Makes a Monster of Self-Referral." The issue of provider-owned facilities is contentious. Five studies were cited demonstrating the costly effects of conflict of interest. Despite the controversy, hospitals are groping for ways to strengthen physician commitment and hospital utilization in an effort to foster physician bonding (Valentine 1990).

Effective physician relations are the foundation of a flourishing hospital. Too much is at stake not to gain perspective from the collective experience of hospitals with successful physician relationship practices. Dozens of tactics have been employed to strengthen hospital-physician relationships. Valentine (1990) has identified a number of physician bonding strategies that hospitals have employed with their medical staffs:

- Assistance in selling practice (retirement)
- Banking relations
- Computer linkages
- Diagnostic screenings of patients
- Educational brochures for physician offices
- Equity joint ventures
- Financial/retirement planning for individual physicians
- Group purchasing
- Grant uniting/research support
- Hospital services director
- IPAs
- Library resources
- Loans at fair market
- Malpractice insurance
- Marketing plans for individual physicians
- Marketing resources (e.g., demographic data and venders)
- Medical directorships/contracts
- Medical staff directory
- Orientation programs for new physicians

- Patient newsletter (physicians send to patients)
- Physician liaisons
- Physician referral services
- Practice efficiency audits
- Practice management assistance
- Reviews of physicians and office staff
- Social functions for physicians
- Seminars for physicians
- Speakers bureau
- Videotapes for patients

Since the mid-1980s, hospitals have initiated a barrage of physician bonding efforts designed to enhance physician commitment and increase referrals. Of these, six have proven especially successful in improving physician loyalty and hospital utilization (Valentine 1990):

1. Routine health screenings (eg., cholesterol) that are free to patients and subsidized by the hospital are an excellent mechanism for generating new patients for doctors.
2. Brochures designed for display in physician offices have multiple objectives. Health education materials oriented to the doctor's specialty can provide consumer health information on specific diagnoses and conditions. Hospital marketing materials can cross-sell a relevant hospital service such as physical therapy.
3. A growing number of hospitals are paying annual stipends of $5,000–25,000 and more to physicians for taking responsibility as medical director for hospital service programs and clinical departments. These stipends in community hospitals may range up to 25 percent of a physician's income. Medical directorships convey responsibilities for participation in management decision making and clinical supervision of the unit or department. The payment of medical directorship stipends has come under criticism arising from situations where physician medical directors were paid for little or no work. This practice has been sharply criticized by Congressman Pete Stark (D-Calif.) and may be subjected to congressional regulation (Burda 1993).
4. A successful medical staff development program must have a responsible staff. Titles vary—physician liaison, physician manager, medical staff coordinator, director of medical staff relations, and assistant to the president are all in use across the nation. In a

large hospital, the physician liaison may be a vice president—for example, vice president for medical affairs. Many physician liaison positions are located in the office of the president/CEO, some are based in marketing, and others are assigned directly to the office of the medical staff. Physicians fill these roles in major medical centers and academic-affiliated hospitals as it strengthens physician awareness of and relationships with the hospital. Functions include preparation of the medical staff development plan, carrying out key programs and activities, monitoring physician effectiveness and satisfaction, and resolving issues arising between physicians and the hospital (ombud).

5. A physician referral service links physicians and patients in need of a doctor. Typically the service advertises an easily-remembered telephone number that patients may call. An operator/marketer assists potential patients in identifying physicians who meet their criteria and then make an appointment. Many physician referral systems are computerized. Successful systems can generate 100–600 new patients per month. Referral systems work best in market areas with high population turnover and rapid growth. Continuing promotion through direct mail, targeted marketing to at-risk groups, and an advertising commitment of at least $40,000–50,000 per year is essential to maintain a high volume of callers.

6. Hospitals have achieved success with nonclinical educational seminars for their physicians and office staff focusing on socioeconomic topics such as financial planning, marketing a professional practice, practice management, HMO billing, guest relations, and other current issues facing physicians.

Looking Forward: Shared Governance and Integrated Organizations

Physician bonding efforts during the 1980s were trendy but scattershot and naive. Some worked; others had minimal impact. The fundamental needs of the medical staff for protection of patients and practice revenues was underappreciated, while the doctors' relationship with the hospital was overplayed. The disturbing reality is that only about one-third of the medical staff really needs the hospital. The rest of medical practice is office-based. New and better physician strategies are needed that are based on the long-term interdependence of hospitals with physicians. Malpractice liability and financial risk will be shared. Managed care and government regulations are forcing hospital-physician collaboration, whether all parties are ready or not.

Teamwork and collaboration must be emphasized by the board. According to Don L. Arnwine (1992), founding CEO of Voluntary Hospitals of America, "Although the board members aren't responsible for selecting and evaluating individual members of the CEO's senior team, they should take a keen interest in how the group is functioning. . . . The board should make sure that incentives are tied equally to team accomplishments and individual performance." Arnwine's (1992) surveys of dozens of U.S. hospitals and health systems have made some key points with regard to the challenges of collaboration and a team approach. He found that: chief executives have a consistently more positive view of team performance than team members themselves; team members and CEOs share a high level of optimism; fatigue and lack of family time are viewed as a significant problem; making decisions efficiently is the biggest challenge; lack of communication often clouds the common agenda; and teams worry about how they are viewed by employees and the medical staff.

Board support of a team concept with management and the medical staff can reinforce a shared optimism and a positive outlook toward the challenges of managing a modern hospital or health system. Open communication and a common agenda are critical to success. The sense of team and collaborative spirit must permeate the entire organization, beginning with the board and senior management team, across the employees and medical staff. Synchronizing business strategies of the hospital and medical staff can further the process of integration (Marks and Woods 1991). Shared vision, high levels of performance, and achievement of desired outcomes can result from strong teams. Even as managed care grows and hospitals and physicians become more competitive in the 1990s, one thing will not change—collaboration and a team approach will be a critical success factor for American hospitals and health systems to create tomorrow's integrated health care systems.

Strategies

1. **Create a culture of cooperation.** The hospital board of trustees can plan a critical role in hospital-physician relations by encouraging the "culture of cooperation" that Shortell (1993, 1991) recommends. While the board sets the tone for hospital-physician relations, its decision-making process must be open to medical viewpoints, and the medical staff leadership must be substantially involved in governance.
2. **Establish physician-hospital organizations.** The new mechanism for building physician relationships in the 1990s is the PHO. Hospitals must increase their efforts to strengthen the practices of their physicians and develop effective organizations (IPA, PPO, HMO) to give their doctors access to managed care contracts. Try new strategies for physican bonding.

3. **Encourage physicians to govern.** Hospitals need more physicians on the board. These "inside directors" should hold up to 49 percent of the seats. Physicians should chair the board on a rotational basis, every other term. Encourage continuity of medical staff leadership with two-term board tenures for physicians. Physician trustees must be elected by the board, not appointed by the medical staff. Rely on educational resources from the American College of Healthcare Executives, the Governance Institute, and Estes Park to train physician leaders in trusteeship and the challenges facing hospitals and health systems.

4. **Develop medical executives.** Every hospital of more than 150 beds should have a full-time physician executive as a member of the senior management group who also sits as a trustee on the board. The vice president for medical care needs to be integrally involved in hospital policymaking and leadership at the highest level. Physician involvement in governance is essential to manage and direct the core business of hospitals—clinical care.

References

Anderson, H. J. 1992. "Hospitals Seek New Ways to Integrate Health Care." *Hospitals* 66 (5 April): 26–36.

Arnwine, D. L. 1992. *The Power of Teamwork in an Age of Collaboration.* LaJolla, CA: The Governance Institute.

Bergman, R. 1993. "A Doctor in the Network: Physician Links Improve Access to Critical Data." *Hospitals* 67 (5 May): 24–26.

Burda, D. 1993. "Looking at Bans in a Different Light." *Modern Healthcare* 23 (31 May): 25–29.

Deloitte & Touche. 1992. *U.S. Hospitals and the Future of Health Care: A Continuing Opinion Survey.* Boston, MA: Deloitte & Touche.

Ewell, C. 1993. "Medical Leadership Institute Offered Practical Tools and Techniques for a Changing Environment." *Medical Leadership Press* 1 (February): 1–5.

Gardner, E., and L. Perry. 1989. "Assessing Computer Link's Risks and Rewards." *Modern Healthcare* 19 (24 November): 20–28.

Glatstein, H. R. 1993. "Physician Organizational Formation." Presentation to the Physician Leadership Conference, Legacy Health System, Portland, Oregon, 3 April 1993.

Goldsmith, J. C. 1993. "Driving the Nitroglycerin Truck." *Healthcare Forum Journal* 36 (March-April): 36–44.

Hagland, M. M., and F. Cerne. 1993. "Fast Forward into the Future: Multihospital Systems Look Toward the Challenges and Opportunities of a Post-Reform Delivery System." *Hospitals* 67 (20 March): 26–28.

Johnsson, J. 1992. "Dynamic Diversification: Hospitals Pursue Physician Alliances, 'Seamless' Care." *Hospitals* 66 (5 February): 20–26.

Marks, N. W., and R. A. Woods. 1991. "Break Down Walls with Business Integration." *Healthcare Executive* 6 (September–October): 23.

Merry, M. D. 1993. "Understanding How Physician Leaders Think." Presentation for the Governance Institute, LaJolla, CA.

Orlikoff, J. E. 1993. "Involving Hospital Trustees in the Quality Management Process." Presentation at the Hospital Medical Staff and Trustee Conference, The Governance Institute, Mauii, Hawaii, 12 January 1993.

Philbin, P. W. 1993. "From the Ground Up: Planting the Seeds of Network Development." *Hospitals and Health Networks* 67 (5 June): 46–52.

Sheldon, A. 1979. *Managing Change and Collaboration in the Health System.* Cambridge, MA: Oelgeschlager, Gunn & Hain.

Shortell, S. M. 1991. *Effective Hospital-Physician Relationships.* Ann Arbor, MI: Health Administration Press.

———. 1985. "The Medical Staff of the Future: Replanting the Garden," *Frontiers of Health Services Management.* 1 (February): 3–48.

Shortell, S. M., D. A. Anderson, R. R. Gillies, J. B. Mitchell, and K. L. Morgan. 1993. "The Holographic Organization." *Healthcare Forum Journal* 36, no. 2: 20–28.

Sokolov, J. J. 1993. "On the Brink of a Third Generation." *Healthcare Forum Journal* 36 (March–April): 29–33.

Valentine, S. T. 1990. *Physician Bonding: Developing A Successful Hospital Program.* Rockville, MD: Aspen Publishers.

9

Physician-Hospital Organizations: Medical Clinic Foundations, Practice Acquisitions, Mergers, and MSOs

> In today's environment, the affiliation between a hospital/health system and one or more medical group practices can be a critical vehicle to retain and expand a primary care base and achieve success in the managed care arena.
>
> —Ross Stromberg (1992)

Physician-hospital partnerships will become a leading strategy for every hospital and health system. For most hospitals, this will mean buying or building a physician organization that can be a magnet for referrals and a partner in managed care contracting.

There will be more changes in the hospital-physician relationship in the next decade than in the past 50 years. The trends for the 1990s are clear but somewhat contradictory (Coile 1991):

- Doctors will move closer to their hospitals and yet compete more often.
- Physicians will move into management yet lose authority over their patients.
- Many doctors will move onto hospital campuses; others will form "outlaw" group practices that are Machiavellian in their hospital affiliations.

Whatever the final shape of the national health care reform plan, these partnerships will be a critical building block. The managed competition scenario envisions the development of accountable health plans between purchasing coalitions and community care networks by America's hospitals with effective physician-hospital organizations (PHOs). The PHOs will provide the integrated delivery system, taking financial and legal risk for providing all health benefits to a defined population of covered lives under a single, capitated payment. The primary purpose of a PHO is to facilitate managed care contracts and provide a structure that will position hospitals and physicians for national health reform (Droste 1993).

The AHA's reform proposal calls for universal access to health care to be provided through local integrated delivery systems called community care networks. Each local system will be different, but each will share the common elements of financial risk, a continuum of care, system integration, outcomes data collection, and clinical protocols (Hudson 1993). These reforms cannot happen without a strong partnering relationship between physicians and hospitals—doctors are too critical to the management of quality and efficiency. Missing also are the medical organizations on which to build the community care networks of tomorrow. Hospitals need a portfolio of approaches and services, including (Coile 1993): a medical clinic foundation for acquiring/merging physician practices; two to three IPAs, at least one of which is capable of taking risk (capitation); primary care network of affiliated primary care physicians and groups for managed care contracts; a "group practice without walls" as a vehicle for solo physicians and small groups to gain the benefits of group practice; on-campus primary care/family practice group; multispeciality clinic located on campus or adjacent to the hospital that is primarily committed to the hospital; long-term exclusive contracts with key specialists for hospital-provided services (pathology, radiology, anesthesiology, emergency); physician management/support organization dedicated to promoting successful physician practice; an integrated information system linking hospital, ambulatory care settings, medical offices buildings, and physician practices; utilization review/quality assurance management function; and a vice president for medical services (full-time physician executive).

The Future Is Now

Hospital boards need to move quickly to develop PHOs. Managed care contracting compels hospitals to develop these relationships, even prior to national health reform.

A signal that the time for PHOs has arrived is the Mayo Clinic buying physician practices. Mayo purchased physician groups in rural Iowa and Minnesota and has plans to acquire others within a 120-mile circle in order to protect its referral patterns in Rochester, Minnesota area. Mayo is not the only hospital seeking strong alliances with organized medical groups. Hospital-physician group practice mergers are in negotiations across the nation, particularly in California and the Midwest (Johnsson 1992). But this trend to physician group acquisition/merger is more widespread according to a national survey by Ernst & Young and *Health Care Competition Week*

(Goldman and Taulbee 1992). More than one-third of hospitals surveyed, 315 short-stay hospitals from across the nation, representative of all hospitals by size, ownership, location, and service mix, had acquired at least one physician practice. The reasons for acquisition cited by hospital CEOs get to the heart of hospital survival in the 1990s: (1) to recruit more physicians, (2) to increase cooperation in cost containment, (3) to increase cohesiveness among medical staff, (4) to enhance quality of care, and (5) to contract with managed care plans.

The survey also revealed that 37 percent of the surveyed hospitals had purchased or created new physician practices (Goldman and Taulbee 1992). Seventy-one percent of these practices were family practice; 33 percent, internal medicine; 23 percent, obstetrics/gynecology; and 13 percent, general surgery. Some hospitals had built/bought more than one type. Hospitals in the 200–400 bed range were most likely to purchase physician practices with the highest level of acquisition activity in the West. Least likely to buy physician practices were smaller hospitals under 50 beds.

Hospitals are moving tentatively to establish closer relationships with their physicians, but only one in ten hospitals has an established PHO. Many hospital executives report having little direct influence over their physicians (Goldman and Taulbee 1992): more than one hospital executive in four (26 percent) of hospital executives think their physician relationships are inadequate for their current needs; 37 percent report these relationships are inadequate for future needs; and 16 percent of the hospitals have established an IPA. Only 38 percent of hospitals who had purchased or built a physician practice since 1990 had a "specific corporate entity" to house those practices. The majority of these corporate entities were tax-exempt (63 percent), governed by a lay board of directors (77 percent), and under the control of the hospital as a sole member (52 percent). Single-specialty practices were more likely to be owned and acquired (52 percent) than multispeciality practices (41 percent) (Goldman and Taulbee 1992).

Purchasing or building practices are only part of a broader array of strategies by hospitals to support physicians. The most frequently provided assistance to physicians includes: setting up a new office practice (78 percent), adding a partner (71 percent), creating a physician referral service (59 percent), marketing office practice (50 percent), and adding a medical waste disposal service (47 percent). Fewer than 20 percent of hospitals reported providing retirement planning assistance. This may be a missed opportunity and an underutilized strategy for identifying physicians who need associates or would potentially join groups and pool their patients.

Gaining the knowledge and undertaking relationship-building efforts in the arena of physician-hospital partnerships is important for trustees. These initiatives must be board-driven, not management-directed. Begin the educational process at the board level and expand medical staff involvement to the entire active staff.

Figure 9.1 Portfolio of Options for Physician-Hospital Relationships

Cooperation   Collaboration   Integration →

Level I	II	III	IV	V
Medical office buildings	Joint ventures	PPO	Clinic foundation	Integrated medical organization
Shared offices	Marketing	Practice management	Practice acquisition	Mayo/Cleveland clinics
Staff leasing	Group practice support	Integrated medical campus	HMO/capitation	Kaiser Health Plan
Practice building	"Group practice without walls"	Management service organization	Hospital-based groups	
Physician referral	IPAs		Medical division	
Ambulatory surgical centers				

Source: Russell C. Coile, Jr.'s "Physician-Hospital Partnering," *Hospital Strategy Report* 4 (July 1992): 5.

A Portfolio of Options

As managed care encourages PHOs, boards will encounter a variety of alternatives for constructing progressively closer relationships, from cooperation to integration (see Figure 9.1) (Coile 1992).

One example of a successful PHO is the Sharp HealthCare System, which acquired the Rees-Stealy Medical Clinic in 1985, a 200-physician medical group practice. Today Sharp HealthCare is emerging as one of three dominant health systems in the San Diego area, with 5 hospitals totaling 1,355 beds, 7 physician group practices, 14 clinics, and 5 skilled nursing facilities. In 1993, with 25 percent of the market, Sharp was responsible for 325,000 covered lives under its 60–70 managed care contracts (8–10 contracts are capitated) (Lumsden 1992). A key factor in Sharp's success in this heavily managed care marketplace is its partnership relations with the seven physician groups in risk-sharing (capitated) contracts. But the Sharp system has a pluralistic relationship with its 2,000 physicians—some are employed by group practices or IPAs, some doctors are salaried by Sharp, and others are independent members of the hospitals' medical staffs.

Collaboratively, physicians and administrators are developing practice guidelines and clinical protocols. Sharp is making a $30 million commitment to integration through 1997 to develop and install a regional information system that will centralize financial and clinical data in a single "electronic medical record."

Physicians Seeking Affiliation

Not all physicians are hostile about affiliating with hospitals or systems. Sometimes they pursue it. The forces that encourage physicians and medical groups to seek affiliation or merger with a hospital are (Coile 1992):

1. Access to managed care patients through the hospital or health system's contracts
2. Capital to expand group or purchase other groups
3. Physician-recruitment incentives and practice guarantees
4. Systems support (such as management information systems), utilization review, and quality assurance
5. Cashing out older, retiring partners
6. Creating equity in the practice by physician owners
7. Investment opportunities in facilities and equipment
8. A strong partner with "deep pockets" for risk-sharing managed care contracts
9. Financial losses to be experienced by the physician group

10. Benefit from a "bandwagon" effect of other groups merging, affiliating, and being acquired.

What kind of doctors should hospitals target for affiliation? Daniel Beckham of Quorum Health Resources has identified four groups of physicians in particular—each with their own set of needs (Beckham 1991)—young physicians interested in personal security (YIPs), physicians exiting practice (PEPs), physicians interested in practice support (PIPs), and physicians independent until they die (PIDs). YIPs are interested in employment opportunities. Some 80 percent of young physicians in residency programs were only interested in working for group- or staff-model HMOs. PEPs are also interested in employment, full- or part-time, but they are even more concerned about retirement security. PIPs are committed to maintaining their independence, but they would like to have some help with the nonclinical business pressures such as reducing overhead. PIDs will maintain their autonomy at any cost; many are successful entrepreneurs.

In the past, most doctors could be characterized as PIDs. Hospitals had to respect this demand for autonomy; any intrusion on PID territory was potentially dangerous for hospital CEOs. Today, doctors make different demands, depending on individual needs. Tomorrow's successful hospitals and health systems will be designed primarily around the needs of YIPs and PIPs. For the YIPs, hospitals will need to encourage group practice development, through support, formation, or acquisition. PIPs need a broader array of support programs such as office practice marketing or managed care contracting. Ultimately, PIPs may also see their future in group practice. Hospitals can be helpful in bringing PIPs together to form groups or creating new models for integration such as the "group practice without walls."

Past Physician-Hospital Joint Ventures

Given what the future will bring, hospitals should terminate most or all of their past physician-hospital joint ventures. Any joint ventures in which physicians have an economic interest will probably be legislated out of existence. Congressman Pete Stark (D-Calif.), whose key Senate subcommittee controls Medicare legislation, has proposed federal legislation to outlaw virtually all forms of physician investment in health facilities or equipment. There may be exceptions for physician group practices, but most other physician-hospital joint ventures are very likely to be legislated for termination by 1995, if not sooner (Burda 1993).

Federal rules in 1992 from the Internal Revenue Service (IRS) and Medicare's amended fraud and abuse "safe harbors" regulations from the Health Care Financing Administration have taken a narrow view of hospital-physician joint ventures restricting those ventures in which hospitals have sold the revenue streams from outpatient services to a joint venture consisting of members of its medical staff. But any types of physician-hospital joint ventures that involve the sale of a hospital's profitable services to physicians must be terminated, or the hospital may face loss of its tax-exempt status (Kenkel 1992).

New Models for Hospital-Affiliated Medical Group Practice

To successfully compete in a managed care marketplace, hospitals will need a portfolio of options for physician affiliation, including: nonprofit medical clinic foundations, management service organizations (MSOs), IPAs, group practices without walls, and faculty practice plans. The development of a tax-exempt medical clinic through the medical foundation model is one form of hospital-physician affiliation that can unite the technological, administrative, and financial resources of a hospital/health system with one or more medical group practices. The MSO can also be an important vehicle to bring capital and other management expertise to medical group practices. The MSO compares favorably in many respects with the medical foundation model, yet allows physicians to retain direct ownership of the group practice.

As developed through a medical foundation or MSO, a hospital-affiliated group practice should be only one component of an overall integrated program of physician practice support (see Figure 9.2). Key elements of hospital/health system support for physician group practice include:

- Managed care—Hospitals and health systems need a strong physician organization to compete effectively in a managed care marketplace. Important additions to a hospital's managed care strategy for physicians include marketing, contracting, capitation management, services to partners (for example, group practices, IPAs, other physicians), and new product development.

- IPA support—IPAs are the most common form of physician organization to arrange provision of medical services in a managed care contract. The hospital or health system typically provides support to its IPAs including management, administrative support services, management information or data systems, financial and accounting, utilization review and quality assurance, claims processing, marketing, personnel, and financial support.

- Physician service organization (PSO)—A number of hospitals and health systems have established medical or physician service organizations to provide practice management and administrative support services, including finance, billing and collections, benefits coordination, strategic planning, marketing, physician/medical office staff education and training, referral services, group purchasing, medical group development, and facility management and consolidation.

- Physician recruitment—Many (82 percent) hospitals and health systems are actively engaged in physician recruitment, providing an array of support services, including recruiting, practice start-up consultation, relocation assistance, income guarantees, loans, medical office building leasing, equipment leasing, and placement assistance such as for a retiring physician (Coplan 1990). Young physicians with more than $25,000 in debt from their medical training are especially likely to enter into group practice arrangements (Cohen et al. 1990).

What will separate the "winners" and "losers" in the new health care environment? It won't be the specific legal structure for integration. It will be what's done with that structure once it's formed. What is done with the foundation, MSO, IPA, or PHO will have much to do with the beliefs of the leaders about what it will take to survive in the future. Under any possible scenario, the prerequisite for winning will be the ability to manage risk, which means managing the delivery of patient care to produce superior clinical outcomes under fixed-dollar capitation payments (Cochrane 1993).

In today's competitive managed care environment, physicians may see several advantages to affiliating with a hospital or health system through a foundation or MSO model. Capital is a major factor where providing capital to a medical group may be the hospital, HMO, or entrepreneur who will then offer financial and strategic support.

Affiliation with a foundation or MSO allows the doctors to practice medicine instead of handling the business, capital, and administrative hassles of managing a group practice (Grant 1991a). The hospital/health

Figure 9.2 Integrated Program of Hospital-Physician Affiliation

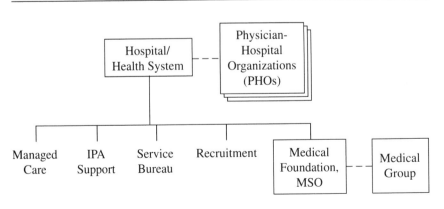

Reprinted with the permission of Ross Stromberg from his presentation, "Hospital-Affiliated Group Practice," 18 September 1991.

system offers a stronger organizational base of management expertise and administrative support services that the group practice could not otherwise develop on its own, such as management information systems. Affiliation also strengthens the group in terms of recruitment, growth, managed care, and other strategic objectives. With foundation affiliation or an MSO, the group practice may be better able to achieve goals such as professional collegiality, enhancing quality of care, lifestyle, and achieving economic stability and security.

The Medical Foundation Model

The tax-exempt nonprofit medical foundation corporation can be organized either as freestanding, an affiliate of the hospital through a common parent organization, or a subsidiary of the hospital. Whether freestanding, affiliated, or wholly owned, all medical foundation models operate the group practice, own the practice sites/facilities/equipment, employ all nonphysician personnel, contract with patients and payers in managed care arrangements, and bill under its provider number. The foundation contracts with a professional corporation that is wholly owned by physicians. The medical group practice may be primary or multispecialty. In California, a medical foundation must have 40 or more physicians in 10 or more specialties, of which two-thirds must be full-time. The physician corporation employs the doctors and provides medical services to the foundation pursuant to a professional services agreement (contract). In most such arrangements, the medical foundation holds a significant amount of the capital assets (for example, land, facilities, equipment, financial reserves), and the professional corporation has relatively few capital assets.

The medical foundation model potentially represents a closer integration of hospital and physician services with a resulting stronger interdependence between participating providers. Options within the medical foundation model (Stromberg 1992) are:

- Freestanding medical foundation, which is not hospital or health system–owned, although it may have close clinical and contractual links with a hospital or system. Freestanding medical foundations are tax-exempt 501(c)(3) organizations that often have a strong research and education purpose. There is limited board overlap with their physician corporation.

- Hospital-affiliated tax-exempt clinic, in which the medical foundation is an affiliate of the hospital or health system. Affiliation may be for managed care contracting or other shared purposes such as to provide a primary care base, operate an ambulatory care center (see Figure 9.3).

- Hospital-owned medical foundation, in which the hospital or health system may directly own the medical foundation (subsidiary), a model that provides for greater control of the medical group practice through the professional services arrangement.

MSOs

The management services organization model provides many of the business and business support services to medical groups but may be perceived as less of a threat to physician independence. The MSO model also presents less of a corporate practice of medicine in that it does not provides services to patients, only to the physicians in the contracting group. Options for MSOs are:

- Freestanding MSO, which is an independent, taxable business corporation whose ownership may be lay (entrepreneur/investor) and/or physician. The MSO furnishes all sites, facilities, equipment and supplies, personnel, and administrative services to a physician corporation. Terms of services and responsibilities are defined in a turn-key management services agreement. The MSO bills in the name and on behalf of the corporation and may also manage other groups and entities. The professional corporation may have a single owner (for example, physician owner of the MSO) or multiple owners (for example, physician participants). The group may be primary care or multispecialty, employing individual physicians to provide services to patients and payers. The corporation owns and operates all clinical aspects of group practice, as well as the charts and patients.

Figure 9.3   Medical Foundation: The Hospital-Affiliated Tax-Exempt Clinic Model

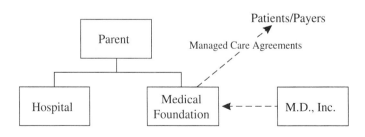

Reprinted with the permission of Ross Stromberg from his presentation, "Hospital-Affiliated Group Practice," 18 September 1991.
    M.D., Inc. = physician corporation.

• Hospital-affiliated MSO, which may be separately incorporated or operated as a division of the hospital or health system (see Figure 9.4). The hospital-affiliated MSO may qualify for 501(c)(3) tax-exempt status, unlike the freestanding MSO, which is a taxable business corporation. The hospital-affiliated MSO provides all sites, facilities, equipment and supplies, personnel, and support services required by the physicians in the professional corporation. The MSO bills on behalf and in the name of the corporation and may manage other groups and entities. The corporation is a professional corporation, wholly owned by physicians, either primary or multispecialty. Unlike the medical foundation model, there is no minimum size requirement under California law. The practice provides services to patients and payers and may be affiliated with an IPA. The corporation owns and operates clinical aspects of the group practice, owns the charts and patients, and employs individual physicians.

Which Model Is Best?

The differences between the medical foundation model and an MSO are both perceptual and real. Both models offer a mechanism to integrate hospitals with physician group practices such as for joint managed care contracting. The key difference is ownership and control. In the medical foundation model, the foundation owns the physician practice and the patients (charts). With the MSO, doctors still own their practice and patients but contract exclusively for support services and facilities. From a day-to-day operational standpoint, no substantial differences exist between the medical foundation model and the MSO, in terms of practice decisions and the

Figure 9.4 MSO–Hospital-Affiliated Model

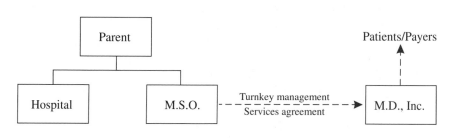

Reprinted with the permission of Ross Stromberg from his presentation, "Hospital-Affiliated Group Practice," 18 September 1991.
M.D., Inc. = physician corporation.

allocation of responsibility and control. However, perceptions are likely to vary widely.

Capital is a major factor in creating either a medical foundation or an MSO. Both the medical foundation and the MSO hold the assets and reserves, not the physician corporation. The medical foundation provides a mechanism by which a hospital can purchase a physician group, with the purchase price thereby providing a return to the physician owners. That capital (purchase price) can also "cash out" retiring physicians or provide an incentive pool to remaining physicians. The MSO model provides a structure for investors (lay, physician, or hospital) to capitalize future growth and development of the physician organization.

Medical foundations may quality for tax-exempt financing, subject to meeting restrictions regarding terms of any agreements with the doctors, as well as limitations on physician participation in governance. It is relatively more difficult to secure tax-exempt status for the MSO, even if it is affiliated with a tax-exempt hospital or health system.

Inurement (financial conflict of interest) is another issue—not for the medical foundation, which is a tax-exempt affiliate of the hospital and directly involved in the provision of health care services, but for the MSO alternative that potentially presents a greater private inurement risk to the hospital. Issues of concern are the level of consideration received by the hospital for services provided (at fair market value), the magnitude of any income guarantees, and aggregate subsidies to the group practice by the hospital. Even with these concerns, there is considerable latitude for a tax-exempt hospital to support group practices through MSO arrangements.

IPAs and Faculty Practice Plans

Operationally and legally, integration is the key difference between the IPA, which is a network of doctors, and the professional medical corporation affiliated with either a medical foundation or the MSO model. The IPA is a partially integrated practice designed as a vehicle for managed care contracting by physicians (Grant 1991b). But the corporation, under either the medical foundation or MSO group practice, is a fully integrated professional corporation. To add complexity to this distinction, however, the MSO could also manage the IPA, and the corporation could participate in managed care contracting as a component of the IPA. The IPA could also have a sponsorship function or otherwise affiliate with a hospital/health system's group practice program. For example, the IPA may have the right to designate seats on the medical foundation/MSO and corporation governing boards. The IPA and the corporation may develop protocols on appropriate utilization of specialists affiliated with the IPA, not only for managed care but also for other patients seen within the group practice program.

Faculty practice plans in academic medical centers are often only a billing vehicle for clinical fees generated by doctors who remain employed faculty of a medical school or teaching hospital. These academic-based physicians are often not employees of a separately incorporated professional corporation. If they were, the medical school or teaching hospital could serve as the medical foundation or MSO and furnish all sites, personnel, and other administrative services required by the legally independent faculty practice group. Sound complicated? It is, but every American hospital will need at least one physician-hospital organization in a managed care/health reform marketplace.

Strategies

1. **Design a portfolio of options for physician affiliation.** Every hospital and health system needs an array of alternatives for physician affiliation, from managed care contracting network (IPA model) to full integration in a staff-model arrangement with salaried physicians. Development of these options needs full board support. Physician-affiliation efforts by the hospital or health system will otherwise be perceived as management-driven by physicians who fear loss of control.

2. **Hire a full-time medical director.** Every hospital and health system needs at least one and, ideally several, physicians on the senior management team. Most important of these positions is the vice president for medical services, to provide high-level management of the medical care provided within the hospital or system. This is a management position, not a liaison role between a hospital and its doctors. The medical director will be analyzing patterns of care with computerized profiles of medical practice, by clinical department and physician. It will be critical to manage the costs and quality/outcomes of medical care, which can only be done by a physician executive.

3. **Encourage physicians to govern.** Hospitals and health systems need to substantially expand physician participation in governance, up to 50 percent of the board. Broad physician involvement is equally important in establishing new physician-hospital organizations. One MSO model appointed a 12-member board with 11 physicians and one administrator. The strong presence of doctors on the board was a signal that this PHO would be physician-driven if the affiliation were to be successful.

4. **Appoint lay trustees on PHO boards.** In establishing new governance structures for these PHOs it is essential to appoint lay trustees to the PHO boards. These outside directors prevent conflict of interest and provide a strong consumer perspective to balance physician viewpoints. For PHOs

to succeed, it will be critical to ensure that they operate to promote community benefit, not physician economic interests. In decisions regarding contracting, pricing, and physician reimbursement, the presence of lay trustees on PHO boards will provide an important public-interest balance to physician professional and economic objectives.

References

Beckham, D. 1991. "Remaking the Medical Staff." *Healthcare Executive* 6 (September–October): 27–29.

Burda, D. 1993. "Looking at Bans in a Different Light." *Modern Healthcare* 23 (31 May): 25–29.

Cochrane, J. D. 1993. "Organizing to Manage Risk." *Integrated Healthcare Report* (May): 1–7.

Cohen, A. B. 1990. "Young Physicians and the Future of the Medical Profession." *Health Affairs* (Winter): 138–48.

Coile, R. C., Jr. 1991. "The 'Medical Piece' of Hospital Strategy." *Healthcare Forum Journal* (September–October): 39–41.

———. 1993. "Physician-Hospital Organizations." *Hospital Strategy Report* 5 (July): 1–5.

———. 1992. "Physician-Hospital Partnering." *Hospital Strategy Report* 4 (July): 5.

Coplan, L. P. 1990. "Developing Contracts and Acquisitions with Physicians." *Topics in Health Care Financing* 16 (Spring): 68–76.

Droste, T. 1993. "Physician-Hospital Organizations." *Medical Staff Strategy Report* 2 (April): 1–3.

Goldman, E., and P. Taulbee. 1992. "Physician/Hospital Organizational Arrangements: Results of a National Survey." *Health Care Competition Week.* (March): 1–16.

Grant, P. N. 1991a. "Alternatives in Restructuring Hospital-Physician Relationships: Management Organization and Tax-Exempt Foundation Models." *Northern California Medicine* 2 (January): 1, 12.

———. 1991b. "Dramatic Developments in IPA, Medical Group Practice, and HMO-Hospital-Medical Group Relations in California." *California Physician* (September): 32–38.

Hudson, T. 1993. "The Race to Integrate: Who Will Be the Leaders?" *Hospitals and Health Networks* 67 (5 June): 25–27.

Johnsson, J. 1992. "Dynamic Diversification: Hospitals Pursue Physician Alliances, 'Seamless' Care." *Hospitals* 66 (5 February): 20–26.

Kenkel, P. J. 1992. "Not-for-Profits Get until Sept. 1 to Shed Questionable Features." *Modern Healthcare* 22 (27 April): 2.

Lumsden, K. 1992. "Sharp HealthCare Integrates Services to Link Patients to Appropriate Level of Care." *Hospitals* 66, no. 7 (5 April): 29–31.

Stromberg, R. 1992. "Group Practice: The Use of Medical Foundations and Management Service Organizations." *Hospital Strategy Report* 4 (July): 1–5.

10

Total Quality Management: A Revolution in Clinical Care and Service Management

The rationale for continuous quality improvement is competitive differentiation through service, cost and value, and image. If health organizations are to be successful in tomorrow's marketplace, they must change their culture fundamentally to focus on quality.

—G. Rodney Wolford (1991)

The quality revolution has arrived in health care; nothing will be the same. Quality will be the driving force in health care, and managers will be paid based on quality indicators of their departments. Physicians will be profiled, rewarded, and privileged (or sanctioned) based on their clinical practice and their patient outcomes. The same scrutiny on quality will be given nurses and nursing units. Insurance companies, managed care plans, major employers, and government will select preferred providers based on quality track records. Consumers will shop for hospitals and physicians based on data on quality made public.

Since *Darling v. Charleston Community Memorial Hospital* (1965), hospital boards have had the legal liability for the quality of their hospital's care. Promoting quality has always had a high priority with hospital trustees. Now there will be a managed process to ensure it and nationally recognized criteria by which boards can measure their success. This process exceeds the medical staff's peer review process. Total quality management (TQM) is both corporate philosophy and management approach that integrates medical staff activities with nursing and the broader hospital organization. A broader definition of quality includes both clinical care and patient satisfaction. TQM gives the board information on quality so that management and caregivers can define standards and continuously measure improvement.

Whether it is called TQM or continuous quality improvement (CQI), emphasizing and managing quality will change the corporate culture of health systems and hospital services. The challenge is global for health care executives: manage the quality of every dimension of performance, prepare to be measured with public data on quality, and never be satisfied with the status quo. Trustee involvement in the TQM program is essential to communicate the board's priority and to inject community values into the TQM process and hospital-defined standards.

Can TQM Work in Health Care?

Although quality management was invented for manufacturing work in the service industry, there is proof today that TQM/CQI is an effective approach that can be successfully applied in a service field like health care. Providing inspiration to America's hospitals is the National Demonstration Project on Quality Improvement in Health Care, which examined 21 projects in hospitals and health organizations across America under a national experiment in technology transfer. Donald Berwick, M.D., was principal investigator for the National Demonstration, which applied the approach and methods of TQM/CQI with technical assistance from the Juran Institute (Berwick, Godfrey, and Roessner 1991). Hospitals learned the language of quality management while students of TQM/CQI learned phrases such as the diagnostic journey. The key lessons for quality improvement in health care were short and simple: (1) quality improvement can work in health care; (2) cross-functional teams are valuable in improving health care processes; (3) data useful for quality improvement abound in health care; (4) quality improvement methods are fun to use; and (5) costs resulting from poor quality are high and savings are within reach.

Leaders in Quality Management

A national survey identified 16 hospitals and health systems as the innovators and demonstrated practice leaders in health care quality improvement in 1991 (see Table 10.1) (Kratochwil and Gaucher 1991). The survey participants were the 21 hospitals, health systems, and managed care plans that participated in the National Demonstration Project on Industrial Quality Control and Health Care Quality, launched in 1987 under a grant from the John A. Hartford Foundation and hosted by the Harvard Community Health Plan. Several of these organizations have won the highly competitive Healthcare Forum/Witt Award for Committment to Quality, an annual competition sponsored by the Healthcare Forum of San Francisco and Witt Associates of Oak Brook, Illinois.

Table 10.1 Leaders in Health Care Quality Management

Hospitals/Health Systems	Location
Alliant Health Systems	Louisville, Kentucky
Atlantic City Medical Center	Atlantic City, New Jersey
Bethesda Hospital	Ohio
Group Health Cooperative of Puget Sound	Seattle, Washington
Harvard Community Health Plan	Brookline, Massachusetts
Henry Ford Health System	Detroit, Michigan
Hospital Corporation of America	Nashville, Tennessee
InterMountain Health Care	Salt Lake City, Utah
Kaiser Permanente	Oakland, California
Meriter Hospital	Wisconsin
Rush Presbyterian/St. Luke's Medical Center	Chicago, Illinois
San Diego Naval Hospital	San Diego, California
SSM Rehabilitation	Missouri
University of Michigan Medical Center	Ann Arbor, Michigan
US Health Corporation	King of Prussia, Pennsylvania

Adapted and reprinted with permission from *The Journal for Quality and Participation* (January–February 1991). © Association for Quality and Participation in Cincinnati, Ohio.

Note: As identified in National Demonstration Project on Industrial Quality Control and Health Care Quality.

Hospital boards should develop relationships with leading hospitals and health systems with which they can benchmark their quality management performance. Benchmarking is a process of systematically comparing results with peer organizations, setting goals based on knowing what has been done by others (Hopkins 1992).

Putting Customers First

A business adage says, "Your customers will tell you what business you are in." Quality Function Deployment (QFD) is a technique for translating customer requirements (expectations) into functional and technical specifications. QFD is a process adapted from the manufacturing environment that is just as applicable in the service sector.

At the St. Clair Hospital in Pittsburgh, Pennsylvania, the process is called QUEST (Quality Enhancement Strategy). A 12-member team used the QFD approach in the emergency room (ER) to determine customer expectations. They learned what customers wanted (Coile 1991) *recognition*—before treatment began, customers wanted recognition as the first component of service, including reassurance, being called by name, comfort measures, privacy, courtesy, and friendly treatment; *organization*—now it was time for the organization's response to customer demands for "zero waiting," a smooth flow of patients, and an easy-to-understand physical layout; *choice/interaction*—in their treatment, patients wanted answers to their questions, for the physician/staff to explain what patients should expect, to have a clear followup, to speak with a physician, and to have a compassionate attitude; *diagnosis and treatment*—customer expectations were simple: accurate diagnosis and treatment; *a well-qualified staff*—patients expected ER staffers who were knowledgeable, skilled, efficient, courteous, certified, dependable, hard-working, and who exuded a positive behavior.

The QFD method analyzes the relationships between customer requirements and existing systems/behavior. The relative weights of all customer requirements are calculated, which exhibits the proportional significance of various customer expectations. It may seem complicated, but the results helped St. Clair focus on which aspects of service delivery in the ER made the most difference in satisfying customers and provided the hospital with a set of benchmark data against which to compare its performance with other hospitals.

Case Study: HCA's West Paces Ferry

Satisfying the customer is the demonstration that industrial quality control can be adapted to health services. Customer satisfaction is the beginning and end-point of the CQI process in the Hospital Corporation of America (HCA), the nation's largest proprietary hospital chain. HCA's West Paces Ferry Hospital has created a quality improvement model that identifies and addresses consumer wants and satisfaction levels before problems occur. Rather than relying on complaints to initiate change, the 354-bed health organization in Atlanta, Georgia, uses sophisticated statistical methods to examine its processes and identify reasons for variation. Then it employs group process techniques to make changes. The focus is on redesigning the process to fit the customer, rather than adding new processes (Caldwell, McEachern, and Davis 1990).

West Paces Ferry executives were determined to focus CQI efforts on those dimensions of service and performance most important to customers. To clearly understand customer values, the health organization regularly conducts a series of customer judgment surveys, using HCA's Hospital Quality Trend reports. A quarterly analysis is performed on surveys from four categories of "customers"—patients, physicians, nurses, and other employees. Over time, the survey data clearly identifies customer service priorities. Physicians, for example, place high value on maximizing available time. Process improvements at this HCA facility to respond to physician priorities have focused on nursing and scheduling.

To foster broad staff participation in CQI at West Paces Ferry, storyboards displaying indicators of quality are posted in the cafeteria and physician lounge. Every clinical and support department at West Paces Ferry rates its ability to meet each key indicator and articulates its role in improving quality throughout the organization. Quality improvement teams of eight to ten individuals take on the identified process improvement opportunities. Continuous monitoring lets HCA executives know whether CQI actions have made a difference in performance at West Paces Ferry.

Trustees should think of the board as a customer focus group for a continuous assessment of service quality. The board should ask for periodic (monthly/quarterly) ratings and comments from consumers on service quality and from the medical and nursing staffs on clinical quality.

The Joint Commission on Accreditation of Healthcare Organizations (JCAHO) has thrown its full support to the quality management effort. Effective January 1994, the Joint Commission completely revised its standards and accreditation manual to incorporate CQI. The Commission considers CQI "the central conceptual framework for more meaningful quality of care evaluation" (O'Leary 1992).

Incorporating CQI into hospital accreditation is one of the major principles of the JCAHO's Agenda for Change, a reform plan to shift the Commission's historic emphasis from quality assurance (structure of care) to quality management (process and outcomes of care). CQI should remedy the negative mindset of quality assurance (QA)—identifying mistakes—to a positive orientation of continuous improvement. CQI broadens quality assurance to look beyond clinical affairs to address customer issues of expectations and satisfaction (Couch 1990).

The Joint Commission will insist on evidence of the board's involvement in quality management. Board leadership is essential to drive an institution or systemwide commitment to quality to ensure that staff are fully dedicated to continuous improvement. The board's priority for quality improvement should be visible across its strategic and policy/operational decisions.

The Pulse of Quality

Newcomers to TQM/CQI often adopt the "busy bee" strategy for quality improvement—flitting from problem to problem. Readers of W. Edwards Deming, the guru of quality management in Japan and America, know that CQI is based on an organizationwide monitoring of all dimensions of quality. Evangelical Health System, a multihospital system in the Chicago area, has utilized a 10-step model for CQI monitoring (Brewster 1991) by assigning responsibility for performance monitoring, delineating the scope of care/service, determining the key aspects of care/service, developing indicators, establishing performance baselines and goals, collecting and comparing actual to expected performance, identifying and analyzing significant performance variation, planning and implementing improvement action, determining the impact of the improvement action, and documenting and communicating results.

Evangelical has used the CQI monitoring process to address issues such as timeliness of medication delivery to nursing units (standard is two hours), reduction of radiology film waste, reduced turnaround time for diagnostic imaging reports, reduction in patient falls with injury, and lower medication errors.

Staff should develop a short set of quality indicators that the board reviews at every meeting, just like financial indicators. Over time, the spotlight of board attention to quality performance indicators should drive improvements in qualitative aspects of the hospital's or system's services.

New Tools for Quality Management

Hospitals are not starting from scratch in TQM/CQI. The private sector has a ten-year head-start from which health care can learn much, particularly from companies like Federal Express, Cadillac, and Ford ("Quality is #1"), and other Malcolm Baldrige National Quality Award winners.

Strategic quality management did not appear overnight. The quality programs being adopted with much fanfare today are remarkably similar in their methods to those that emerged 20 years ago that focused on "zero defects," the cost of quality, interfunctional coordination, and statistical quality control (Couch 1991). Frederick W. Taylor's scientific management programs of the 1920s were quickly adopted in the manufacturing environment. Now health care is learning about the benefits of TQM/CQI. Managing quality has a language of its own with a toolbox of specialized methods for charting symptoms and identifying root causes. Participants in the National Demonstration Project on Industrial Quality Control and Health Care Quality devised the learning curve with regard to management of quality. These sophisticated organizations demonstrated the range of methods hospitals can apply in managing quality (see Figure 10.1) (Kratochwil and Gaucher 1991).

The tools do work. A seven-year problem was solved at one hospital in a few months once staff knew the methods of CQI. A task force had worked in vain for seven years to solve the continuing problem of expediting patient discharges. Despite identifying dozens of bottlenecks, no solutions made much difference. The hospital bought more wheelchairs, hired transportation staff, but nothing worked. Patients continued to occupy beds for hours or even days after they were supposed to be discharged and out the door—until CQI. After undergoing CQI training, the hospital staff conducted a fresh

Figure 10.1 Use of "Total Quality" Tools in National Health Care Quality Projects (1990)

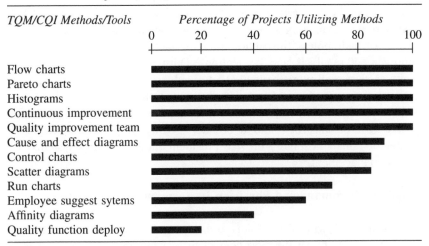

TQM/CQI Methods/Tools	Percentage of Projects Utilizing Methods

Flow charts
Pareto charts
Histograms
Continuous improvement
Quality improvement team
Cause and effect diagrams
Control charts
Scatter diagrams
Run charts
Employee suggest sytems
Affinity diagrams
Quality function deploy

Reprinted with the permission from *The Journal for Quality and Participation* (January–February 1991). © Association for Quality and Participation, Cincinnati, Ohio.

study of the problem—they interviewed patients. The answer was simple—lack of a ride. Consequently, the discharge planning system was modified to include transportation planning, beginning several days before the likely date of discharge (Coile 1991). This experience exhibits the power of managing quality in the 1990s.

Use the board's community connections to gain access to the private sector for advice and experience in quality improvement. The board should invite private sector companies in the community, or from other comparable markets, to discuss their quality management programs. These board exchanges will create staff-level interchanges for peer networking. This is an opportunity for community networking and goodwill. The board is a liaison to the wider community of business and government organizations who are equally concerned about quality (King 1990).

The Future of TQM/CQI: Five Trends for the 1990s

Tomorrow's hospitals and health networks will be selected and paid based on their quality of care. Patient outcomes and customer satisfaction will be continuously monitored by managed care buyers and future HPIC coalitions of employers. Managed care plans are applying strong incentives to follow practice guidelines and demonstrate quality (Sandrick 1993). These are the key trends that will drive the process of quality management in America's hospitals and health organizations.

Trend 1: From Bad Apples to Process of Care

In an issue of the *New England Journal of Medicine*, Donald Berwick (1989) predicted that managing health care quality would have to shift from a "theory of bad apples" (inspection after the fact) to a theory of continuous improvement (analysis and prevention). During the 1990s, hospitals and health systems will move beyond QA to analyze, manage, and continuously improve their processes of care. In the transition, functions such as peer review, risk management, infection control, accreditation and utilization review will be absorbed into a broader TQM/CQI program, headed by a director (small hospitals) or vice president (large hospitals/systems) for quality management.

Trend 2: Micromanaging Physician Performance

Most hospital TQM/CQI programs to date have focused on those areas over which management has the most control such as nursing, admitting, business office, and food service. The greatest challenge facing TQM/CQI in health care is managing the clinical practice of medicine (Kralovec 1990). This must be a process where doctors manage doctors. TQM will succeed in medicine if physicians recognize quality management as a useful tool that will allow them to improve the care they deliver. But if doctors believe that TQM is a mechanism by which hospital management will control their actions, expect physicians to "dig in their heels" and resist the quality movement. Brent James (1991), a physician who heads Intermountain Health Care's Institute for Health Care Delivery Research, has suggested a number of principles hospitals should understand as they involve doctors in TQM/CQI.

- Quality improvement is not new to clinicians.
- Many physicians have a deep distrust of clinical measurement projects initiated by management.
- For clinical products, physicians are already organized into clinical teams.
- Independent physicians need to devote most of their time to their own practices.
- Structure clinical management projects within existing medical staff meetings.
- Do not impose consensus protocols generated by outside organizations on the medical staff.
- Support in-house research efforts by which the medical staff can develop their own data on which to prepare their own practice guidelines.

To guide the management of patient care, physicians will develop critical paths, which are guidelines to move patients through a hospital as effectively and efficiently as possible, by managing length of stay, intensity (and cost) of resources, with continuous attention to quality and outcomes.

Doctors fear there will be national practice standards dictated by government. At first, critical paths will develop on a hospital-by-hospital process. Health systems can leverage this process using multihospital teams and corporate research support. At Alliant Health Systems physicians have focused on frequently performed, high-cost procedures such as mastectomy and lumbar laminectomy. Alliant's Methodist Evangelical Hospital has saved 1.1 patient days and at least $1,254 in cost savings per case (Wolford 1991).

Trend 3: Quality Is Public Information

Data on health care quality will be public. Hospital mortality data already is regularly disclosed by HCFA. The data is crude but widely publicized in the media. More sophisticated data bases on hospital and physician quality will be mandated by insurance companies and government. By 1995, hospitals should expect Medicare to adopt a universal system for measuring quality, such as the MedisGroup System from MediQual (Watham, Massachusetts) or the Iameter system (San Mateo, California). Already two states, Pennsylvania and Iowa, require all hospitals to install quality monitoring systems and report the data to the state. These states are issuing hospital-by-hospital comparative reports on selected diagnoses.

Trend 4: Contracting Based on Quality

Today's marketplace is characterized by a "let's make a deal" mentality. Price is the driver. Despite lip-service to quality, insurance companies and managed care plans are still contracting for hospital and physician services based overwhelmingly on price. That is what happens at a time when buyers have little information on hospital quality or physician outcomes to apply in selecting preferred providers. In the future, major employers will utilize quality criteria to differentiate among competing managed care plans. Peter Boland (1991) of Boland Healthcare has predicted that "managed care plans—HMOs, PPOs and managed indemnity plans—will be rated and selected on quality. They are only as good as their numbers!"

Trend 5: Outcomes Defining Quality Performance

Hospitals will certainly be judged on their outcomes—the tangible results of provider services as measured in terms of the health status of patients. This will not be easy. Defining quality is a slippery slope of professional judgment with few nationally accepted standards. Paul Ellwood, M.D., (1988) issued a challenge to the medical profession and health services research, calling for the development of a ten-year research and development program in outcomes management. The goal was to create national criteria for defining clinical outcomes.

To manage clinical outcomes, hospitals need standardized data systems. Susan Horn, a nationally recognized expert from the Johns Hopkins University, is the originator of severity-indexed systems for measuring patient health status (Horn 1991). Using systems like Apache, which was developed by Horn, each hospital and health system will use outcomes to guide their search for the most efficient and effective processes of care. Providers will document actual patient outcomes against "optimal" standards and use this evolving data base to advance the state-of-the-practice of medicine. Patient outcome information will be used to demonstrate (to the institution, purchasers, and patients) that effective and efficient care has been provided.

What is an outcome? Some examples from the Surgical Intensive Care Unit's 1990–1991 Quality Assurance Plan, developed by the Moses Cone Memorial Hospital (1991) are:

- "Cardiovascular and pulmonary and neurological complications (i.e., respiratory arrest fatal arrhythmias) are minimized."
- "Physiological stabilization as soon as possible. As indicated by: Patient is able to maintain physiological functions without increasing medications and technological support within an optimal time period (2–24 hours)."
- "Dependency upon life support is minimized as soon as possible. As indicated by: Patient weaned from life support measures and medications within optimal time period (24–48 hours)."
- "Physiological and psychological stability is established as soon as possible allowing for transfer to a recuperative unit. As indicated by: Transfer order written within optimal time period (48–60 hours)."

Failure to manage outcomes performance could ultimately cost a hospital its Medicare certification. HCFA began publishing data on patient outcomes in 1986, and despite much controversy, it has continued to publicize mortality data as one indicator of hospital quality. But HCFA has moved beyond disclosure of data. Since 1989, HCFA has taken action against 78 hospitals with profiles that showed an excess overall mortality for two years in a row.

Trustees must prepare for the time when the hospital's quality data will be made public (Hofmann 1990). First, the board should know how good its quality really compares with peer hospitals and with national standards. The board, medical staff, and employees should regularly see reports on clinical outcomes and customer satisfaction. Trustees should review Medicare quality data as reported by the HCFA on hospital performance compared with other hospitals in the community and state. Staff should create indicators from the HCFA/Medicare data and regularly report to the board.

Alliant Health Systems: A Model for TQM

Alliant Health Systems of Louisville, Kentucky, is a model for total quality management. The 1991 National Healthcare Quality Conference was cosponsored by Alliant with the Healthcare Forum. Alliant's philosophy is that CQI is "competitive differentiation through service, cost and value, and image" (Wolford 1991). If hospitals are to be successful in tomorrow's marketplace, they must fundamentally change their culture to focus on quality (Wolford 1991). Alliant's TQM program integrates values, quality principles, and quality policy in a systemwide effort across Alliant's three acute care hospitals and 950-bed system. Alliant's mission is short and clear: "to be the leading provider of value-driven, superior quality health care in Louisville and the surrounding region."

Alliant's commitment began in 1987 after a year spent researching quality management. Three full-time staff visited leading companies in the private sector, including Hewlett-Packard, Xerox, and L.L. Bean. One of the first steps taken was promotion of the vice president for quality to COO. This led to decentralization of decisions, empowering of middle and first-line managers, and a new visioning process at all levels.

The TQM program at Alliant has been a stimulus for change. Alliant has a "creative tension" in never being satisfied with its quality, and its vision statement's emphasis on "superior quality" has driven the strategic planning process at all levels of the organization, as outlined in Figure 10.2 (Wolford 1991).

TQM is a comprehensive framework for managing hospitals and health care systems. Alliant's TQM program includes:

- Mission/vision—The system strives to be the "leading provider of superior quality care."
- Education/training—Alliant has taken three years to learn the language and the methods of TQM. Every employee has been trained.
- TQM teams—Every department has a TQM team that meets monthly; more than 100 TQM self-directed work teams conduct quality improvement projects across the system.
- CEO commitment—The CEO and senior managers plan to spend 20–30 percent of their time on managing quality in the first year.

Figure 10.2   Alliant Health System's Vision-Driven Planning Process

Adapted and reprinted with the permission of G. Rodney Wolford from his presentation, "Alliant Total Quality Management (TQM) Overview and Strategy" at National Healthcare Quality conference, 30 September 1991.

Alliant has established a Quality Council chaired by the CEO that reviews quality performance.

- "Walk the talk"—TQM cannot be delegated by the CEO or top management who must be role models and continuously demonstrate interest in managing by walking around.
- Customer focus—The focus must always be satisfying the customer —patients, visitors and family, payers, and other departments and caregivers.
- Physician involvement—To complement the CEO's Quality Council, a Physician Quality Council regularly analyzes clinical and service quality.
- Critical pathways—The medical staff develops critical pathways for efficient quality care, with a focus on the most frequently performed procedures and managed diagnoses.

Pennsylvania's Health Care Cost-Containment Council

The "Pennsylvania experiment," the Pennsylvania Health Care Cost-Containment Council (HCCCC), may determine whether detailed data on hospital quality will be made widely available to government, purchasers, and the public (Shanahan 1991). The Council is a national model—a similar health quality/cost disclosure system has been adopted by Iowa, and other state legislatures are considering imitating the Pennsylvania program.

Created in 1986, the Council was intended to help reduce health costs through collection and public dissemination of data on hospital costs and quality. After more than three years of organizing and collecting data, the first public report was issued in 1991 using 1989 data (Pennsylvania Health Care Cost-Containment Council 1991). A series of annual reports is planned that will profile health costs by major DRGs in nine service regions across Pennsylvania. In a controversial move, the Council began to publish provider (physician)-specific data in 1992.

Designed to create "informed purchasers" in the health care marketplace, the Council serves all hospitals in Pennsylvania over 100 beds that are required to collect clinical information about patient hospitalization. In creating a uniform statewide data base, hospitals utilized MedisGroups, an automated severity-of-illness indexing system. Data is collected by quarter, grouped by nine geographic regions and analyzed by selected DRGs. Pennsylvania data is compared with a broader sample of 106 hospitals in MediQual's data base (which includes 43 Pennsylvania facilities).

Hospital Effectiveness reports with a full year's 1989 data were published for all nine regions. The three most important indicators in the HCCCC tables are deaths (mortality), the medically unstable during first week (major morbidity), and average charge. Actual payer data shows costs of care per discharge so purchasers can begin to differentiate among hospitals in the same market area.

Expect payers and large employers like Hershey Foods and John Deere to use HCCCC data to select preferred providers for HMO/PPO networks and for exclusive provider arrangements (EPAs) for specialized services such as cardiac bypass surgery. The Council's comparative data provides a base for insurance companies, managed care plans, and major employers to identify which hospitals and physicians have the best cost and quality track records.

Looking Forward: The Value Equation

The health care marketplace is beginning to witness the signals of a paradigm shift in the relationship between buyers and sellers (Sanger 1991). Quality will become the primary criterion for health care purchasers because patient days and procedures are commodities in health care's mass-market transactions between providers and very large buyers (insurers, HMOs, government); virtually every provider in today's health marketplace will discount charges or fees; buyers can contract with the most prestigious medical centers and top-reputation physicians at commodity prices; managed care is rapidly replacing indemnity insurance—only 10 percent of the market will be held by indemnity products by the year 2000; and if buyers can contract with any provider at preferred prices, purchasers will shift to quality as their second criterion for provider selection.

Provident Life and Accident Insurance Co. has contracted with ten hospitals that have been selected for exclusive contracting for transplants under its quality centers program (Sardinha 1992) some employers are contracting directly with hospitals for specialized services, and Blue Cross–Blue Shield of Michigan recently became the first insurer to adopt a quality-based payment strategy that contractually ties hospital reimbursement to quality standards. With a 35 percent marketshare, Blue Cross–Blue Shield "carries a big stick" in Michigan. The Blues plan to track every aspect of hospital care from admission to discharge, continuing the quality surveillance post-discharge to review aftercare outcomes.

Health care buyers want value for their substantial health benefit expense (Garvin 1988). The nineties equation for success in the health care field will be value equaling quality divided by costs. Research confirms this equation. A study that appeared in the *Journal for Quality and Participation* found strong relationships between hospital quality and profitability (Sepielli and Klausner 1991). Using PIMS (Profit Impact of Market Strategies), a much-cited quality data base, researchers found that hospitals providing the highest quality care for cancer surgery had a $276 contribution margin per Medicare discharge, while the lowest quality group lost $1,100 per patient.

Good medicine *is* efficient as well as effective. Hospitals and their medical staff must know their quality as well as their costs, and they must seek to maximize the value equation for their buyers, and the community.

Strategies

1. **Be leaders of quality management.** Think of the board as TQM Task Force. Put the board in charge of TQM, not as a passive observer. Inject board values into TQM standards. The board represents the community—and patients—in protecting quality. Trustees should receive training on the methods of TQM and use TQM approaches in problem analysis and decision making. Hospital boards have the legal liability for their institution's quality, and now they will have the tools by which to manage that responsibility.
2. **Evaluate the CEO on quality.** When the board evaluates CEO performance, quality should be the priority criteria. From the board's perspective, managing quality should be one of the CEO's most significant tasks. Allow the CEOs to spend 20–30 percent of their time on TQM/CQI in the first year—much will be reading and research. Then the CEO should be ready to set TQM goals and the board can measure progress.
3. **Track quality like finance.** Management and the medical staff should deliver regular reports on quality performance, just like financial reports.

The board should adopt a set of key indicators of quality and assess these with as much attention as they give the financials.

4. **Make a long-term commitment to TQM.** There will be no easy victories; TQM is a long-term investment. The first three years are basically a learning process for management and the medical staff. Over time, the process of TQM will become ingrained into problem-solving, while the commitment to quality will become an ingrained value in the organizational culture.

References

Berwick, D. M. 1989. "Continuous Improvement as an Ideal in Health Care." *New England Journal of Medicine* 320: 53–56.

Berwick, D. M., A. B. Godfrey, and J. Roessner. 1991. *Curing Healthcare: New Strategies for Quality Improvement.* San Francisco, CA: Jossey-Bass.

Boland, P. 1991. *Making Managed Care Work.* Rockville, MD: Aspen Publishers.

Brewster, C. 1991. "Performing Monitoring and Measurement in a Quality Improvement Environment." Presentation at the National Healthcare Quality Conference, Louisville, KY.

Caldwell, C., J. E. McEachern, and V. Davis. 1990. "Measurement Tools Eliminate Guesswork." *Healthcare Forum Journal* 33 (July–August): 23–26.

Coile, R. C., Jr. 1991. "The Quality Revolution in Health Care." *Hospital Strategy Report* 4 (December): 1–7.

Couch, J. B. 1990. "Getting Aggressive about Quality." *HMQ* 12, no. 4: 23–25.

———, ed. 1991. *Health Care Quality Management for the 21st Century.* Tampa, FL: American College of Physician Executives.

Ellwood, P. 1988. "Shattuck Lecture: Outcomes Management: A Technology of Patient Experience." *New England Journal of Medicine* 318: 1549–56.

Garvin, D. A. 1988. *Managing Quality: The Strategic and Competitive Edge.* New York: Free Press.

Hofmann, P. 1990. "Coming Forward." *Healthcare Management Quarterly* 12, no. 4: 2–5.

Hopkins, J. 1992. "Benchmarking: Beating the Best." *QRC Advisor* 8 (July): 1–3.

Horn, S. D. 1991. "CSI and CQI: A Natural Link." Presentation to the National Healthcare Quality Conference. Louisville, KY.

James, B. C. 1991. "How Do You Involve Physicians in TQM?" *Journal for Quality and Participation* (January–February): 42–47.

King, B. 1990. "Healthcare as a Quality Trendsetter." 33 *Healthcare Forum Journal* (July–August): 17–18.

Kralovec, O. J. 1990. "Clinical Quality Improvement." *Healthcare Forum Journal* 33 (July–August): 33–34.

Kratochwill, E. W., and E. J. Gaucher. 1991. "National Demonstration Project on Industrial Control and Health Care Quality." *The Journal for Quality and Participation* (January–February): 32–34.

Moses Cone Memorial Hospital. 1991. Surgical Intensive Care Unit. 1990–1991. *Quality Assurance Plan.*

O'Leary, D. 1992. "Continuous Quality Improvement and the JCAHO Agenda for Change." Presentation at the Estes Park Conference for Trustee, Medical Staff, Administration. Amelia Island, FL.

Pennsylvania Health Care Cost-Containment Council. 1991. *Comparative Hospital Costs and Quality in the State of Pennsylvania.* Harrisburg: The Council.

Sandrick, K. 1993. "Managed Care Helps Push Quality Guidelines Forward." *Hospitals* 67 (5 May): 30–31.

Sanger, M. 1991. "Assuring Quality Healthcare... A Gigantic Feat." *Journal for Quality and Participation* (January–February): 48–52.

Sardinha, C. 1992. "Provident Signs 10 Facilities as Transplant Centers of Excellence." *Managed Care Outlook* 5 (6 November): 9.

Sepielli, R., and A. Klausner. 1991. "New Quality Challenges for Healthcare." *Journal for Quality and Participation* (January–February): 54–58.

Shanahan, M. 1991. "Pennsylvania's HCCCC: Cost/Quality Watchdog or Paper Tiger" *QRC Advisor*. Rockville, MD: Aspen Publishers.

Wolford, G. R. 1991. "Alliant Total Quality Management (TQM) Overview and Strategy." Presentation at National Healthcare Quality conference, Louisville, KY.

11

Hospitals of the Future: Becoming a Patient-Centered Healing Environment

Imagine a place which creates a sense of restfulness, revitalization and connectedness! A place where you find restoration and balance. A healing microcosm is a space which reflects and connects us with these environments. It is a space which is naturally therapeutic.

—Leanne Kaiser Carlson (1992)

The hospital of the future is a high-tech tower, an urgent care center, a medical office building, a nursing home, a health education center, even an ambulatory surgery center with overnight beds. It is a campus of vertically integrated services, linked by computers into a seamless web of care. To adapt to health care reform, patient demands, payment limits, and new technology, the hospital of tomorrow will be all these things and more. In the hospital of the future

- Fewer acute beds will be needed—perhaps 25–35 percent fewer inpatient beds, as managed care channels patients to lower-cost settings.
- Ambulatory care will be the entry point into the system.
- Medical offices will house 35–50 percent of the medical staff.
- Long-term care facilities will be immediately adjacent or will reuse former inpatient units for skilled and intermediate nursing care.
- Home care will be coordinated by hospital-based case managers using high-tech in-home monitors.
- Emergency rooms will focus on the truly emergent patient, while routine urgent care will be provided in walk-in clinics and on-campus physician offices.
- The ambience will be that of a small, fine hotel.

- The campus setting will feature skyway bridges, thousands of parking spaces, and a primary access point with valet parking.

It may seem too good to be true, but it's possible. The hospital of the future will be patient-centered, organized for the care and comfort of patients. Routine services will be conveniently located to patients; a mini x-ray department will be on the orthopedics unit or a mini-lab will be near oncology patients. Tomorrow's hospitals may have a dozen different entrances—and their own parking lots—for patients of specialized programs.

But tomorrow's hospitals will have to be designed for efficiency as well as comfort. Layouts will be restructured for cost-effective deployment of scarce staff. Computers will be everywhere, from bedside to the housekeeping department (Lumsden 1993). Patient care will be managed intensely, with shorter hospital stays and more ambulatory visits. Longer-stay patients will be transferred to on-campus nursing homes or monitored in home settings as an extension of hospital care. A new world of hospital design is coming, and the board of trustees is its "master design team." The board provides patient care philosophy, sets strategic direction, creates guidelines for design of facilities and amenities, authorizes the capital, and is the top consumer research panel on all design issues.

The Three Pavilions

Hospitals of tomorrow will look deceptively like hospitals of today—the familiar profile of patient care towers superimposed on a sprawling one-story base is likely to be as prevalent in the year 2000 as today. But the hospital of the next century will differ from its 1990 counterpart, much as the room-size computer of the 1960s compares with today's lap-top supercomputers.

Contrary to some opinion, hospitals will exist in the twenty-first century, but they will be organized and managed on a three-pavilion concept. Tomorrow's hospital will be constructed of three semidetached units with an allocation of space for acute (40 percent), long-term (30 percent), and ambulatory (30 percent) care. Each pavilion will be built for its specialized role and functions. Nonacute facilities will not need to meet hospital code requirements, or pay inpatient-level construction costs or operating expenses. The three-pavilion concept recognizes the future roles of high-tech, high-acuity inpatient care, separately organized and delivered from ambulatory care for routine family health needs and long-term care for providing chronic care to the elderly.

The core hospital acute inpatient facilities will become increasingly specialized in the year 2000, a 300-bed intensive care unit. Futurists like Jeff Goldsmith (1992) predict that although the number of acute inpatients will be smaller by at least 15–25 percent, they will be older and more seriously ill.

To continuously assess their fragile health conditions, telemonitors will be widely used. Patients requiring less complex care will not stay in the acute hospital unit. Current trends in rising acuity and severity of hospitalized inpatients have already led some hospitals to adopt this mode of service.

What will be new for hospitals is that related facilities—pavilions for ambulatory and interim care—will be attached by skyways to the acute care pavilion. These semidetached structures will house the expanded functions of the modern hospital. Nonacute pavilions will be built for efficiency in the delivery of their specialized functions and lower-cost in construction and operation because they do not have to meet hospital standards.

Four Levels of Care

Within the integrated health systems of the future are four distinct levels of facilities and service (see Table 11.1). Hospitals will be at the hub of the three more advanced levels, 2–4, while the ambulatory-oriented "integrated medical campus" comprises the level 1 of care, complemented by a 20 to 30–bed postsurgical recovery center (PSRC) for brief stays of one to three days.

Hospitals of the twenty-first century will be mini-systems of multiple levels of health services that will require substantial land (Mayer 1992). A multiacre campus concept will integrate the location of acute, long-term, and ambulatory care facilities on sites of 60–100 acres. More than 75 percent of future hospital facilities will be located on the same campus, with another 25 percent of hospital-sponsored services in satellite locations for ambulatory care, imaging and ambulatory surgery centers, and long-term care campuses.

Hospitals should purchase land 10–20 years in advance, where possible, to obtain the benefits of location, site, and price. Hospitals should identify their long-range land use needs for a time frame of 20–30 years and begin to purchase land and seek land donations well in advance of potential construction. Early planning and purchase will give hospitals a strategic position for the future by preempting competitors and establishing early relationships with local governments to coordinate land-use planing.

Hospitals are advised to buy as much land as possible. Surplus land can always be sold for future profit, and the hospital can influence the use of the excess property. New hospitals and those considering relocation and replacement should look for sites with at least 30–50 acres. Regional medical centers may need 60–100 acres or more. These megasites not only provide room for expansion but buffer the institution from future neighborhood concerns of noise, traffic, and congestion as development fills in around the hospital campus.

Not many health campuses of today have 50 acres. In these crowded facilities, staff constantly wage "space wars" to expand their square footage.

Table 11.1 Levels of Care in Tomorrow's Hospitals, Year 2000

Level	Hospital Configuration	Ambulatory Care	Interim Care	On-Campus Physicians
1	Comprehensive ambulatory center • No acute beds	25,000–100,000 square feet	20–30 Postsurgical recovery center	15–40 MDs, part-time chief
2	Community hospital • Nonteaching • 1–2 centers of excellence • 80–120 beds • 10–15 ICU beds	50,000–120,000 square feet	40–75 Skilled nursing facilities	40–100 MDs, full-time chief
3	Regional medical center • Residencies • 3–5 centers of excellence • 150–300 beds • 30–40 ICU beds	75,000–150,000 square feet	50–100 Skilled nursing facilities, TCU, Rehabilitation, Behavioral Medicine	75–150 MDs, full-time chief, part-time departments
4	Superregional health sciences center • Teaching • > 6 centers of excellence • 250–400 beds • 40–60 ICU beds	100,000–250,000 square feet	75–125 Skilled nursing facilities, TCU, Rehabilitation, Behavioral Medicine, Postsurgical recovery center	150–400 MDs, vice president of clinical care management, full time department, chiefs

Hospitals must find innovative ways to create land from the small sites crowded with preexisting buildings. Some hospitals can expand vertically, with multistory patient care towers or vertical ambulatory care facilities/ medical offices. But many of today's space-short facilities must reprogram existing space for higher uses and priority needs using the modern engineering principles of "patient-focused care" (Lathrop 1991). For hospitals with smaller sites, nonpatient "back office" support services will be located off-campus in lower-cost space, housing functions such as finance, information systems, materials management, marketing, public relations, and other administrative activities.

Small and rural hospitals will also need more land in the future, at least 15–25 acres if possible. These micromedical centers will be the hub of local multiservice health campuses, including acute care, ambulatory care, emergency/urgent care, long-term care, medical offices, related health services (pharmacy, optometry, physical therapy, retirement housing) (McKahan 1990). One architectural design for a 120-bed hospital created a "spine" of core facilities to which patient care modules could be added as community and hospital grow in the future. Some small-hospital campuses will also host local public health agencies and voluntary health agencies such as a cancer society, heart association, or Red Cross.

The far-sighted hospital board will acquire land well in advance, purchasing property years, even decades, before it is needed. Every board needs to develop a 30-year long-range development strategy that anticipates future needs into the far horizon. Then it must pursue acquisition strategies to purchase or achieve donation of land in desired locations for future growth. Follow the "double-it" rule—whatever the planners say will be adequate for the future, acquire twice as much.

Hospital Construction in an Era of Health Reform

The rising concern over national health costs is likely to have a chilling impact on facility construction in the middle to late 1990s. Uncertainty about future controls may have just the opposite in the short run. While the health reform debate continues, hospitals and health systems may binge on capital spending, building new facilities and upgrading old ones before a limit may be placed on capital investment by federal or state governments. During the early 1990s, health facility construction was one of the few active sectors of building activity on the national scene. Even with the economic recession, constructing and replacing health facilities has been one of the strongest sectors of the construction industry. Hospital construction spending dropped in the mid-1980s, after Medicare introduced DRG-based reimbursement (Figure 11.1) (*Health Facilities Management* 1993). Despite uncertainty over phase-down of Medicare's capital passthrough, hospital spending on construction has come back strongly, increasing from $10.1 billion in 1989 to an estimated $11.3 billion in 1993 (Hemmes 1993).

Where is all this construction money going? Most (77.2 percent) of health care construction projects are renovations, exceeding new construction projects by more than three to one (*Health Facilities Management* 1993). The top reasons for renovation projects, reportedly, are to: enlarge existing space (61.3 percent), update existing space (58.5 percent), accommodate new technology (32.1 percent), meet consumer demands for new services (31.2 percent), maintain or increase physician loyalty (24.1 percent), and facilitate diversification (21.7 percent).

Medicare's "capital fold-in" policy is the real wild card in future hospital construction. If Medicare eliminates hospital capital payment by blending it into DRG reimbursement, hospital construction spending could drop by $1–1.5 billion per year during the mid-1990s before hospital financial confidence returns and hospitals develop new sources of capital. Uncertainty about Medicare funding may stretch the planning and construction cycle from five to seven to seven to nine years, with more projects planned and implemented in stages.

Investing major capital in future health facilities is a gamble in the face of health reform and Medicare's phase-down of capital payments. The hospital of the future burdened with $50–100 million of debt may be unable to break even on Medicare/Medicaid and tightly negotiated managed care payments. On the other hand, government health reforms may restrict future facilities construction and capital spending. Because this is one of the most

Figure 11.1   Hospital Spending on Construction (1982–1993) (in billions)

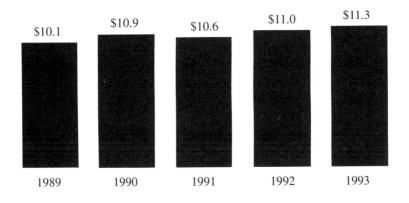

Source: 1992 Health Care Construction Report, *Health Facilities Management* (September 1993).

challenging issues hospital boards will face in the next three to five years, they are advised to take on only as much construction debt as can realistically be repaid under stringent financial scenarios.

The Integrated Medical Campus

Ambulatory care is ready for the next stage of development—the integrated medical campus (IMC). Not a larger ambulatory care center, it will provide community-based, ambulatory and chronic care for the majority of patients who do not need custodial care, serving a population base of 150,000–200,000 (Goldsmith and Miller 1990). The organization's philosophy is that an IMC is more than a medical office, better integrated than a medical mall, and built with physicians not for them. A typical IMC project is a $20–30 million all-ambulatory care complex that will house 36 physicians and a cluster of high-tech services to treat patients, including ambulatory surgery, diagnostic imaging, sports medicine and rehabilitation, clinical laboratory, and pharmacy.

The first IMC was built in 1987 for Denver's Presbyterian St. Luke's Medical Center to serve a new and rapidly growing of suburban Denver. That project, the Centennial Healthcare Plaza, served as the IMC prototype. IMCs are best suited to areas where ambulatory care demand is growing rapidly and hospitals want to develop medical office space in collaboration with physicians. Not all IMCs will be built off-site; some will be constructed on a hospital campus.

Physicians on Campus

There will be many physicians on site in these three-pavilion hospitals of the future. Enough office space will be provided in the ambulatory care pavilion and convenient medical office buildings that 25–40 percent of a hospital's medical staff will practice on campus or immediately adjacent within the hospital's medical zone. Hospitals need a medical staff development plan to predict the configuration of the future medical staff, group practices, and office needs (Anderson 1992).

Hospitals will need more medical office space on the health care campus of the future. Perhaps twice as many physicians will work full-time for hospitals in the year 2000. Some 15–20 percent of a hospital's physicians may be on the payroll as consultants, such as in the laboratory or radiology, or as hospital-based providers in the emergency room, or in ambulatory care. Although all hospitals will share the trend toward hospital-salaried physicians, their prevalence will be much more pronounced in the level 4 hospitals (20–30 percent), and relatively less common in level 3 (15–20 percent) and 2 facilities (5–10 percent).

Consequently, boards should invest in on-campus office space for physicians with the goal of building group practices. Every hospital will need medical group practice partners in managed care contracting. Design on-campus medical office buildings and off-campus satellites to be used by group practices, not solo practitioners.

High-Potential Facilities

Which type of health care facilities will receive most capital investment during the 1990s? The short answer is "hospital-based ambulatory care," according to a 1991 survey by *Modern Healthcare* (Scott 1992). Freestanding ambulatory care facilities were the second-ranked choice for future construction investment, and retirement and long-term care facilities are also expected to experience increased capital spending well into the 1990s (see Table 11.2) (Scott 1992). Ambulatory care will clearly continue to be one of bright spots for health facility expansion and construction in the 1990s: The 75 percent of architects and construction experts ranked ambulatory care first in potential (Scott 1992). The reverse of this trend may also be true—the need for more intensive care units. Architects advise hospitals that have emphasized ambulatory care expansion and have delayed renovating critical care units will need to make major capital investments in upgrading intensive care units in the future. Architects and design/build firms reported a total of 528 projects in intensive care units in 1992, involving nearly one in ten of America's 6,000 community hospitals (Scott 1993).

However, the building boom may have ended for specialty health facilities. Because of major expansion during the 1980s, the market of psychiatric and rehabilitation services appears saturated. Psychiatric hospitals especially are suffering from excess capacity and declining utilization, as

Table 11.2 Which Building Types Offer the Greatest Opportunities?

Facility Type	Percent of Respondents
Hospital-based ambulatory care	74.7
Freestanding outpatient care	8.1
Retirement communities with health facilities	5.1
Long-term care facilities	5.1
Inpatient beds	2.5
Psychiatric hospitals	1.0
Rehabilitation hospitals	0.5
Other facilities/no choice	3.0

Adapted and reprinted with permission from *Modern Healthcare* (23 March 1992). © Crain Communications, Inc., 740 N. Rush Street, Chicago, IL 60611.

skeptical buyers and managed care plans reduce admissions and cut length of stay. Rehabilitation facilities now serve a smaller niche market. The merger of HealthSouth and Continental, two of the nation's largest rehabilitation for-profit companies, was evidence that the rehabilitation market is ripe for consolidation. In mid-1993, Continental announced it would drop plans to build 30+ new facilities, citing uncertainty about the future health care environment (DeLafuente 1993).

Hospitable Design

Hospitals of the future will be more hospitable. Ultimately, they will become healing environments as architects and interior designers rethink the design of health care facilities (Ruga 1992). Most important, designers are considering patients ahead of providers in making design recommendations. "Racetrack" floor plans and light-weight privacy curtains have become obsolete. The traffic flow of staff that competes with patients' needs for privacy will be reevaluated to recognize that the curative function is to lift morale as much as to repair bodyparts (Ulrich 1993). Gone also is the gloomy half-light that resembles neither night nor day. To brighten hospitals visibly, designers will flood hospital corridors and patient care areas with sunlight. One architect has specifically ordered designs to "seek natural light. Break the confinement and monotony of ordinary halls and rooms. Puncture walls and roofs; draw light along floors and stairs, at rooflines, in ridges, at corners, even at peaks. Catch the dawn and the sunset. Then spaces will be vibrant" (Bush-Brown and Davis 1992).

The patient-centered design concept is based on the simple premise that "the goals of design must be to enhance the quality of life experience through hospitable design" (Ruga 1992). Some designers have grasped the concept so well that the hospitals resemble country clubs. At Baptist Hospital of Miami, for example, a wealthy donor left the hospital $1 million and land to establish the facility, on the stipulation that the new hospital resemble the Boca Raton Country Club. The result was a hospital that parallels a premier hotel and has been featured in *Architectural Digest*. At Baptist Hospital of Miami, obstetrics patients enjoy candlelight dinners in one of the LDR/Hotel (Labor/Delivery/Recovery) 48 private rooms (Bush-Brown and Davis 1992). Successful hospitals in the future should model Baptist's philosophy—"To provide quality healthcare in a hotel setting" by recruiting designers and ideas from the hotel and hospitality industries.

As a design team trustees should visit as many facilities as possible for a hands-on assessment of proposed design approaches. Architects should give the board a thorough orientation in modern concepts of health facility design and provide the latest research on healing environments. In designing future facilities, the board is the surrogate for the community and the first line of consumers testing design concepts, plans, layouts, and materials.

Planetree's Healing Revolution

A quiet revolution is taking place in a handful of hospitals that is altering the traditional concept of a hospital. Planetree is a philosophy of consumer-centered health care that breaks established rules regarding the patient's physical environment, encourages patients to become active partners in their own health care, shatters the tradition of the confidential medical record by allowing patients access to their own charts, elevates the role of nurse to educator/trainer and health counselor, involves family and friends in the care process, even to giving medications, provides a new balance in the patient-physician relationship, and may change how administrators calculate the real "bottom-line" of health care.

A small but growing number of hospitals and health systems are opening a window of change by adopting the Planetree program. Planetree's first consumer health library and 13-bed model hospital unit opened in San Francisco's California Pacific Medical Center in 1985. Now the experimental program is being installed in a half-dozen progressive hospitals, from 1,000-bed medical centers to small rural hospitals. One executive from Planetree's parent company has explained that "consumers have a fair amount of choice in other goods and services they purchase in America, and health care should be the same" (Weber 1992).

As a symbol of healing, the Planetree idea dates to the fifth century B.C. Hippocrates, the father of modern medicine, taught his students in the shade of a sycamore, or plane tree. In the 1980s, Planetree became a symbol of medical and spiritual healing Angela Thieriot found lacking in local hospitals. Thieriot gathered a group of 15 other socially committed individuals that conceived of an alternative form and philosophy of health care (Jurow and Schweitzer 1992). Planetree's "model hospital project," a 13-bed medical/surgical unit in California Pacific Medical Center brought the Planetree philosophy inside a hospital.

Upon entering the facility, visitors are immediately struck by the curving walls and wood trim. Patterned bed linens, fresh flowers, and artwork from the San Francisco museum have been added to create a fresh, friendly interior. What's missing is the nursing station—the "bunker" that provides a defensive position for hospital staffers has been replaced by a simple desk for nurses and a small writing table for doctors. In place of the nursing station is a family room, with a kitchen, where patients, friends, and family are invited to relax. A VCR and films such as "Splash" and "It's a Wonderful Life" illustrate the Planetree spirit. Patients and family can cook simple meals or warm up a pizza. There is wine in the refrigerator. Some patients have the option of a drink instead of a sleeping pill.

The Planetree philosophy is more important than its design innovation (Jurow and Schweitzer 1992). Planetree's healing philosophy includes an extensive education of patients in their own disease and therapy. "Information therapy" reduces patient anxiety and improves compliance with doctor's orders. Planetree patients are allowed access to their own medical records and write their own "patient progress notes." Now, more than 25 states have passed laws guaranteeing patients access to their own records.

Planetree may be the first wave of a "healing revolution" in health care design and service delivery. Robin Orr, Planetree's original director for hospital projects, remembers when terms like "healing environments" and "patient-centered care" were viewed with suspicion or worse (Lumsden 1993). Architects, executives, and trustees are now looking at the facility from the patient's perspective. Traditional hospital units are being redesigned to ease levels of patient stress and give them more control over their environment. In the future, patient rooms will be larger to accommodate visitors, while technology will be less conspicuous, often hidden in built-in storage units. Room decor and lighting will be more homelike. Artwork, paint, and textures will be cheerful but not "busy." Patient servers wil link rooms to hallways with pass-through shelves for supplies. Bedside computers will provide electronic access to the latest patient data, combining high-tech with high-touch. Tomorrow's health facilities have no choice but to become customer-centered. As consumers, the responsibility of the board is to imbed a patient-focused orientation into every design and program decision for the health facilities of the future.

Hospitals Adapt to the Age Wave

Tomorrow's health facilities will also have to be designed with the elderly in mind because within ten years more than half of all consumers will be 50 years or older. Those over age 65 will be the most frequent users of hospitals and health facilities. To compensate for the age wave: doors will open with paddles, not handles; directional signs will be in large print and repeated frequently for reassurance; corridors will be well lit, but without glare, to take advantage of high-tech lighting and optimum use of natural light; hospitals will be "step-less"—nothing but flat walkways or ramps for patients and visitors; hallways and restrooms will be equipped with reassuring handrails.

Another benefit of the demographic changes ahead may be the expanded role of volunteers in tomorrow's hospital. Record numbers of retiree volunteers should be available for hospital service, a benefit of the age wave. Hospitals will rely on volunteers as staff substitutes in more professional roles and responsibilities: Retired bankers may work on finance projects and fund development programs. Retired physicians and nurses may provide medical care to the poor and homeless. Retired computer scientists may rewrite hospital software and help program special applications. Retired workers from construction and trades may help remodel hospital space or community health facilities. Retired salespeople may revamp the gift shop or provide concierge services.

Design Challenges

Futurist Leland Kaiser (1993) declares that the challenge of the twenty-first century will be design: community-based design will be the solution to community-generated problems. Design for patient-centered care health facilities of the future must meet the challenges of patient focus and staff productivity. Designing health facilities for cost-effectiveness recognizes the multiple demands of health and safety codes, productivity, efficiency, and user satisfaction by patients and staff. Factors that will contributing to cost-effective design include productivity, work flow, space utilization, durability of materials, cleaning expenses, maintenance costs, energy expenses, flexibility for future uses, patient satisfaction/repeat business/referrals, and staff satisfaction/turnover.

Patient-centered units will be designed for efficiency and productivity. The new 72-bed patient-centered care pavilion at 604-bed Norfolk General Hospital opens in April 1994 at a cost of $26 million (Scott 1993). The central nursing station has been divided into several subunits, saving steps (and labor hours) because staff are closer to patients. Frequently used ancillary services are located on patient floors, saving hours in transporting patients and staff from remote centralized support departments. Patient rooms in another hospital of the future are 40 percent larger, but some, architects included, believe the overall hospital will shrink, due to smaller centralized services and by moving patient care out of the hospital (Scott 1993).

Boards should consider the long term in investing in tomorrow's health facilities. Most facilities will not be remodeled for 15–20 years, and many facilities will be in use for 30–50 years. Never skimp on space or materials— these facilities will only need major upgrading in five to seven years, and at greater cost.

Invisible Changes

Not all advances of form and function in the hospitals of the future will be obvious to patients or staff. Many changes will be invisible in tomorrow's hospitals.

- Electronic computer networks across all patient care units and clinical offices will interconnect on-campus and satellite facilities as well as physician offices and wherever clinical work stations are located.

- Medical artificial intelligence and expert systems for real-time management of costs and quality with recordkeeping by computer will make the hospital substantially paperless.
- Physician executives in management positions and hospital-salaried doctors will consult and care for patients.
- Group practices will be colocated with the hospital for convenient management of HMO/PPO patients.
- Continuous quality will be monitored, from critical care to central supply, conducted widely across the long-term care and ambulatory pavilions. New staffing patterns will emphasize collaborative nurse-physician practice and flexible use of a variety of nursing extender personnel.
- Service orientation will be geared to satisfying expectations of patients and families at every level of care.

The Look of Tomorrow's Hospitals

Envision the hospital of the future: gracious interiors and cozy spaces designed for comfort (and healing) at the hub of a 60–100 acre medical campus of multiconnected buildings, with parking, or at least a valet to remove parking as a barrier to patients and the visiting public. The service-first attitude of hotel chains or country clubs will be written into customer policies for hospital employees, as hospitals imitate the look of traditional wallpapers, wing chairs in vestibules, and over-scale flower arrangements. Floral sheets will be coordinated with the decor. Comfortable chairs will be found everywhere. Chairs in patient rooms will be "sleepers" for overnight visitors. In addition, hospitals will be quiet—indeed, serene. There will be no more public address announcements. Staff will be discretely summoned by electronic pagers. Carpeted hospital hallways will muffle footsteps and traffic. Natural light will infuse interiors and patient rooms. All patients have windows because patients recover faster (shorter length of stay) when they can see a tree through a window. Hallway clutter—waste bins, spare gurneys, and wheelchairs—will be banished to built-in storage units. Waste bins in patient rooms and treatment spaces will be in-wall units. Even potentially infectious red bag trash will be disposed in built-in containers.

The hospital will be a community art gallery. Art is therapy. Tomorrow's hospital corridors will be lined with art. Volunteers will bring an art cart to newly arriving patients to select one or more pictures to brighten their temporary home-away-from-home. All this is part of a strategy to humanize health care interiors and to give patients some sense of control over their environment. Patient rooms will be single-occupancy; semiprivate rooms will be obsolete in the year 2000 to accommodate patient preferences and hospital flexibility in patient assignment. Converting semiprivate units to private is one solution to the problem of excess beds.

Hospitals of the twenty-first century will continue to be unique combinations of social institution and business enterprise. They will adapt to the changes for society and the health field. By some estimates, another 500 hospitals—10 percent of U.S. community hospitals—may close their doors in this decade, driven out of business by financial pressures and inadequate reimbursement. That prediction underestimates the leadership and resiliency of American's community hospitals. Although 10–15 percent of U.S. hospitals today are characterized as financially troubled, most will find ways to reduce costs and regain financial stability.

The aging of the population is propelling a paradigm shift from acute to chronic care, and from an intervention to health maintenance orientation. The concept of short-term care recognizes a growing number of services and facilities that fall somewhere between acute and ambulatory on the continuum of care. This underlying shift will slowly influence the practice of American medicine and the design of tomorrow's hospitals. And as the industry reforms its payment scheme, hospitals have the opportunity to design integrated health systems and facilities that are patient-sensitive, efficient, and healing environments.

Strategies

1. **Put the patient first in planning for the future.** Use the Planetree program as a model of customer-centered care. Envision a hospital stay, emergency room visit, or surgical procedure as a "designed experience" that will satisfy patient hopes (and relieve fears). When architects planned a children's hospital, they walked around on their knees through a full-size mockup of a patient unit. One result was "scoops"—cutaways in the countertops of nursing stations—to enable smaller customers to see the staff without standing on tip-toes. Trustees are the hospital's touch-stone to customer sensitivities.

2. **Develop a long-range master facility plan.** Trustees need to lead a process of planning for the health campus of tomorrow. Most often that means a fundamental updating of the hospital's master facility plan, a physical layout of the buildings and major blocks of services and programs that will be needed over the next five to ten years. Work with the architects in the planning process. Plan for the community's future service and program needs.

3. **Consider services within a community framework.** Grand designs for a hospital's future must to be shaped by a more global perspective that recognizes the role of the individual institution in the larger community

care system. No hospital is an island any more. Trustees need to take a communitywide perspective with their own institution. All hospital plans for growth and development must be prepared in a community context. In a spirit of collaboration, neighboring hospitals should share long-range plans and reduce duplication where possible, especially of high-cost and underutilized services. Antitrust barriers to collaboration may be eased during the 1990s as policymakers realize that antitrust is actually contributing to higher health costs when hospitals cannot share expensive equipment or realign services.

4. **Create healing environments.** In an ideal future, all health facilities will be designed as healing environments that contribute to well-being. Early research findings show that windows, light, color, space, texture, and layout all influence patient moods and recovery processes. Make the hospital a laboratory for innovative design that enhances the health of all patients as well as the productivity of the staff. Better yet, make it a premier hotel that provides quality health care at the same high standard.

References

Anderson, H. J. 1992. "Hospitals and Medical Staffs: The Concept of Planning Takes on New Meaning." *Hospitals* 66 (20 October): 22–26.

Bush-Brown, A., and D. Davis. 1992. *Hospital Design for Healthcare and Senior Communities*. New York: Van Nostrand Reinhold.

Carlson, L. K. 1992. "Creating Designs that Heal." *California Hospitals* (May–June): 11–14.

DeLafuente. D. 1993. "Continental Medical Drops Plans to Build 30 Facilities." *Modern Healthcare* (28 June): 8.

Goldsmith, J. C. 1992. "The Reshaping of Healthcare." *Healthcare Forum Journal* 35 (July–August): 34–41.

Goldsmith, J. C., and R. Miller. 1990. "Restoring the Human Scale." *Healthcare Forum Journal* 33 (November–December): 22–27.

Health Facilities Management. 1993. "Health Care Construction: Where It's Headed in the 1990s." 6 (September): 95.

Hemmes, M. 1993. "Health Care Construction in the 1990s." *Health Facilities Management* 6 (September): 18–22.

Jurow, A., and M. Schweitzer. 1992. "Planetree Patients Come First in Health Care." *California Hospitals* (May–June): 14–16.

Kaiser, L. 1993. "Design Challenges." *Healing Healthcare* 4 (Summer): 2.

Lathrop, J. P. 1991. "The Patient-Focused Hospital." *Healthcare Forum Journal* 34 (July–August): 17–21.

Lumsden, K. 1993. "The Clinical Connection: Hospitals Work to Design Information Systems that Physicians Will Use." *Hospitals* 67 (5 May): 16–26.

McKahan, D. C. 1990. "The Healing Environment of the Future." *Healthcare Forum Journal* 33 (May–June): 36–39.

Mayer, D. 1992. "Hospital Design of the Future." *California Hospitals* (May–June): 8–11.

Ruga, W. 1992. "Breakthrough Thinking in Healthcare Design." *Healthcare Forum Journal* 35 (September–October): 17–19.

Scott, L. 1992. "Annual Construction and Architects Survey." *Modern Healthcare* (23 March).

———. 1993. "Construction and Design Survey." *Modern Healthcare* 23 (15 March): 29–44.

Ulrich, R. 1993. "How Design Impacts Wellness." *Healthcare Forum Journal* 35 (September–October): 20–25.

Weber, D. 1992. "Planetree Transplanted." *Healthcare Forum Journal* 35 (September-October): 30–37.

12

Community Health: The Social Responsibility of American Hospitals

The hallmark of tomorrow's successful hospitals and health organizations will be measurably healthier communities. Health care organizations and their leaders should serve as catalysts for healthier communities—from our own corridors to the larger society we serve.

—Kathryn Johnson (1993b)

Healthy communities, let these be the symbols of the best hospitals in America during the 1990s. Define a hospital's success not only on its financial bottom line, but equally by its success in improving the health of the community. The concern for healthy communities is part of the "greening" of America, a social consciousness that begins with the environment but includes many social causes, which is recapturing popular opinion. Social and environmental activist trustees are leading their hospitals to address a wide range of community and ecological issues. These trustees have recognized that unless hospitals participate, the future of public health in America could be grim in the decades ahead. Despite having the best medical technology in the world, the United States faces such dramatic problems as infant mortality, AIDS, and vast numbers of medically uninsured that will worsen during the 1990s. Public health agencies lack the money, staff, and organization to effectively address many public health problems. Greater portions of public health dollars will be spent to direct medical care for the poor, not to immunization, prenatal care, health education, and prevention. Neglecting these basics is creating public health "time bombs" for this decade.

The 1990s is poised to be a renaissance of ideals and social commitment. The baby-boomers who were tempered by the socially conscious 1960s have reached their middle years and now hold positions of authority. The community-spirited hospital trustees and executives of this generation in particular are making social issues a priority. Symbolic of this change of direction in the health field, the Healthcare Forum has refocused its mission on "healthy communities." At its 1993 annual meeting, the Healthcare Forum convened an international summit on healthy communities, with participants from proclaimed "healthy cities" in Europe, Asia, Australia, and the United States. Participants received a "Healthier Communities Action Kit" that shared lessons from communities where hospitals, health professionals, voluntary health agencies, and government formed coalitions targeting local health issues such as smoking, obesity, and teenage pregnancy (Johnson 1993a). Examples from the United States include St. Paul, Minnesota; Dalles, Oregon; and Palo Alto, California.

In St. Paul, the five hospitals of HealthEast have brought together other community hospitals and public agencies to address the unmet health needs of the East metro area, such as loss of health insurance by the temporarily unemployed.

In Dalles, a rural community 70 miles east of Portland, the Mid-Columbia Medical Center has pledged to "tithe" 10 percent of its profits for community health projects, such as a jogging trail along the Columbia River and an Olympic-size swimming pool.

In Palo Alto, doctors at the Stanford University Medical Center have created a network of communitywide smoking-cessation and health education programs for small towns in coastal and central California.

Community health is a partnership process. Hospital trustees must initiate the collaborative efforts with local health agencies in order to successfully address unmet health needs and introduce prevention programs. In the 1990s providing charity care alone will not be enough.

Goals for the Year 2000

Imagine an America with lower infant mortality, fewer preventable deaths due to auto accidents or violence, and improvements in dozens of indicators of individual and community health. This is a visionary future advanced in *Healthy People 2000*, a voluminous report advanced by the Bush administration's Department of Health and Human Services. More than 200 goal statements were set for the year 2000, covering a broad range of health conditions and behaviors. Many of the goals focused on improvements in lifestyle and behavior. Some, such as AIDS, require medical breakthroughs.

The Clinton administration hopes that many desirable community health objectives in *Healthy People 2000* can be met in this decade through enactment of universal coverage. Under the Health Security Act of 1993, health promotion services such as mammograms, immunizations, preventive dental services for children, and health education classes would be covered benefits. The Clinton reform initiative also calls for increased funding of public health programs.

Oregon is an example of a state that has created its own agenda, becoming the bellwether state for community health issues. Oregon established a grass-roots consumer organization called "Health Decisions" during the mid-1980s to lobby elected officials on community health and ethical issues. The group conducted a series of town meetings on health issues all over the state, identifying problems and consumer concerns first-hand. The result was the ground-breaking decision by the Oregon legislature to shift funding priorities from high-technology to maternal and child health. In Oregon, the state Medicaid program no longer reimburses costly organ transplants. The Oregon legislature has permanently reprogrammed the $1 million into health promotion for children and prenatal care for women. Based on the success of Health Decisions, more than a dozen and a half similar grass-roots groups have mobilized in states across the county. In 1993, the Clinton administration granted Oregon a waiver to continue its rationing program for the state's Medicaid population.

Oregon's own Health 2000 project is a statewide effort to improve the health outlook for Oregonians and their children. Its report defines the basis for its strong community health orientation:

> Preventable injuries, disease and premature death have extracted their toll from our society for so long that we have come to accept them as being inevitable and beyond our control. With few exceptions, we have been surprisingly willing to tolerate high rates of poor health and to expect only the most gradual improvements. It is time for a radical change in our expectations, and for new vigor in our efforts to promote health. (State of Oregon 1988)

Developing "Oregon Health 2000" was a community affair. Representatives from 20 organizations collaborated in analyzing problems and developing action recommendations. Most participants came from public health agencies or consumer organizations. Only two providers participated, a public health nurse and a physician. This was a missed opportunity for hospital leaders—they were not officially represented.

Oregon's Health 2000 is a call for action rather than a blueprint. Each of the 13 objectives set are for the year 2000 (see Table 12.1). For each goal area, indicators were identified with which to measure progress. A statewide rate or level provides a benchmark for today, along with a projection for the year 2000 that foresees dire circumstances if nothing changes to improve reaching the health objectives.

For each goal area, the Oregon Health 2000 report specifically identifies the health objectives for the year 2000, with indicators, baseline statewide rates, and 2000 projections; the 1988 status and trends in Oregon; the health implications on significance and health impact; recommendations for specific action that identify relevant public and private groups to take

Table 12.1   Oregon's Health Objectives for the Year 2000

Goal	Current Status	Selected Year 2000 Indicator
1. Healthy babies	5.1	4.5 low birthweight infants per 1,000 live births
2. Physically fit children	No data	66% of children grades K–12 meet health-related fitness levels
3. Unintentional injuries	1,296	683 years of potential life lost due to unintentional injury deaths/100,000 population
4. Intentional injuries	6.8	6.0 deaths due to homicide per 100,000 population
5. Drug & alcohol	19.8	14.8 deaths resulting directly from the effects of drugs and alcohol per 100,000 population
6. Sexually transmitted diseases	150.8	75 gonorrhea cases per 100,000 population
7. HIV infections	20.8%	30 percent prevalence of HIV infection among gay males
8. Cardiovascular diseases	281.5	145.9 deaths due to cardiovascular diseases per 100,000 ages 45–64
9. Tobacco-caused diseases	190.0	222.2 deaths due to lung cancer per 100,000 population age 45+
10. Cancer	198.2	148.7 deaths due to cancer per 100,000 population
11. Immunizable diseases	3.2	0.3 incidence of haemophilius influenzae meningitis per 100,000 population
12. Environmentally caused diseases	No data	Identify indicators, develop baseline data
13. Independent living	44%	90 percent of mentally ill served by independent living programs

Source: State of Oregon Office of Health Policy, as printed in its *Health Objectives for the Year 2000*, 1988.

a leading role; and data needs to fill major gaps in existing knowledge. Strategic planning and futures research techniques were utilized to prepare the report. First, an extensive data base was developed for projecting health-related trends in the environment, technology, demographics, and socioeconomic factors. From this futures research, a scenario for the remainder of this century was painted, and strategic directions for health identified. From these broad directions resulted the 13 specific objective areas. Measurable health outcome goals or process objectives were set, with action recommendations and identified lead agencies. Progress toward each of the 13 objectives is monitored; a mid-course report will be released by 1995.

Public Health at a Watershed Moment

American public health is in crisis. After 20 years of neglect and underfunding, America's public health programs are progressively unable to maintain basic inspection and immunization programs and are floundering in their efforts to provide direct medical care to the poor and medically uninsured. Federal, state, and local public health programs were lambasted in a national study by the prestigious Institute of Medicine (IOM). Published in 1988, "The Future of Public Health" (1988) was an early warning that America's public health infrastructure was crumbling. The report opened with this observation: "There is a widening perception that America has lost sight of its public health goals and has allowed the public health system to fall into disarray." The report is critical of the sad state of America's public health infrastructure:

> An impossible responsibility has been placed on America's public health agencies: to serve as stewards of the basic health needs of the entire populations, but at the same time avert impending disasters and provide personal health care to those rejected by the rest of the health system. The wonder is not that American public health has problems, but that so much as been done so well, and with so little. (Institute of Medicine 1988)

The IOM study produced tremendous ferment within the public health community. It galvanized the professionals and health-disadvantaged groups to counterattack in preventing further cutbacks in public health funding. In California alone, it prompted seven position papers in formal response, which were presented in a conference that re-energized California's public health agencies.

To conduct its assessment of public health, the IOM constituted a 22-member committee drawn broadly from public health officials, academics, physicians, elected officials, and individuals representing the private sector. This group gathered data and conducted site visits to six states and their local health agencies. A broad base of data and testimony on the status and future of public health was gathered. The result was a highly influential study that has catalyzed reform movements in a number of states to revitalize public health programs.

The Healthiest Population

America's hospitals should take the lead in voluntarily addressing local health issues. After all, hospital trustees are community stewards. As corporate citizens, hospitals have a civic responsibility. Every hospital's trustees should include in their long-range strategic goals the improvement of specific community health problems.

Looking to the 1990s, America should have the healthiest population on record. Isn't the medical care in the United States considered the finest in the world? While the public's health may be improving in some areas, progress is lagging in many others. Major threats to the public's health loom ahead, but the capacity of the public health system to address them is seriously limited. Since the scathing report of the Institute of Medicine in 1988, a set of more than 200 health goals for the year 2000 were announced. But setting goals does not address the problem of funding and program capacity of public health agencies at all levels of government falling behind urgent public health needs.

Can the nation's public health respond effectively to the public health problems of the 1990s? Unless America's hospitals and physicians volunteer to help, these public health problems will only worsen. According to the IOM these are the key threats to the public health that must be addressed in the 1990s.

* AIDS—More than 1 million people have been infected with HIV, resulting in 200,000 deaths in the United States (Haason 1993). AZT appears to slow the onset of AIDS symptoms, but the AIDS virus is spreading among thousands of intravenous drug abusers whose care will be acute and costly. The question for the future is whether a cure and vaccine will be developed before this disease reaches epidemic proportions. In the meantime, public hospitals in New York and other affected metropolitan areas are struggling to cope with growing numbers of seriously ill AIDS patients.

* Access for the indigent—Between 35 and 40 million Americans do not have basic health insurance. But the problem of access is deeper than insurance coverage. About 43 million Americans, or 18 percent of the population, do not have a physician, clinic, or hospital as a regular source of care. The proportion of those below the federal "poverty line" who do not have Medicaid coverage has increased to 54 percent. This is a national problem. Since 1980, more than 20 states have appointed commissions to study the issue of access for the medically indigent.

* Injuries—Health injuries are an underrecognized problem affecting more than one in three Americans. Each year, more than 140,000 people die from injuries and another 70 million sustain nonfatal injuries. It is the leading cause of death for children and young adults. Motor vehicle accidents are

the leading cause of severe injury and death, causing 3.2 million injuries and one-third of fatalities, according to a 1985 study by the Committee on Trauma Research. (Institute of Medicine 1988)

- Teen pregnancy—Almost 500,000 babies are born each year to teenage mothers in the United States. Births to teenage mothers are about 13 percent of all births. For example, 15-year-old girls in the United States are five times as likely to become pregnant than their counterparts in any other industrialized country. Pregnant teenagers have higher rates of miscarriages, complications, stillbirths, and infant and maternal deaths. Low-income teenagers are more likely to have premature deliveries. Teenage pregnancy is linked with school dropout, contributing to low future incomes and poorer health in later years for mothers and children.

- High blood pressure—A key factor in stroke and heart disease is high blood pressure. Some 60 million Americans are affected by high blood pressure. A national campaign begun in 1972 to identify those with high blood pressure levels was helpful in lowering the incidence of stroke, but level of community involvement has been a factor. Noncompliance with medical advice is a persistent problem. Even those who know they have hypertension may not be controlling their condition with diet, exercise, and medications. Up to two-thirds of hypertensives in a 1976–1980 study were not in control programs. In 1986, blood pressure control levels ranged from 25 to 60 percent.

- Smoking—According to recent statistics, 25 percent of American adults are addicted to cigarettes. So are 17 percent of high schoolers. Smokers have a 70 percent higher death rate from all causes than do nonsmokers. Smoking is the single greatest cause of premature death in this country with 400,000 deaths estimated every year. It is estimated that smoking contributes to as many as 225,000 deaths from coronary heart disease, 100,000 deaths from cancers, and 20,000 deaths from chronic obstructive lung disease each year. Another 10 million Americans suffer from debilitating chronic diseases caused by smoking. If that was not enough, smoking is the major identifiable cause of residential fire deaths and injuries. In the 20 years since the initial Surgeon General report on smoking and health, there has been progress: Smoking was down from 33 percent of adults and 27 percent of high school students in 1979. Antismoking measures are working. In California, a three-year-old initiative has funded a $100,000 million advertising smoking prevention campaign.

- Substance abuse—Despite public fears about drugs and crime, America has made some progress against substance abuse. Alcohol consumption has remained steady since 1978, at slightly under three gallons per person over age 14. During the late 1970s and early 1980s, drug abuse remained stable and even declined for some illegal substances. About 16 million

Americans smoke marijuana, 1–2 million use cocaine, 1 million misuse barbiturates, and thousands are addicted to heroin. Problems may be growing. Cocaine use doubled during the 1980s. Teenage occasional "binge" drinking increased from 37 to 41 percent in a five-year period in the 1980s. Then there are the related health problems: Alcohol is a factor in 10 percent of all deaths and is frequently associated with auto fatalities. Intravenous drug abuse is increasingly associated with AIDS transmission. The three habits of smoking, alcohol, and drug abuse are consistently related to poor pregnancy outcomes.

- Toxic substances—This problem has come into greater focus as the public learns the dangers of hazardous wastes, pesticides, chemicals, and carcinogens. Pollution of ground water supplies is a serious threat to public health. At one acid pit, ground water was still being contaminated 13 years after the dump site closed and five years after the pits were capped. A National Academy of Sciences report in 1987 focused on 28 of 53 pesticides classified as carcinogenic; more than 80 percent exceed the Environmental Protection Agency (EPA) standards. The National Institute of Occupational Safety and Health has reported that 4 million American workers are exposed to mercury, aluminum, and other metals that can cause chronic kidney disease.

- Aging and Alzheimer's—As many as 2 million Americans suffer from Alzheimer's disease, resulting in severe, disabling intellectual impairment. While the exact causes are unknown, the disease is clearly associated with age. More than 20 percent of those over age 80 are believed to have the disease. The number of Alzheimer's cases is expected to increase dramatically over the next several decades as the number of elderly increases. The problem will be especially visible in those over age 85, the fastest-growing segment of the population today.

California's Community Coalition on Future of Public Health

A new coalition has formed in California to reenergize public and private health initiatives. The IOM report has had a tremendous influence on state and local public health. To address the future of public health in the nation's most populous state, a broad coalition of more than 40 California health organizations convened a statewide conference in 1990. The coalition was formed to unite California public and voluntary health agencies in seeking higher visibility and funding for public health programs.

In response to the grass-roots initiative for public health, the State of California issued its own report, *The Year 2000 National Health Objectives: The California Experience* (1991). The report indicated that more than 20 objectives were met in areas such as cancer, heart disease, and stroke; but it also signaled that minority populations, especially blacks, still were not meeting health objectives. California has encouraged its local health departments to focus on health status improvements, and the state is monitoring progress with regular public reports (California Department of Health Services 1993). Progress is being made, according to a report jointly developed by the State of California and the California Coalition for the Future of Public Health (1992).

California demonstrates how effective a public-private coalition can be in promoting healthy communities. Since 1988, the California Healthy Cities Project has recognized local health improvement efforts in dozens of California cities from rural Aracata to West Hollywood (California Coalition for the Future of Public Health 1992). The project is jointly sponsored by the Western Consortium for Public Health, State Department of Health Services, and California Wellness Foundation. The success of the California Healthy Cities Project has occurred because it introduces innovative ideas and resources, according to Consortium Director Joseph Hafey, and brings together people who are committed to community improvement.

The Healthy Cities concept was originally promoted by the World Health Organization, which has now recognized hundreds of cities for their health initiatives (Tsouros 1992). To build healthy cities, says public health consultant Len Duhl, M.D., "You must change the business and social policies that run society" (Flower 1993). Duhl's 1985 paper "Healthy Cities," which was presented at a Toronto conference, launched an international movement. In the United States, the National Civic League launched a program to encourage American communities to promote community health (National Civic League 1993). More than 100 local cities and towns have been cited by the National Civic League for their health promotion efforts.

Hospital trustees need to take a leadership role in supporting coalition-building among public and voluntary health agencies, much like those in California. The goal is to develop innovative voluntary responses and find new financing for underfunded public health programs like immunizations, prenatal health, teenage pregnancy, tuberculosis, AIDS, and medical care for uninsured.

Partners in Prevention

San Diego's Partnership in Prevention demonstrates the impact of community hospitals who develop public-private partnerships for community health. Paradise Valley Hospital, located a few miles south of San Diego, convened business, education, government, social services, and health agencies to improve the health status of this inner-city community. The coalition targeted women's breast cancer and launched a mobile breast screening program, "Mammography on the Move." In its first year, mobile detection revealed four cases of breast cancer in 700. Some 60 percent of the women had never been screened before. With a grant from the California Wellness Program, the mobile screening program was extended into 1994 (*Star-News* 1992).

Paradise Valley's partnership coalition is now looking for new health promotion priorities. Data has been developed by surveys of physicians, community health providers, "key informants" and community leaders, and community residents. The hospital has analyzed morbidity and mortality data, seeking more unmet needs. Many community residents lack access to primary care due to a lack of health insurance, awareness of health care issues, and some cultural barriers. Now the partners coalition is setting new targets for its next community health initiatives, convinced that national health reform will not solve all the health-related issues that confront local residents (Walker 1993).

The Growing Uninsured Population

The debate over national health reform recognizes what America's hospitals know well—that too many consumers have little or no health insurance coverage. Estimates by the U.S. Bureau of the Census place the number of uninsured at over 37 million in 1993. Each year of the 1980s, the medically uninsured grew by about 1 million. Public hospitals, city and county health departments, and state governments cannot keep up with these types of demands. America's voluntary community hospitals—not the government— have become the "safety nets" for the poor and uninsured, subsidizing their care as well as covering the costs of underfunded government Medicaid and Medicare programs. Revenue deductions of 20–35 percent are commonplace among community hospitals for community care, bad debts, and unpaid costs of care to government beneficiaries.

Inner-city hospitals are trying to fill the gaps with community-based programs for the poor and uninsured. America's hospitals are strengthening their community health efforts to revitalize inner-city neighborhoods and address local issues such as drugs, illiteracy, and teen pregnancy. And hospitals hope such efforts will preserve their tax-exempt status, especially if national health reform eliminates "charity care." A growing number of community hospitals support neighborhood health centers and similar programs for the poor (Pellarito 1992). Seedco, a nonprofit community development organization provided grants to 13 community partnerships that included hospitals.

Some public-minded hospitals have taken a proactive approach to improve the public's health. In Columbus, Ohio, for example, a campaign to reduce infant mortality in the one area is being spearheaded by Riverside Methodist Hospitals. A coalition of more than 20 community businesses, churches, and voluntary health organizations have joined together to provide programs in prevention, education, family planning counseling, outreach for early prenatal care, and expanded prenatal services. Methodist Hospitals and their Foundation have donated substantial funds and volunteer staff time to establish a clinic that opened in early 1993 (Matheny 1992).

And in Chicago, a collaborative effort has tackled the problem of access to health care in disadvantaged Chicago neighborhoods. The Chicago Health Initiative (CHI) was launched in 1991 under the leadership of the Lutheran General HealthSystem, which had funded early projects with its own money and has also built a community partnership with the local business community and neighborhood organizations (McGrath 1992). A committee has developed guidelines for support of community-based projects that have the potential to reinforce and improve weak links in the community health delivery system, respond to community health needs, and build on and strengthen existing health care resources. Projects already underway include a church-based community health program in an Hispanic parish, joint funding of a maternal/child health coordinator in a City Department of Health clinic, and a women's health fair.

Trustees can learn from these examples. Hospitals need to renew and expand their community outreach efforts. It is not enough to provide charity care in the emergency room and to write off hospital bills for those who cannot pay. Every hospital needs to be a visible symbol of community care, with mobile screening programs and gap-filling programs for underserved population groups.

Making a Commitment to the Environment

Hospitals that establish a reputation for preserving the environment can reap a harvest of savings and stature. Unfortunately, America's hospitals have a reputation as corporate polluters. Waste disposal is a case in point. Hospitals produce as much solid, liquid, and nuclear waste as many industrial companies. The methods used by hospitals to dispose of radioactive and infectious waste, including HIV-tainted "red bag" trash, have been widely criticized. Beaches from Maine to Florida have been awash with syringes and medical waste. The public suspects that hospitals have been quietly dumping trash and medical disposables at sea or slipping untreated medical waste into public landfills. Hospital incinerators for infectious waste have been "lightning rods" for public protests. Disposing of medical waste is an immense and costly problem. Medical waste represents only about 10–15 percent of all hospitals' waste stream, but only part of that is truly infectious and requires incineration. Reducing the volume of hospital wastes is good business as well as being "environmentally correct."

Some hospitals have made commitments to recycle paper, aluminum, silver, and cardboard, and to ask vendors and suppliers to cut back on materials in packaging their products for hospital use. What about disposables? Should hospitals return to recyclable products like surgical drapes, gowns, and diapers? As hospitals become more environmentally concerned, the widespread use of disposables is becoming a high-visibility concern. This is not a simple issue. The cost of dumping disposable materials must be compared with the costs of cleaning and repackaging reusable products. Patient safety is a concern, as is staff labor, a high-cost item. The issues and costs of recycling vary from community to community.

Cogeneration of steam and electricity is another area where hospital investment can reduce operating costs and lower energy consumption. Some hospitals tried cogeneration during the 1980s and were disappointed with operational breakdowns. A new generation of cogeneration devices for the 1990s offers more durable designs with minimum maintenance requirements. Some low-cost cogeneration devices use natural gas to cost-effectively generate both steam and electricity.

Hospitals will find savings in energy conservation, recycling, and waste reduction, but first they must make an investment. Hospitals should expect to spend money in the first two years before seeing net returns from environmental programs, but the increased community stature and regard are well worth the investment. Environmental responsibility is good "corporate citizenship."

Now more than ever, there is a need for hospitals to take a leadership role in addressing community health problems. This is a call for social responsibility by the U.S. hospital industry. Public health agencies are struggling to meet the needs, and public-private partnerships can help raise community health levels. America's hospitals must set a higher goal for their efforts in the 1990s than profitability in the 1990s, or they will have done little to prevent the possible regulation a national health system would bring.

Looking Forward: Hospitals' Social Conscience

As part of America's revival of environmental concerns, hospitals need to become more invested in community health. America's hospitals have been preoccupied with competition and declining reimbursement for the past ten years. In the era of health reform, hospitals must turn outward to the community. If hospitals do not act to support their local and state health agencies, lower rates of prenatal care and renewed breakouts of tuberculosis, measles, and other communicable diseases are likely.

Ten steps hospitals can take toward healthier communities in the 1990s are to:

1. Adopt a problem. Every hospital should identify a local health issue and make it a cause.

2. Collaborate with voluntary agencies. Find common goals with local voluntary health agencies and work actively with them to address local health issues.

3. Take policy positions. The hospital should take a visible policy stand on local and state health issues. Provide educational assistance to local and state legislators on health problems. Take public stands on health-related problems.

4. Make community service a job requirement. Every hospital manager should be a director of a local health agency, and every hospital staffer should volunteer time at least once each year to a chosen health cause. Add it to job descriptions.

5. Donate funds to good causes. Use the hospital's philanthropy to support of needy community health programs.

6. Plant seeds. As a major corporate citizen, the hospital could provide "seed funding" for community health projects.

7. Create a community service plan. Conduct a community health assessment and develop a community service plan that identifies the hospital's role in charitable care, uncompensated service, and support for community health programs. This should be a board activity in collaboration with the Foundation board.

8. Require community service for medical staff privileges. The board and executive committee of the medical staff should ask the medical staff to donate time and services to the poor, medically underserved, and special needs populations as a condition for maintaining privileges at the hospital.

9. Adopt a school, special needs group, or neighborhood. Every hospital should identify a needy subset of its population to which it will reach out and assist to raise health levels.

10. Look after your own. Assess the hospital's employees, looking for workers and families in distress, and assist them in their times of need.

Strategies

1. **Make community health a hospital responsibility.** Hospitals must now stand up for the public's health. If America is to achieve many of the high goals set by the federal reports such as *Healthy People 2000*, hospitals must take a leadership role. This is a time for collaboration. Hospitals can play a catalytic role in convening other hospitals, local health agencies, consumer organizations, and government in new consortia approaches to solve pressing community health issues. Hospitals cannot replace public

health agencies, but they can be a good "corporate citizens" and partners in collaboration.

2. **Set higher goals beyond competitive survival.** During the 1980s, hospitals were intensely preoccupied with survival—coping with Medicare DRGs, managed care, and competition. Hospitals lost sight of community health issues. While hospitals lobby Congress to protect their institutions under national health reform, hospitals could lose their tax-exempt status if government officials perceive there is no more charity care. Hospitals need to turn to their communities and actively pursue public health problems.

3. **Wear values "on the sleeve."** Communicating this broader interest in community health is essential for hospitals in the 1990s. Health care organizations must be social institutions first, business enterprises second. The language is symbolic of underlying changes, as America's hospitals and health systems must refocus on a more idealistic and public-spirited set of goals. Nothing will do more to improve the image, and the impact, of hospitals and health care systems than to take on responsibility for their health of their communities and make a measurable difference.

4. **Ensure that community health is the essence of hospital governance.** Providing community care, protecting environmental health, and improving the well-being of patients—this is the essence of hospital governance. Hospitals and health organizations can do much to provide leadership in collaboration with other hospitals, voluntary health agencies, and government to promote community health improvement. The 1990s will be a time for values and ideals. America's hospital trustees should be clear in their commitment to creating healthy communities. Follow the rule set by Riverside Methodist Hospitals, where before any decision is made, the trustees ask: How does this decision benefit the community? and What community needs are being addressed?

References

California Coalition for the Future of Public Health. California Healthy Cities Project. 1992. "Awards Presentation." Sacramento: The Coalition.

California Department of Health Services. 1993. *Year 1993 County Health Status Profiles.* Sacramento: California Department of Health Services.

———. 1991. *The Year 2000 National Health Objectives: The California Experience.* Sacramento: California Department of Health Services.

Flower, J. 1993. "Building Healthier Cities: A Conversation with Leonard J. Duhl, M.D." *Healthcare Forum Journal* 36 (May–June): 43–54.

Haason, J. 1993. "AIDS Task Force To Tackle Red Tape." *USA Today,* 1 December.

Institute of Medicine. 1988. *The Future of Public Health.* Washington, DC: National Academy Press.

Johnson, K. 1993a. *Healthier Communities Action*. San Francisco: Healthcare Forum.
————. 1993b. "Through the Bonds of Community." *Healthcare Forum Journal* 36 (May–June): 6.
Matheny, P. 1992. "Community Collaboration—A Model for Change." *InterHealth Links* 8 (Fall): 3.
McGrath, A. F. 1992. "The Chicago Health Initiative." *InterHealth Links* 8 (Fall): 3.
National Civic League. 1993. *The Civic Index: A New Approach to Improving Community Life*. Denver, CO: The League.
Oregon Office of Health Policy. 1988. *Health Objectives for the Year 2000*. Portland: The State of Oregon.
Pellarito, K. 1992. "Providing More Than Just Care to Neighborhoods." *Modern Healthcare* 22 (3 August): 59–64.
Star-News. 1992. "Hospital Awarded Wellness Grant." 1 November.
Tsouros, A. 1992. *World Health Organization Healthy City Project: A Project Becomes a Movement*. Copenhagen, Denmark: World Health Organization.
U.S. Department of Health and Human Services. 1990. *Healthy People 2000*. Washington, DC: U.S. Government Printing Office.
Walker, C. 1993. *Partners for Prevention: Synopsis of Needs Assessment*. National City, CA: Paradise Valley Hospital.

13

Health Care 2001: Anticipating and Managing the Future

It is in the future where our greatest leverage is. . . . Anticipation provides you with the information that allows you to be in the right place at the right time with your excellent innovative product or service.

—Joel Barker (1992)

The future of health care—what will it bring? This is a volatile and uncertain time for America's hospitals as they adjust to the era of health reform. Politicians and consumers are badly split with regard to how the American health system should be changed and improved. What does the future hold for the year 2001? A better question for America's hospitals and their trustees is which future would they prefer because there are many possible futures. The challenge of leadership is for each hospital and health system to define a preferred future for its twenty-first century health organization.

Bridging the Leadership Gap

Health care executives, medical staff leaders, and trustees overwhelmingly believe there is a leadership gap between how America's hospitals and health systems are managed today and the types of leadership competencies and values that will be needed in the next century (Johnson and Berger 1992). A nationwide survey on leadership for the next century, conducted by the Healthcare Forum Leadership Center and supported by a major grant from the Eastman Kodak company, revealed that American health care needs a new direction; it needs a "New Civilization," a far-reaching scenario that study participants strongly preferred (87 percent support) in preference to the "High-Tech" and "Government Leadership" alternatives. Kathryn Johnson has said, "If we can predict the future, then we can manage it" (Johnson and Berger 1992) The "Bridging the Leadership Gap" study provided new specifics on the 18 dimensions of leadership competencies and values that will be needed in the year 2001 and beyond.

The Leadership Gap study posed four questions about managing health organizations in the year 2001.

1. What will twenty-first century health care organizations look like?

While the future cannot be predicted with certainty, three possible scenarios for health care in the year 2001 were ranked. Participants strongly preferred the "New Civilization" over two others, yet were not certain which possible future was most likely. The first future—"Continued Growth/High-Tech" envisions a health care system that expands with the national economy, taking 17 percent of the GNP by 2001. Technology has provided cures and extends lives but at a high cost. Poverty and unequal access to health care persist. In "Hard Times/Government Control," a persistent economic recession leads to a political revolt in the mid–1990s over rising health care costs. The result is a frugal Canadian-style national health insurance system with services rationing, especially the high-tech, based on cost-benefit and outcomes research. In the preferred future (or "New Civilization" scenario), social change is global as the health of the community and environment become major societal concerns. National health reform that ensures basic coverage for all is enacted with an emphasis on individual and community health promotion. Hospitals and doctors align with social HMOs (SHMOs), which become the primary vehicle for improving individual and community health.

Whichever scenario the future brings, America's hospitals and health systems are about to be revisioned and reinvented. The twenty-first century health organization, under a variety of possible scenarios, is likely to be a regional network of hospitals, doctors, and other health providers linked by integrated information systems. Future medicine will be cost effective and anticipatory, using computers and expert systems as pathways to faster learning to predict and manage disease. Hospitals and physicians will be integrated in long-term customer relationships that emphasize "value" (cost plus quality) to patients and major purchasers. Technology will be cooperatively regionalized among once-competing hospitals with a shared vision by all creating healthy communities (Bezold 1992).

2. What new demands will be placed on our health care leaders?

Health care leaders don't know whether to expect the "High-Tech" or "Hard Times" scenario. Both were rated as somewhat likely, but neither one was dominant. The survey results really mean that nobody knows what will happen to health care in the next decade. There is no consensus on the direction of change, only that some significant change is ahead.

Managing tomorrow's hospitals and health systems will require a paradigm shift in leadership styles and strategies. Health care's current management paradigm of "business enterprise" will become obsolete. Thinking for the short term, maximizing profits, and aggressive marketing against competitors will be much less important among hospitals of the future. In the twenty-first century, health care leaders must think long range, must put community service first, and must build new learning organizations that can manage continuous change. Future health organizations will be more flexible, with cross-functional structures and a pervasive team approach to problem-solving and learning.

3. What competencies and values will be needed to lead twenty-first century health care organizations?

The five most important leadership competencies/values for the twenty-first century health care leader as ranked by survey participants are mastering change, systems thinking, CQI, shared vision, and serving the public community. *Mastering change* views change as opportunity by focusing on innovation and the up-side potential, by supporting risk-taking by mid-level management, and by fostering innovation and experimentation to find new approaches as the environment shifts. *Systems thinking* systemically analyzes problems, looking for leverage points, developing innovative solutions to complex patterns, and designing long-range interventions that address root problems. *Continuous quality improvement* (CQI) is a never-satisfied attitude about quality coupled with an organizationwide process to improve service and clinical outcomes. *Shared vision* creates a common picture of the future that builds alignment and a sense of shared purpose among key "stakeholders"—hospital management, physicians, major employers, government, and the public—to manage rising costs and provide quality service. *Serving the public/community* is the bottom-line for health care organizations in the twenty-first century, balancing social mission with profit margin to create healthy communities, in a future where hospitals and doctors will be measured on the health of their patients. Board members are the futurists and philosophers of their organization. The board must establish the dominant paradigm for the organization. In the coming age of health reform, every board must prepare to make radical shifts in its paradigm. New concepts such as physician partnering must be accommodated in this paradigm shift.

Predicting Health Care's Future

Forecasters and futurists do not share one view of the future of American health care. This chapter highlights the predictions of America's leading forecasters and futurists—Kenneth Abramowitz, Clem Bezold, Jeff Gold-smith, Leland Kaiser, Gerald McManis, and John Naisbitt.

Kenneth Abramowitz

Few market analysts are more direct, or more accurate, than Wall Street's Kenneth Abramowitz. The senior health care analyst for New York-based Sanford Bernstein & Co. has been an early and strong supporter of HMOs as the primary tool of market reform in the U.S. health industry. Abramowitz predicts that 100 (or so) privately owned managed care companies will cover 85 percent of all Americans by the year 2000. Government will provide coverage for the other 15 percent who are medically indigent. In the Abramowitz scenario, the U.S. health care market moves 250 million "retail buyers" (individuals) into 100 "corporate buyers" (HMOs), moving health care from a retail market to a wholesale market. The shift implies margin declines and consolidation for providers. Quality will improve as HMOs refuse to do business with low-quality providers. Weeding out the highest-cost and most ineffective 20 percent of providers will raise quality. Getting discounts from the other 80 percent of providers will lower health costs.

If Abramowitz is right, the nation's employers will conclude that HMOs—not a government takeover—is the best solution to rising costs and uncertain quality in health care. Privately owned HMOs will do a better job of controlling costs than the federal government could do under a national health insurance system.

Employers will use financial incentives to steer employees toward HMOs. Otherwise, employees can pay extra out-of-pocket costs to join any other plan. Hospitals will convert government health programs with mandatory HMOs for Medicaid. The shift to managed care will not happen overnight. Managed care companies need more practice as they learn to appropriately control costs and quality. Providers will slowly accept the managed care imperative. Physicians will embrace managed care only when competition forces them to either participate or lose patients. Financial pressures will bring hospital costs and excess capacity under managed care control. Ultimately, HMOs are the future of U.S. health care; they are the equivalent of putting the country on a budget. Eventually America will come to its senses, Abramowitz (Souhrado 1991) believes, and realize that it has no choice but to accept budgeted health care.

If Abramowitz is right and "the future is an HMO," every hospital will need a managed care strategy. More fundamentally, hospitals must make the paradigm shift from a "revenue center" trying to make a profit by expanding services to a "cost center" that is only one of a continuum of services provided under a capitation contact with "covered lives."

Clem Bezold

Clem Bezold is America's leading designer of alternative futures. His non-profit organization, the Institute for Alternative Futures, has worked with dozens of hospitals and health organizations to envision their futures. Bezold relies on scenarios to sketch possible futures as a way to convince organizations to create a strategic vision.

Bezold has been involved in major studies of the future of the health field, on the topics of leadership, nursing, pharmacy, and the future and health. In each, he created alternative scenarios to provide images of the future, focusing on the most plausible images but encouraging the field to consider more transformational possibilities of ideal futures.

From Bezold's perspective, health care's future will be shaped by three major streams of change.

- Health promotion—Through a combination of lifestyle improvement and medical technology, experts envision a "compression of mortality." Assuming that the onset of chronic diseases can be delayed through health-promoting behavior, then death (morbidity) can be compressed into a relatively brief period before the end of the life span. A compression of morbidity could lower health costs by 15 percent, as "successful aging" decreases the need for acute care and high-cost medical interventions would be reduced.

- Information technologies—While health care will be infused by a number of technologies in the future, information technologies will be among those with the greatest impact. Consider how much of medical care is really information analysis and information therapy. Electronic medical records will integrate health information between hospital and doctor, with the ability to link medical knowledge and patient observations virtually anywhere. Expert systems will aid diagnosis, providing a computerized second opinion and treatment plan. The "hospital on the wrist" is a combination of electronic monitor and self-regulating device—a personal health system—linked by telecommunications to a community care system. Ultimately, with genetic information and electronic networks, the health system will have the capacity to provide biochemically unique health and promotion services customized to each individual.

- Smarter markets—The health care marketplace of the future will be improved with public data bases on cost and quality. Activist consumers will take a more involved role in managing their own health. Outcomes research will provide new data and sophisticated measures of care effectiveness. Informed consumers—individuals, employers, insurance companies and managed care plans, and government—will select providers and treatments based on efficiency and effectiveness.

It is the role of the board to shape the long-range global vision that will drive the future of the hospital. As a committee of community futurists, the board takes the lead in exploring future scenarios and defining its preferred future.

Jeff Goldsmith

Credit Jeff Goldsmith for the concept of "predict and manage." If an organization can predict its preferred future, then it can create a management plan to achieve that vision (Goldsmith 1992). Managing the future means working backward from the desired future to the present. The Chicago-based consultant is national advisor to Ernst & Whinney, and president of his own company, Health Futures. His book, *Can Hospitals Survive?* threw out a challenge to the nation's hospitals and health systems to become more competitive.

His *Harvard Business Review* article (Goldsmith 1989), "A Radical Prescription for Hospitals," called for a reorientation away from expensive acute inpatient and refocusing on ambulatory and chronic care services. Goldsmith believes that hospitals today can be characterized by declining margins, excess capacity, mature product portfolio, bureaucratic overburden, poorly planned and executed diversification, and rapid CEO turnover. The larger health care environment is marked by soaring health costs and premiums and rising consumer discontent. The hospital as we know it, Goldsmith asserts, is too costly, too unwieldly, and too inflexible to survive. By concentrating on the revenue side of operations and traditional—and costly—institutional care, administrators and their boards have ignored the possibility of fundamental changes in hospitals' product and philosophy.

In the short term (three to five years), Goldsmith suggests four key strategies:

1. Physician collaboration—Hospitals and doctors must reinvigorate their collaboration by controlling how the hospital's resources are used in treating patients. Medical staff must use hospital services sparingly, and administrators must make meaningful cost reductions.

2. Productivity—Because health services are so labor-intensive, cost-conscious hospitals must look for ways to use employees. The ratio of white-collar workers (marketing, finance, information systems) to line workers (nurses, technicians) is too high. Goldsmith calls for simplifying management structures and eliminating layers of "administrative cellulite." Cross-training caregivers will add flexibility

and reduce full-time equivalents. Sophisticated cost and clinical information systems can reduce clerical costs while supporting productivity.

3. Ambulatory/chronic care—Although hospitals have staked major positions in ambulatory and home care, Goldsmith believes they did so for the wrong reason—to produce more inpatient volume. He argues that ambulatory and chronic care is the business of tomorrow's hospitals, while demand for inpatient care will decline.

4. Managing for medical value—The real goal of quality management is "value," whether a medical procedure or stay of care benefits the patient given its cost. Increasingly, buyers will ask whether the procedure could have been eliminated or the expenditure saved without compromising the medical outcome. Hospitals must prepare for a future market of smart buyers. By the mid-1990s, government, insurers, and employers will have systems that measure efficacy of various treatment patterns and will be able to compare the value of provider services.

Over the long term, acute care will be concentrated in a small number of high-tech regional centers treating traumatic and chronically ill patients. Community hospitals will continue to provide some acute care, like obstetrical services and surgery. Most of this care will be ambulatory. The community hospital will decentralize its services. Increasingly, the chronically ill will be treated at home or in settings remote from the traditional hospital facility. The challenge to hospitals as the American population ages will be to relocate resources from acute to chronic care.

As health care heads toward the next century, Goldsmith's "predict and manage" strategy will ultimately be driven by the emerging science of genetic analysis and therapy. As genetically informed medicine becomes more widely available, doctors will have the capacity to predict each person's genetic predispositions and genetic trigger-factors for chronic illnesses. New genetically engineered pharmaceuticals will target therapies directly to the molecular level. Medicine will be able to intervene much earlier in the advent of disease, and the result should be life extension, compression of morbidity, and higher quality of life. High-cost "heroic" medicine will become obsolete. The result of this genetic revolution in medicine will be declining health costs and improving community health levels.

Trustees must think of the future of the hospital and health system as an opportunity to "predict and manage." Note Goldsmith's strong views that America's hospitals must shift from an acute to chronic care focus. The board should reconfigure its hospital to expand ambulatory care and downgrade heroic high-cost interventions.

Leland Kaiser

Leland Kaiser says: "I just got back from the future! There's nothing there except infinite possibility waiting to happen. And what it's waiting for is you, because you are futurist. You are an architect of the destiny of your organization. You are a designer, and the future is waiting for you." Thousands of trustees have heard this message from, arguably, America's best-known source for inspiration about the future of health care.

Kaiser believes the single most determining characteristic for a health care facility's future is the collective mind-set of the people who work there. The future must exist in their imagination before it can exist in reality. Kaiser admonishes health care's trustees, medical leaders, and managers to take the future into their own hands. The future is too important to forecast or predict. It's the job of trustees to invent a new reality; the task of managers is to manage that image.

Too often, Kaiser tells health care audiences, their organizations believe that the "drivers" of the future are outside forces—their competitors, the regulators, the multihospital systems, market forces. These assumptions can limit, or enable, an organization's future.

Kaiser envisions the future not through predictions but preferences for health care's future in the twenty-first century (Kaiser 1992).

- High-technology will enable health care to extend life to 100 years of high-quality life through molecular-level medicine.
- America may spend 22 percent of the nation's GNP on health in the year 2001, with wide social benefit.
- Improving community health will be the true bottom-line of tomorrow's health care organizations.
- Health care providers will focus on lifestyle more than clinical interventions.
- Every child at birth will be imprinted with a hologram that will key a universal health record.
- Computerized sensors will assess body systems, read vital signs, make a diagnosis, and plan treatment.
- Health facilities will become healing environments that encourage regenerative health and a sense of well-being.
- A health care organization should be a research and development laboratory for continuous experimentation in clinical science and customer service.
- Health care will be redefined as "potentiation"—helping all human beings expand their full facilities as physical, mental, moral, and social persons.

The future is a design project, and the board, medical staff, and employees are the design committee. Recreating hospitals in Kaiser's spirit will result in "healing environments" whose goal is to assist all members of the community to achieve their optimum well-being and quality of life. Healing health care is a paradigm change and requires an about-face for many traditional health professionals and their institutions (Kaiser 1992).

Gerald McManis

Gerald McManis is one of America's most intuitive observers of the health care scene. His market and strategic insights have shaped the strategies and management of hundreds of America's hospitals and health systems. As a Washington, D.C.–based consultant heading McManis and Associates, he understands the interplay of market forces and government policy in the health field. In the past ten years, few have been right more often in spotting health care's trends. McManis was one of the first to see that Medicare's shift to prospective payment and DRGs in 1983 would impel hospitals to become market-competitive. He encouraged health care providers to organize into clusters to provide an integrated delivery system, a strategy ahead of its time.

McManis (1990) makes these predictions for health care in the year 2000.

- Recognition of limits to spending for health care will result in "rationalizing" delivery systems to get rid of excess capacity.
- Refocusing on prevention, wellness, and early diagnosis will deemphasize acute care.
- Some 70–80 percent of physicians will be members of integrated health care delivery systems.
- Health care systems will revolve around natural markets where most services will be available with 15–60 minutes driving time.
- Most major metropolitan areas will be dominated by two or three major provider systems.
- Consumers will become sophisticated buyers of health care services, with better cost and outcomes information.
- Medical technology and information systems will refocus on promoting patient health.
- Managed care will be replaced with "managed health," an approach oriented around the patient rather than the provider or the payer.
- Nonprofit health care foundations will be organized to balance the power between hospital and physicians in management of hospitals and regional delivery systems.

- Society will be unwilling to spend large sums of money on patients' last months of life.

Boards should be dreamers, but they must be realists as well. If society is unwilling or unable to spend 15–20 percent of America's GNP for health on health care, hospitals must take the lead in developing local health systems (the "cluster" concept) that cost-effectively provide the benefits of healing and health promotion.

John Naisbitt

John Naisbitt's *Megatrends*, published in 1982, was one of the most influential books of the 1980s. *Megatrends 2000: Ten New Directions for the 1990s*, which Naisbitt coauthored with his wife, Patricia Aburdene, says: "We stand at the dawn of a new era. Before us is the most important decade in the history of civilization, a period of stunning technological innovation, unprecedented economic opportunity, surprising political reform, and great cultural rebirth. It will be a decade like none that has come before because it will culminate in the millennium, the year 2000."

The megatrends for the 1990s are drawn on a larger canvas against a global perspective and multinational in their interaction. Five of the ten megatrends 2000 are global in scope while the other five are more uniquely American, identifying shifts in the U.S. society, economy, and technology.

The ten megatrends are summarized below, with suggested strategies for trustees during the 1990s.

Megatrend 1: The global economic boom of the 1990s. If Naisbitt and Aburdene (1990) are right, the 1990s will be a period of sustained economic growth. This worldwide prosperity will result from a confluence of factors, including global peace, economic interdependence, synergistic effect of growth feeding demand, lowering of trade barriers toward free trade, telecommunications and 24-hour global markets, and economic barriers overcoming political factors. Naisbitt and Aburdene's predictions for a global economy suggest that American health care executives

- Prepare for foreign competition. The 1990s may see the first wave of invasion by foreign-based companies into U.S. services industries, including health care. Pedus, the West German food service firm, has entered the U.S. contract service field to hospitals and nursing homes.
- Beware of international acquisition of U.S. companies. U.S. drug, biomedical, and genetic engineering companies are targets of foreign buyouts. German and Japanese investors are reportedly assessing investment opportunities among U.S. health care companies.

Megatrend 2: Renaissance in the arts. Art could replace sports as the primary leisure activity during the 1990s as box-office trends support the expansion of demand for theatre, music, and the arts. In 1968, citizens spent twice as much on sports activities as compared to arts. In 1988, however, $3.7 billion was spent on the arts, while only $2.8 billion was spent on sports. During the period 1983–1987, box-office dollars increased 21 percent while sporting activity gate receipts decreased 2 percent. This is a global trend. Japan has built 200 museums in 30 years while Germany has opened 300 museums in the past decade alone. Workforce affluence is the cause, driven by an educated, professional, and increasingly female workforce. Baby-boomers are leading this trend. Blockbuster art shows and multimillion dollar music tours demonstrate the economic power of the arts. Art becomes a global market as Japanese and other buyers price single works of art over $50 million. The direct participation of major corporations is the only factor Naisbitt and Aburdene (1990) believe necessary to solidify the preeminence of arts over sports as society's top leisure activity in the decade ahead.

An arts renaissance would encourage American health care systems to

- Link art to hospital philanthropy. Next year, hospitals should sponsor an art event as well as a 10K race. Look for cultural opportunities to cultivate philanthropic sources.

- Sponsor the arts. As a major employer and corporate citizen in their communities, hospitals should undertake sponsorship of selected arts programs and events, making art accessible to the community, the bed-ridden, handicapped, and disadvantaged.

- Become a healing space. Invite design professionals to make the hospital a healing environment, through use of color, light, space, and art. Use "competition by design" to differentiate the hospital as a patient-friendly environment.

Megatrend 3: Emergence of free-market socialism. If Boris Yeltsin and the heirs of Gobrachev's liberalism survive their current political crises, the most fascinating socioeconomic experiment of modern times will be staged—the retroconversion of socialism to a free-market economy. Yeltsin's dismantling of Russia's welfare state is another instance of the emergence of "free-market socialism." The former Soviet Union is engineering the conversion of its centrally planned economy to one infused by competition, despite considerable opposition.

For U.S. health firms, the conversion of once-socialist economies to a free market could

- Create new opportunities. The privatization of socialist health systems could offer new business opportunities for U.S. health care providers and hospital systems, through management contracts or by providing a private sector alternative to socialized medicine. Newly liberated Eastern European nations may be a prime market for American health firms.

Megatrend 4: Global lifestyles and cultural nationalism. A new international lifestyle is emerging due to the world economy, expanding global telecommunications, and a consumer-driven revolution in styles and tastes. As the world becomes more cosmopolitan, the global acceptance of consumer products like Perrier, McDonalds, Honda, Coke, and Sony suggests these world brands are resulting in a new set of worldwide consumer patterns. American TV programs (and dubbed reruns) dominate world home entertainment. English is the global language.

Globalization of culture and lifestyle is a major opportunity to:

- Work to keep American medical technology the best in the world. In a global marketplace, American medical technology is the "gold standard" to which consumers will flow.

- Organize for global marketing. America's premier medical centers should organize for marketing high-tech medical specialty services on a global basis. Hospitals in Houston, Dallas, New York, Miami, Honolulu, and Los Angeles are reaching out to a world of potential consumers.

Megatrend 5: Privatization of the welfare state. Privatization is a global trend. America's free-market economy is the inspiration for a shift from the socialized governmental controls to enterprise models. This trend is most dramatically evident in Britain, where the Conservative government has been systematically dismantling England's nationalized industries. Dozens of industries and companies have been denationalized. Home ownership in Britain has risen from 62–75 percent of all households. Reforms begun under Margaret Thatcher have been expanded under the Major government to inject market incentives into Britain's national health system.

In the United States, privatization means converting garbage collection, prisons, and public hospitals to private-sector management. With the inroads of Federal Express and UPS, mail delivery is already well along a trend to privatization. Thirty-nine states have enacted "workfare" programs to get the unemployed off welfare rolls and into private-sector jobs.

For health care, the shift to privatization may mean the industry must

- Think deregulation, not reregulation. If privatization is the global trend, then deregulation, not reregulation, should dominate public policy for health care in the United States. Perhaps the United States is out of step. While America looks at Canada as a future model for a national health system, other European and socialist countries are looking for ways to privatize their health services to improve services and provide private capital.

- "Sunset" health care regulation. Research from the RAND Corporation makes it clear that regulation increases, not reduces, health inflation. Providers should keep up the pressure on state legislatures to eliminate all remaining regulatory programs such as certificate of need, capital expenditures review, and rate control.

Megatrend 6: Rise of the Pacific Rim. The Pacific Rim is emerging like a dynamic young America, but on a much grander scale. This global shift needs little embellishment. Naisbitt and Aburdene note that the economies of the Pacific Rim are growing five times faster than the United States grew during its industrial revolution a century ago. Although Japan is the leader today, China and the "four tigers"—South Korea, Taiwan, Hong Kong, and Singapore—may eventually dominate.

With the growth of the Pacific Rim economies, American health care should

- Consider the Pacific Rim market. America's Pacific Rim states are well positioned to capitalize on the shift into the Century of the Pacific. Hawaii's Queens Medical Center has set a long-term goal of becoming the premier medical center of the Pacific Rim.
- Recognize the aging of a global market. Japan is experiencing an age wave comparable to that of the United States. Care of older Asian adults may be a growth market opportunity for American long-term care providers. Japan may export its elderly to America, due to high land prices and limited housing supply. Japanese investors are reportedly exploring potential for building retirement communities for elderly Japanese in the United States.
- Prepare for biomed competition. Japanese and Asian companies are investing heavily in biotechnology and genetic engineering. These companies will be a major competitive force in the 1990s for U.S. biomed manufacturers, drug companies, and suppliers.

Megatrend 7: The 1990s—Decade of women in leadership. The 1990s will be the decade of women in business. For the past two decades, women have taken two-thirds of all new jobs. Today about 74 percent of all men work, but 79 percent of women who have no children under the age of 18 are in the workforce. More than half of all professionals are women. Women constitute 30–50 percent of the workers in American companies, and they are starting new businesses twice as fast men. *Working Woman* outsells all business publications except the *Wall Street Journal.*

The rise of women in the workplace and in society requires that systems

- Welcome women hospital executives. Women will hold all levels of executive and management positions in U.S. hospitals during the 1990s. More than half of the average hospital's senior management team will be women before the year 2000 because in 1992, 75 percent of the hospital workforce is women. Watch for directors of nursing to move into the chief operation officer position as they advance to CEO.

- Encourage flexibility in the workplace. Hospitals will be flexible to accommodate women as they balance the demands of career and home. To do well, hospitals must provide flexible hours, compensation, child care, and support services. Part-time workers now fill 35–40 percent of many hospital positions. During this decade, as many as 50–60 percent of women may be part-time workers in health care.

Megatrend 8: Age of biology. If the twentieth century was the century of physics, then its successor will be the century of biology. Mapping the human genetic structure should be complete by the year 2000, and it will bring a wave of artificially engineered pharmaceuticals. A new generation of vaccines and therapeutics is in development. These new diagnostics and drugs will be cellular and site-specific, targeted directly to the virus or cancer. Disease-prone persons will be identified. Anticipatory medicine will use genetic probes and family histories to predict disease years before symptoms show.

With biotechnology an enabling technology, health care executives should

- Prepare for the onset of biotherapeutics. Artificial insulin and tPA, the clot-dissolving drug, are just the first of a broad wave of new genetically engineered pharmaceuticals. If there is a cure for cancer in the 1990s, it will probably be genetically engineered. Biotherapeutics could radically alter medical care.

- Support new diagnostics. With genetic probes, physicians will pinpoint disease sites and early symptoms. Hospitals should support this research because it may reduce hospital length of stay by one or two days.

Megatrend 9: Religious revival of the next millennium. At the turn of the new millennium, there are signs of a worldwide religious revival. Some baby-boomers are returning to the church or joining the New Age movement, while others fear the end of the world.

A rising consciousness about religion and values will demand that the health care field

- Recognize spiritual needs. Medical care must recognize the spiritual needs of patients, a principle aligned with that designated by Naisbitt and Aburdene (1990) as high-tech/high-touch. As a result, some hospitals have revived their chaplaincy programs.
- Establish bioethics programs. More than two-thirds of U.S. hospitals have bioethics programs. Every hospital should identify the ethical and social issues it faces in the 1990s and establish policy positions.
- Become value-driven. Like the most successful American companies, hospitals should make their values prominently known within the hospital and community, and let them drive their strategic decisions.

Megatrend 10: Triumph of the individual. A new respect for the individual is underlying many of the megatrends identified by Naisbitt and Aburdene (1990). The environmental, women's, antinuclear, and New Age movements represent a return to the idea of the individual as the building block of societal change. Collective structures such as unions, political parties, big business, cities, and government have lost power.

Naisbitt and Aburdene end *Megatrends 2000* (1990) by recognizing the individual as the thread connecting every trend described in the book. The new responsibility of society is to reward the initiative of the individual. Today, the future is in the hands of individuals, empowered by information, who can shape the emerging reality of the next century. This means that health care organizations must

- Put patients first. Naisbitt's "high-tech/high-touch" admonition is clear: Put patients first, and treat them with humanism and dignity. Hospitals cannot exist without patients.
- Improve quality and productivity. The key to productivity and quality in health care is through committed individuals who share the values and ethics of the organization. Seek out those individuals for executive and board positions.

Looking Forward: What Other Megatrends Will Influence the 1990s?

Despite the broad reach of *Megatrends 2000*, inevitably some trends were omitted. The missing megatrends may be among the most important influencers for the health industry in the 1990s: aging of the population, environmental protection and health, disappearance of the middle class, consumerism, euthanasia and new attitudes abut death, labor shortages, functional illiteracy and the high-tech work site, quality-of-life issues, resetting national priorities (from guns to butter), and the baby-boomers reaching middle age.

Some of these changes are global in scope while others are more uniquely American, suggesting that other potential megatrends exist simply to reinforce the complexity of managing in the 1990s.

Like Naisbitt and Aburdene, who undoubtedly had a difficult time determining which ten megatrends to discuss, every organization's strategy must narrow the base of its strategic assumptions to a workable number defined as the most critical success factors. In a time of transition, it would be dangerous to shorten that list too much by omitting a factor that may be essential for organizational success. Never limit key assumptions to those from within the health field. Outside factors may be even more important.

Trustees should watch which U.S. hospitals are closing. Hospital financial failure is widely blamed on changes in Medicare payment, but the reality is that local economic conditions have driven more hospitals out of business than Medicare. Texas, which lost more than 50 hospitals in the 1980s, still has a turbulent economy due to the low price of world oil and the cause of these failures is global but the impact is local. As a result, hospital trustees and their executives must maintain a global and wide-ranging perspective as they set strategy for the future. It is a changing world for hospitals, medical groups, health systems, employers, insurers, and regulators of all health and related services. However, the changes ahead for health care providers will not be limited to those we read about in the pages of *Modern Healthcare*, *Hospitals*, or *Healthcare Forum Journal*. The health field is only part of a wider world that is a swirl with change. Keep a weather eye on these megatrends for the year 2000; they will influence us all.

Strategies

1. **Be a futurist.** As Leland Kaiser has admonished, every hospital trustee, executive, and medical staff leader must be a futurist. Collaboratively all must reach a consensus on the desired future—Lee Kaiser's "design party"—and then build it. America's hospitals have a special access to wide-ranging expertise from their trustees, representing many fields and experiences. That collective wisdom, pointed toward the future, should illuminate what comes next for their institutions.

2. **Think globally, plan locally.** Remember that most futures will be local, not national. Here the experts are local—trustees, medical staff, management, employees, community leaders, elected officials, and the public. No national expert can know the community's prospects better than

these local futurists. Each hospital and health system exists in a unique environment. Often these local dimensions will be more important than any national megatrend in shaping the future of the organization. Strategic plans should be tailored to unique and local factors that will drive the future of the community and health care service area.

3. **Consider the future a resource.** Think of the future as a resource to be managed. The potential of leaders to imagine, or envision, a different future is powerful. A vision of the future charts new directions (strategy) and provides symbols (values) that stir emotional commitment to the goals. Trustees are "keepers of the flame." It is their leadership charge to ensure that visions are value-driven. Management's task is to translate the organization's vision into plans and objectives. Images of the future provide a strategic framework through which key stakeholders can align their plans.

References

Barker, J. A. 1992. *Future Edge: Discovering the New Paradigms of Success.* New York: William Morrow and Company.

Bezold, C. 1992. "Five Futures." *Healthcare Forum Journal* 35 (May–June): 29–42.

Goldsmith, J. 1989. "A Radical Prescription for Hospitals." *Harvard Business Review* 67 (May–June): 104–11.

———. 1992. "The Reshaping of Healthcare." *Healthcare Forum Journal* 35 (July–August): 34–41.

Johnson, K., and J. Berger. 1992. *Bridging the Leadership Gap.* San Francisco: Healthcare Forum.

Kaiser, L. 1992. "Our New Look." *Healing Healthcare* 3 (Summer): 2.

McManis, G. 1990. "Who Will Decide the Future of Health Care?" *Hospitals* 64 (5 May): 72.

Naisbitt, J., and P. Aburdene. 1990. *Megatrends 2000: Ten New Directions for the 1990s.* New York: William Morrow & Co.

Souhrado, L. 1991. "Three Experts, Three Visions of the Future." *Hospitals* 65 (5 April): 41–43.

About the Author

Russell C. Coile, Jr., is a futurist specializing in the health industry. He is the President of the Health Forecasting Group of Santa Clarita, California, which provides market forecasts and strategic advice to a wide range of U.S. health care organizations. He is the author of *Revolution: The Future of Medicine under Health Reform* (1993), *The New Medicine: Reshaping Medical Practice and Healthcare Management* (1990), and *The New Hospital: Future Strategies for a Changing Industry* (1986). He is the editor of the *Hospital Strategy Report* and a member of the editorial advisory boards of *Modern Healthcare, Managed Care Outlook*, and *Healthcare Competition Week*. His columns "The Leading Edge" and "21st Century Physician" appear regularly in the *Healthcare Forum Journal* and *Northern/Southern California Medicine*. Coile holds a B.A. from the Johns Hopkins University and an M.B.A. in health care administration from the George Washington University. Prior to forming his own consulting firm, he established the first corporate futures program in the health industry for the Lutheran Hospital Society of Southern California where he was director of the Center for Health Management Research. He is a frequent speaker with the American College of Healthcare Executives, the Governance Institute, the Healthcare Forum, the American Hospital Association, and other national health care organizations.